THE
SAN JUAN
ISLANDS
AFOOT & AFLOAT

THE
SAN JUAN
ISLANDS

✦ AFOOT & AFLOAT ✦

THIRD EDITION

Marge & Ted Mueller

THE
MOUNTAINEERS

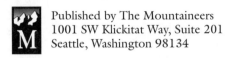

Published by The Mountaineers
1001 SW Klickitat Way, Suite 201
Seattle, Washington 98134

First edition 1979. Second edition 1988. Third edition: first printing 1995, second printing 1996, third printing 1998, fourth printing 2000, fifth printing 2002

Published simultaneously in Great Britain by Cordee, 3a DeMontfort Street, Leicester, England, LE1 7HD

Manufactured in the United States of America

Edited by Scott Stevens
Maps by Marge Mueller
All photographs by Marge and Ted Mueller unless otherwise noted
Cover design by Watson Graphics
Book design and layout by Gray Mouse Graphics

Cover photographs: Aerial view of Shaw Island Cove, San Juan Islands (photo: © Randy Wells/Allstock); *insets:* a Washington State ferry prepares to dock at Friday Harbor (photo: Marge and Ted Mueller), kayakers on Orcas Island (photo: Marge and Ted Mueller), child examining shell (photo © Phil Schofield/Allstock)
Frontispiece: Heavy-weather sailing in San Juan Channel; Cattle Point beyond

Library of Congress Cataloging-in-Publication Data

Mueller, Marge.
    The San Juan Islands, afoot & afloat / Marge & Ted Mueller. -- 3rd ed.
        p.   cm.
    Includes bibliographical references and index.
    ISBN 0-89886-434-8 (pbk.)
    1. San Juan Islands (Wash.)--Guidebooks. I. Mueller, Ted. II. Title. III.
Title: San Juan Islands, afoot and afloat. IV. Title: San Juan Islands.
    F897.S2M79 1995
    917.97'74--dc20   94-44878
                                                        CIP

CONTENTS

Kayakers explore Sucia Island's Echo Bay.

PREFACE

As its title indicates, this book deals with a broad spectrum of good, clean, healthy, active, and largely nonpolluting recreation available in the San Juan Islands, either on land or on water. Yet the reader thumbing through these pages for his or her favorite sport will soon note that island recreation does not divide itself into two neat categories, for some hikes and campgrounds are accessible only by boat, fishing can be from either boat or land, scuba diving can be boat- or shore-based, and many beaches can be reached either by land or by sea. And to achieve a catchy title, bicycling was not implied at all, although it certainly is one of the most delightful pastimes in the San Juans, and one that is frequently mentioned in these pages.

In addition to these active types of recreation, this book includes take-it-easy, stop-and-smell-the-flowers diversions. The islands aren't very big; one could rush through the three larger ones in a day and claim to have "seen" the San Juans. We urge the reader to stop and think about the history of the Indians who first arrived here in long cedar canoes, and the Spanish and English explorers who came later in sailing ships. Take time to notice the unique birds, flowers, and animals, and the special quality of the clouds piled high above the long, horizontal reaches of the islands. The more you look, the more there is to see.

While this is a guide to recreation rather than facilities, at the same time it is recognized that any visitor to the San Juans needs to have at least a general idea of what to expect in the way of amenities. Commercial facilities listed in this book are mentioned primarily on a "need-to-know" basis, such as where to find food, lodging, fuel, moorage, and other necessities. When fees are charged for services such as moorage and boat launching, we have indicated that. For visitors interested in specifics regarding island facilities, a number of tourist and commercial publications, including one by the authors, *The Essential San Juan Guide*, are available that list names, addresses, and phone numbers of businesses in the islands.

The places in the book were surveyed over a period of several years, and rechecked just prior to publication. Changes to facilities do occur, however. The authors and The Mountaineers Books would appreciate knowing of any changes so future editions can be updated. Please address comments to:

Marge and Ted Mueller
c/o The Mountaineers Books
1001 SW Klickitat Way, Suite 201
Seattle, WA 98134

INTRODUCTION

Tucked away in the northwest corner of the state of Washington lie the San Juan Islands—a cluster of emerald gems set in a shimmering azure sea. The islands, tops of an ancient mountain range that over eons settled and became inundated by the sea, were sculpted by massive glacial ice sheets that completely covered them, grinding off the tall peaks, gouging out watery channels and estuaries, and depositing great piles of gravelly debris.

Only the granite heart of the mountains remains, still bearing the marks of the glaciers' southward journey. Soft glacial till in lowlands has fostered the growth of forests, thickets, and meadows. The buffeting of wind and water on mile upon mile of coastline has formed myriad shapes, ranging from wide, bay-bottom tide flats and long, curving, golden sandspits to narrow, wave-cut bedrock benches.

By definition, the San Juans are generally accepted as being those islands lying north of the Strait of Juan de Fuca, south and east of the Canadian boundary and west of—aye, there's the rub! Where do we draw the eastern boundary? San Juan County uses Rosario Strait as its line of demarcation, but islands eastward ache to be called San Juans, too, and with some justification. But holding to bureaucratic boundaries, this book covers those islands lying within San Juan County. Outlying islands are described in another book, *North Puget Sound, Afoot and Afloat*.

The Skagit County islands of Fidalgo, Guemes, and Cypress serve as an entrance to the San Juans because a majority of the traffic passes among them, either on the ferry from Anacortes, or through Deception Pass or Swinomish Channel. It is here that the visitor first sees the forested hills reaching down to placid bays, and the rock buttresses enclosing narrow, silvery channels that characterize this ultimate melding of land and water.

The Book of the San Juan Islands, which is published by the *Journal of the San Juan Islands*, reports that San Juan County boasts 375 miles of saltwater shoreline—more than any other county in the United States, and nearly as much as the Pacific shorelines of Washington and Oregon combined.

And how many San Juan Islands are there? As difficult as the territory may be to define, it is even harder to catalog. Figures range from 172 to more than 700! If that seems a startling discrepancy, consider: When is an island merely a rock? How many rocks make a reef? Is a reef an island? What about tidal changes that cause rocks and reefs to appear and disappear and split apart or join together? The problems are legion.

The figure of 172 theoretically includes all of those named islands or groups of named islands within San Juan County, but don't try to count them—you'll never come out with that number. For now let's say "around 200," and go on to other things.

The Fly in the Ointment

Most paradises have their flaws, and unfortunately the San Juans have theirs, for they are loved almost too much and they can be crowded—exasperatingly crowded! Long ferry lines can mean up to a three-hour wait for car passengers, and in extreme cases a four- to five-hour delay. Foot passengers rarely have extensive waits. Overnight accommodations can be filled, marinas can be congested, and parks can be overflowing with people from June to September.

Is it worth it? You bet it is! But you must be prepared to be patient and relax (that's one of the great secrets of the island magic). If the ferry leaves you at the dock, there's always another one soon, and no matter how many people there are, the scenery is big enough for everyone to share.

So be forewarned—if visiting the islands in summer, expect waits in the ferry line, crowded accommodations, and filled campgrounds. Signs attempt to notify prospective campers of campsite availability before they board the ferry in Anacortes. After Labor Day the tourist crowds almost magically disappear and, except for an occasional sunny winter holiday, the islands are returned to their grateful residents.

Does that mean that the islands aren't any good off-season? Shhh—that's the best kept secret of all. They're often better. The mobs are gone (but won't be if the secret gets out), and although the weather is cooler and a bit more unpredictable, on a crisp fall day when Indian summer paints the forests, or on a blustery winter day when waves lash furiously at beaches, or on a damp spring day when wildflowers fill hedgerows and lambs cavort in fields, the islands truly show the many subtle nuances of their beauty.

Some Economic Facts

Some visitors to the San Juans have squalled loudly when they discovered that some prices are higher than for comparable goods on the mainland, a few miles away. In a few cases prices can run 20 percent higher. Residents are *not* out to gouge the summer visitor—residents have to pay those prices too.

A row of bicycles waiting for the ferry at Orcas Landing

The problem is that the islands produce relatively few hard goods, and it is tough to earn a living here. Many of the people who live here are retired; a few others make a living by commuting to mainland jobs; some are writers, artists, and craftspeople whose jobs are not dependent on local suppliers. Only a few people in the county are engaged in full-time farming, and the fishing industry is but a shadow of what it once was; only around 2 percent of the islands' work force is engaged in farming, forestry, or fishing; aquaculture holds some promise for the future. Tourism is the leading industry here, and as such it must pay for itself. The people who live here and provide services for the tourists still have to pay taxes and feed their families all year, even after the tourists have gone home.

On the other hand, you can make some excellent purchases in the islands. Resident artists and craftspeople offer superb works of art for sale at local stores or in their own shops. All three major islands have artists' cooperatives that represent a number of artists and display a wide selection of items. Pottery, porcelain, fiber arts, wood arts, gallery photographs, and jewelry are among the offerings, as well as paintings, sculpture, and limited edition art prints. Some people make a point of adding a few pieces of art to their collection each time they visit, and of course island art makes wonderful gifts.

The available public lands (especially parks and campgrounds) are heavily used by tourists, and there is a constant cry for more. Unfortunately, every bit of land that is put in the public trust for recreational use narrows the tax base, placing a greater financial burden on those remaining landowners. Additionally, the more tourists that arrive, the greater the burden on public utilities such as power, water, and sewer, and public services such as road maintenance, fire protection, and law enforcement—all of which are paid by local taxes.

Consider also that nearly all goods that are consumed here must be brought in by ferry. Gasoline, for example, is brought by tanker trucks on special night runs, after regular passenger runs, due to its hazardous nature. After carrying fuel the ferries must be completely hosed down to eliminate any possible danger from spilled fuel. The cost of this special service must be passed on to the consumer. Although this is one of the more extreme examples, it illustrates the reasons goods and therefore services often are more expensive on the San Juan Islands.

The people who live year-round on the islands do so because they love it here—but they aren't making a killing on the tourists. With this in mind, don't resent it if residents expect a fair price for their goods and services or expect to be paid for use of their property.

Of "No Trespassing" Signs and Other Aggravations

One of the most negative aspects of the San Juans—and most noticeable to those of us devoted to good, clean public recreation, and lots of it—is the proliferation of "No Trespassing" signs on every fence post and every beach, screaming, "Stay away, this is mine, and I don't want you here!" Under such duress the meek become paranoid, and the feisty grow defiant.

San Juan residents aren't unfriendly—in fact they're some of the nicest folks around, and many of them feel that tourism is a vital function of their islands. These people are simply tired of boorish boaters who come ashore to relieve themselves and their dogs on private beaches, leaving feces and toilet paper strewn about; they're tired of fences ripped down and campfires built in dry timber and grasslands by campers; they're tired of farm animals shot and children endangered by overzealous hunters; they're tired of ignorant disregard of privacy and outright vandalism and thievery.

The horror stories are plentiful—enough to make fellow tourists ashamed of their breed. But we know we're not all like that, in fact few of us are, so don't take "No Trespassing" signs as a personal affront. Instead, heed them and respect the rights of the people who own the property, who keep the islands functioning with their tax money, and who are doing their best to keep it unspoiled for the future.

Even if lands are unposted, do not assume they are public or that no one cares if you trespass. Unless clearly designated as public land, *stay off*—somebody owns it. The growth of public recreation in the San Juans lies largely in the hands of the residents. More lands are available for development now, and more could become available in the future, but it will take a favorable position by these residents, convinced that tourism is really good for the economy, before there is any marked increase in public recreation facilities.

Problems in Paradise—and How You Can Help

San Juan County has trouble coping with pressures created by its own residents and newcomers, let alone hordes of visitors. Many ask, how far can the islands stretch? With an educated, cooperative attitude, tourists can minimize the impact on these islands, and somewhat ease the pressures.

Water. "Water, water, everywhere, but not a drop to drink" may soon become the theme of the San Juans. At the present there's barely enough to go around. Some of the small marine park islands have none at all, and wells at several of the other parks frequently run dry by midsummer. Even in the towns water is at a premium, with new construction of homes and businesses limited in some areas by unavailability of water hookups. Heavy demands on wells and catch basins are causing these water resources to be depleted.

As ridiculous as it may sound, when visiting the San Juans, *bring water!* Fill up camper and boat water tanks at home or at the last mainland stop, and once you're there, take it easy. There's enough water at present to assure reasonable cleanliness for everyone, but don't let faucets run unnecessarily at campgrounds, don't use a gallon of water when a quart will do, and don't rinse down boats with fresh water at marinas. During times of water shortage, washing boats may be strictly prohibited, with a stiff fine imposed on those who do.

Fire. Going hand-in-hand with the water problem in the islands is the problem of serious fires. There are no convenient fire hydrants on every street corner (and very few street corners). In remote areas reaching a fire is very difficult, and putting it out more so. By late summer roadside grasses and thickets

A faucet at Spencer Spit underscores water concerns.

can be tinder dry, so please be extremely careful with matches, cigarettes, and campfires.

Pets. It may come as a surprise, but good old Fido is not exactly welcome in the San Juans. In this largely rural county, city dogs and farm animals often do not mix well, and every year there are tragic incidents of domestic animals being slaughtered by dogs roaming free. The perpetrators were not vicious watchdogs, trained to attack, but friendly, sit-by-the-fire family pets. The San Juan County dog ordinance states that any unlicensed dog found at large in rural areas may be shot. This applies to dogs of residents and visitors alike. Leave your pet at home or keep it on a leash at all times. Several boarding kennels are available for the use of those who have brought their animals.

GETTING AROUND THE ISLANDS IS HALF THE FUN

A watery highway system of broad straits and fjordlike channels links the San Juan Islands. Gleaming white state ferries cruise the waters, busily "busing" people, cars, bicycles, trailered or car-top boats, and a startling range of other conveyances from island to island. All state ferry routes begin at the city of Anacortes on Fidalgo Island and usually stop at four of the larger islands—Lopez, Shaw, Orcas, and San Juan—and occasionally continue on across Haro Strait to Sidney, British Columbia, on Vancouver Island. Two smaller, private passenger ferries operate from Bellingham and Anacortes.

On the state ferries, passengers enjoy what is advertised as "the most scenic ferry ride in the world" from picture windows in the comfort of the ferry's interior or from breezy open decks resembling balconies above the water. At times the vista is a broad panorama of sparkling sea and receding layers of gray-green islands backed by distant snowcapped mountains. Other times rugged rockbound shores seem within touching distance as the ferry threads through narrow passages.

Depending on the season and the luck and sharp eye of the observer, jumping salmon, curious seals, soaring eagles, flocks of migrating waterfowl, or even a group of orca whales may be seen. At each time of day, each change of weather, each advance of season, the islands are painted in infinite variety: the vivid hues of a perfect summer day, the drifting mists of a springtime fog, the blaze of a sunset.

Of course private boats, too, travel these waterways—do they ever! Seeking nirvana in salt-scrubbed air and crystal water and tranquil anchorages, they arrive, drove upon drove. Unfettered by such things as stodgy ferry schedules, they wander freely among all the islands, visiting big and little, and particularly frequenting the numerous boat-in marine state parks.

But the non-ferry-served islands are not reserved for affluent yacht owners alone. Even a kayak, canoe, or rowboat will do to reach some, for several of the state parks lie on protected bays within paddling distance. Islands across broader channels can be reached by boats brought via the ferry to launching spots on the larger islands; marinas within the San Juans offer a wide variety of boats to be rented for the hour or day, or chartered for extended cruises. Charters are also available at the nearby cities of Anacortes, Bellingham, and Victoria. Skippered charters that leave the navigation to an experienced captain and the relaxed sightseeing to the guests are also available. Some specialize in wildlife viewing, fishing, or scuba diving.

Many tourists leave their automobiles at a fee parking lot at the Anacortes ferry terminal, or at a lot off SR20 east of Anacortes, take a free shuttle bus to the ferry terminal, and walk onto the ferry with bicycle or backpack and hiking boots. Roads on the ferry-served islands are gently rolling, traffic is light, and the slow and quiet traveler will see far more wildlife and far more beauty than those who rush from here to there in automobiles.

In recognition of the increasing interest in human- and wind-powered boating—kayaks, canoes, rowboats, and day-sailors—the Washington Water Trails Association and various state agencies have cooperated to create the Cascadia Marine Trail, a series of camping and access sites stretching from Olympia to the Canadian border. These sites are reserved for persons paddling the water trails to facilitate this unique way to experience and enjoy the beautiful marine environment of Puget Sound and the San Juan Islands.

For a speedier trip to the islands, air flights are available; in good weather this is an especially scenic way to go. San Juan, Orcas, and Lopez islands have small airports; West Isle Air and Harbor Airlines maintain a regular schedule year-round from either Bellingham or Anacortes to and from San Juan, Orcas, and Lopez airports, with added flights in the summer. Kenmore Air offers daily scheduled seaplane flights to Orcas, San Juan, and Lopez islands. Other air services based at San Juan Island, Anacortes, and Seattle charter either small land or seaplanes for flights throughout the islands. Seaplane floats are maintained at Friday Harbor and Roche Harbor. Many of the other islands have single-landing-strip airfields used by private planes or charters.

So You've Decided to Take the Ferry...

For the novice ferry user, the system may at times seem bewildering; even experienced ferry commuters accustomed to cross-sound runs will find the procedure in the San Juans is different. In addition, the system can change from season to season, and year to year, depending on the demand, operating funds available, and new ideas to streamline the operation.

Three types of ferry runs operate through the islands: the *domestic*, the *inter-island*, and the *international*. In the summer, departures are about hourly; however, not all ferries stop at all islands. Confusing? It certainly can be. Just remember: it is up to you to be sure you are on the right ferry for your destination. Read the ferry schedule carefully, and when in doubt ask the ticket agent.

At Anacortes, tickets for the domestic runs are sold only as round-trips, eliminating the need for collecting fares for the return trip. If you buy a ticket for an early stop, such as Lopez Island, and then later decide to continue west to a different island, an additional fare will be collected. The inter-island runs are on a smaller ferry traveling only between San Juan, Orcas, Shaw, and Lopez islands, with no direct service to the mainland.

The international run travels to Sidney, B.C. in spring, summer, and fall. Reservations for vehicles destined for Sidney are accepted on this trip, so space for San Juan-bound vehicles on that ferry may be very limited. Travelers headed to Sidney purchase one-way tickets. If you travel from Anacortes to the San Juans you do not go through customs, even if you are on the international run; however, if you should happen to catch the international run on its return from Sidney on Vancouver Island you will be slightly delayed by the customs inspection in Anacortes.

Ferry schedules (which, by the way, change quarterly) are available at the various ferry terminals and at many businesses in ferry-served cities. Schedules and other information can also be obtained by writing to Washington State Ferries, Pier 52, Seattle, WA 98104, or by telephoning the number listed in the back of this book.

Walk-On Passengers

Riding the ferry is a simple matter if traveling by foot: simply buy a ticket and walk on board when the boat arrives, relax by a window, and enjoy the beautiful ride—no hassle, rarely any wait, and very inexpensive. You can spend the day cruising through the islands, watching the changing scene from the breezy decks or enclosed cabins of the ferry. Maps posted on one of the main decks show the route through the islands. A coffee shop on board sells snacks, sandwiches, and beverages.

Loudspeakers announce destinations as the ferry approaches them. Although foot passengers embark and debark via an overhead ramp at Anacortes, at island destinations they use the car deck; watch where other passengers are headed. If you arrive on the auto deck once unloading has begun, use extreme care to avoid moving vehicles.

With the exception of the vessel that makes the inter-island run, facilities for the physically disabled are available on all the San Juan ferries. At Anacortes, persons in wheelchairs can load via the foot passengers'

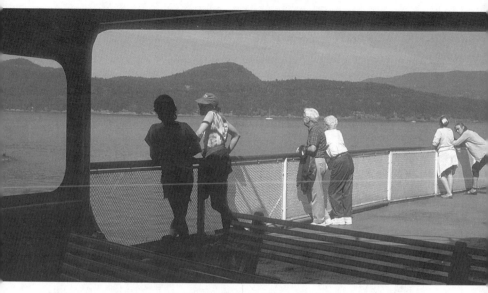

Visitors can see many of the San Juans' 172 islands from the comfort of the Washington State ferry.

overhead ramp to the observation deck. For disembarking at any of the islands, a small elevator operates between the upper decks and the car deck. At Friday Harbor, the facilities of the town are within a few blocks, and streets are reasonably level. On Lopez and Orcas they are some distance away, and the exit roads are quite steep.

By car, if you are physically disabled or are traveling with a disabled person and want to leave your vehicle to go to the observation deck, inform the attendant when you purchase your ticket. The crew will attempt to see that your vehicle is parked near the elevator with room to unload.

Bicycles and Hand-Carried Boats

These increasingly popular modes of transportation are also readily accommodated on the ferries, although some people wonder if the day won't come that a ferry will be so filled with bicycles and kayaks that there won't be any room for cars. There is a small charge for bicycles in addition to the regular foot passenger fare. Passengers are responsible for loading and unloading, and for the safety and security of their own equipment.

Bicycles are usually loaded and unloaded as a group, ahead of other vehicles; follow the directions of the ferry crew. After leaving the boat, be aware that a long line of cars with some possibly frazzled drivers is coming right behind you. Stay well to the side so you don't hold them up.

Paddlers have recently added a leaf to the Indians' book on portaging by carrying canoes and kayaks onto the ferries, then launching them from nearby public access for tours of the islands. These boats are loaded and unloaded along with bicycles, and there is a slight charge in addition to the foot passenger fare. There is no additional charge for bicycles or kayaks that are attached to vehicles.

Vehicles

Oh, you want to take your *car*? Well, that's another matter. The first question is—won't you reconsider? Will you really need it on the island? Call ahead and see what transportation arrangements can be worked out, for there are many alternatives: if you are visiting friends, perhaps they will pick you up at the terminal; many resorts will meet their customers and drive them to their destination. If you are chartering a boat, the same arrangements may be possible. Car rentals and taxi service are available on Lopez, Orcas, and San Juan islands; bicycles and mopeds can be rented on San Juan, Orcas, and Lopez. Or consider carpooling with a friend. If you have reservations for lodging at a motel or inn, inquire if they provide pick-up service at the ferry; many do.

However, if you're convinced your car or camper is necessary, remember that ferry travel by vehicle can be a delight or an aggravation—it depends largely on the frame of mind of the traveler. Off-season, arrive a minimum of 15 to 20 minutes ahead of the time of departure to allow time for purchasing tickets and obtaining information.

Peak hours are in the early morning and early evening. Busiest days are Friday through Sunday and, of course, holidays. If possible, avoid these times. During periods of peak traffic it may be wise to arrive at the terminal even earlier, because cars are loaded in order of arrival. As noted earlier, you may have a wait of up to three hours due to heavy travel.

On the ferries there is an extra charge for large RVs and trailers. In addition, only limited space is allotted for large vehicles, so it is possible that during peak hours you may have a longer wait if you drive this type of camper. Ferry attendants try to load as many customers as possible. As the ferry approaches capacity it is easier for them to shoehorn in six Volkswagens and Toyotas than one large pickup camper pulling a boat.

Also be aware that you may be asked to *back* your vehicle on or off the ferry, depending on how it is loaded for inter-island stops. To some drivers, negotiating an unwieldy car-and-trailer combination up a ramp in close confines may present a problem.

Purchasing tickets. At Anacortes and Sidney tickets are purchased at a toll plaza, prior to parking. At other locations drivers who are westbound to other island destinations must park first and walk to the ferry landing to purchase tickets. Eastbound travelers do not need to obtain tickets. On the islands the ticket office may be closed until just shortly before the arrival of a ferry.

Lane assignment. To achieve smooth and quick unloading, cars are assigned lanes at the landing when purchasing tickets. The lanes are usually signed by destination; however, if you are uncertain check with the agent to see that you are correctly parked.

Do not be upset if later-arriving cars are assigned to shorter lanes. Space on the ferries is apportioned, depending on typical traffic, with more spaces allowed for Orcas and San Juan islands, and fewer for Lopez and Shaw. The system is as fair as possible. At times the ferry will leave the dock with cars still waiting, but open space still obvious. This is done only when it is necessary to save room for cars already waiting on another island.

Most important of all—don't try to crash the line. In addition to being in very bad taste, it can be injurious to your health. After waiting in line for an hour or more, motorists have been known to become pretty irate at people who do not play by the rules, and fistfights have occurred. While this type of retaliation is not recommended, be fore-warned: it can happen.

The word is *relax*, be patient and courteous, stay alert, and follow directions. Ferry employees have a monumental task in properly load-ing cars for the various destinations and assuring that space is fairly allo-cated to all. Don't hassle them—they know what they're doing. Aside from genuine medical emergencies, they cannot grant special favors to passengers.

Stopovers. The ferry agent will ask your destination; tell the agent your *first* planned stop. If you plan to stop at one island before continu-ing on to another, be sure that you are parked in the lane for your *first* destination, not your final one.

Overloads. There will be times when there are too many vehicles for a particular ferry to hold. Those waiting will be given priority on the next available boat. Sometimes additional boats will be put in service, if they are available. The ferries will keep running until all waiting traffic is handled.

If you anticipate waiting in line, take along a book to read (this one is highly recommended), a pillow to take a nap, or a deck of cards to play games with the kids. (Drain the dog in the bushes, please.)

Get out of your car and walk around, browse through nearby shops, but don't stray too far, for at times during peak traffic hours an extra ferry may be put into service, and can appear without warning. Ferry schedules are often loose during times of heavy traffic, as the boats hurry to provide maximum service. Be alert for ferry arrivals and departures. If you are parked in a ferry-loading lane, and you are not in your car when the ferry begins loading, you can be fined and your car impounded and towed.

Friday Harbor and Orcas have restaurants or cafes overlooking the terminal where passengers can eat while waiting; Anacortes and Lopez have snack bars. If you plan to dine in a restaurant, find out from a ferry attendant when your boat is due, and when you order inform your waitress or waiter what your time schedule is. They may be able to hurry your service along if necessary.

A reservation system would be the ideal solution to ferry waits; unfortunately, no workable system has yet been devised that would be fair to both residents and visitors, taking into account the complexity of loading for multiple destinations.

Wheewh!

Now that you've made it on board you may leave your car and go topside to enjoy the scenic boat ride. The loudspeaker will announce when your destination is near, giving you ample time to return to your vehicle.

RECREATION IN THE SAN JUANS

Boating

Boating in the San Juans is such a broad category, indulged in by so many people in so many different ways, that it becomes difficult to discuss. Cruisers have one point of view, sailors another, anglers another, and kayakers yet another. The authors of this book are sailors, and thus are especially concerned about such unpleasant things as scraping keels across rocks, running aground, and encountering strong tidal currents (this perhaps also accounts for our take-it-easy point of view).

Comments regarding boating are as general as possible, touching on as many situations as possible; however, in no way can this book take the place of a *good nautical chart* and boating know-how. Charts covering the San Juans are listed in the back of this book.

There are many hazards, both in the islands and inherent to boating. Before attempting any cruising, boaters are urged to take a boating safety course. The U.S. Power Squadron's classes in small boat handling are excellent; information regarding the course can be obtained through the U.S. Coast Guard.

In many places throughout the text cautionary comments refer to "small boats," a vague category including dinghies, rubber rafts, canoes, and kayaks, or, in general, any watercraft that is paddled or has minimal power. These cautions can also apply to boaters in larger boats who have had little experience in handling adverse conditions, for they too should use extra care when navigating here. Personal watercraft (PWCs), such as Jet Skis, are banned on all San Juans waters.

Many kayak and canoe trips are possible in the San Juans, ranging from quiet paddles around protected bays to extended open-water excursions. Paddlers should have training in ocean traveling before attempting any open water trips, and *any* boater, before beginning any trip, should check on local weather conditions. Unpredictable winds, strong tidal currents, and tide rips common in some San Juan waters can raise havoc with paddle-powered boats.

Rocks and shoals. Most hazardous rocks and shoals lying in well-traveled areas are marked with lights, buoys, or similar navigational devices. In less-frequented places these hazards may be unmarked, although they will be shown on large-scale charts. Local boaters will occasionally mark notorious keel-killers with a vertical pole; these aids are not always maintained and do not show on charts. Another warning of a rock or reef is long streamers of bull kelp floating on the surface; approach any bed of kelp cautiously.

The tidal range in the San Juan Islands is about 14 feet, except for extreme tides. The lowest of low tides run about minus 4 feet, the highest of high about plus 12 feet. During extreme low tides, rocks and shoals that are normally well covered suddenly are close enough to the surface to cause grief to the unwary skipper. During times of minus tides, use special care to consult navigational charts, and if mooring check tide tables to be sure the night will not find you mired on the bottom.

Tidal current. Tidal currents in the San Juans vary from one to six knots, with the strongest currents usually occurring in Spieden Channel. The more severe currents can cause small boaters serious problems, and a strong beam tide can even create difficulties for larger boats navigating in a dense fog.

Tidal current *is not the same as the tide*, although one does give rise to the other. Tides measure the vertical distance water rises and falls above the sea floor due to the gravitational attraction of the sun and moon as well as more obscure forces. Tidal currents represent the horizontal flow of water resulting from this rise and fall of the tide.

Tidal current tables (*not* tide tables), which are printed annually, are keyed to station points on the small craft portfolio of charts. The approximate time of maximum velocity of the current can be computed by referencing the tidal current tables to the station point. Although many other factors enter into the actual surface velocity and even the direction of the current, general knowledge of the predicted current is invaluable to safe navigation.

Tide rips. Navigational charts typically bear notations of "tide rips" off points of land between channels. Tide rips are caused by either the impact of tidal currents meeting from differing directions or the upwelling of currents as they meet underwater cliffs. In either case the surface appearance is the same: the water appears to dance across an area in small to moderate choppy waves, and the water appears to swirl like a whirlpool. A boat crossing a tide-rip area may have difficulty maintaining course as erratic currents spin the vessel first one way and then another. Kayakers and persons in small boats may find rips an uncomfortable experience—one that should be avoided. The positive aspect of tide rips is that the upwelling current also brings to the surface food-chain elements that attract game fish; therefore they are ideal fishing spots.

Choppy water. A phenomenon peculiar to long open channels such as Rosario or Haro straits is a very short, steep wave form that generally occurs when a strong breeze comes from the direction opposite to the tidal current. Long, relatively shallow channels with moderate to strong tidal currents build this wave form, in contrast to the broader swells built in the deep channel of the Strait of Juan de Fuca or the open ocean. These short, choppy waves chew away at forward boat speed and provide persons prone to seasickness an excellent opportunity to head for the lee rail. Passage for small boats can be downright dangerous in choppy seas, as they can be swamped or overturned. A close watch on weather reports and tidal current predictions can help a skipper avoid these unpleasant experiences.

Weather. One of the reasons the San Juans is such a prime vacationland is that it is much sunnier and drier than the rest of Puget Sound. Vancouver Island and the Olympic Mountains to the west and southwest protect the region from storms off the ocean, while air rising over the mountains deposits much of its moisture on the west of the mountains before flowing over the islands. Winds, however, can be strong and unpredictable here. Steep terrain that forces the wind along waterways produces an effect called *channeling*, which can cause the speed of the wind to double in a short distance. These channeled or gap winds are a special concern in East Sound.

The price often paid for warm sunny summer days is morning fog created by the temperature differential between the sun-warmed land masses and the perpetually chilly waters of Puget Sound. Fog generally lifts by mid-day, but early departure plans should also include a well-plotted compass course to destinations that may disappear in the sea-level morning mist.

Fishing, Scuba Diving, Seafood Harvesting, and Beach Foraging

Fishing seasons vary by year and location; be sure to check state regulations for open seasons, possession limits, and other restrictions. A few of the lakes in San Juan County are open year-round; others have seasons. A brochure published by the state Department of Fish and Wildlife lists all regulations and seasons. Lakes within the state parks are subject to these same restrictions.

Numerous publications are available that give suggestions on digging clams and catching crabs and shrimp. Several are listed in the back of this book. A state Department of Fish and Wildlife license is required, and the license tag must be displayed on the outside of clothing when harvesting clams, crab, other types of shellfish, and seaweed. To many, capturing fresh food for the dinner table is one of the greatest delights of a visit to the beach. Unfortunately this resource is not limitless, and heavy use can seriously deplete areas.

Will there be a pot of fresh clams on the galley stove tonight?

Empty seashells, small rocks, and driftwood may be taken by beach-combers, except in state parks, although many of these beach finds may harbor tiny marine life. Check to see if it's inhabited before taking it home. Overzealous beachcombers are often seen hauling off buckets of beach treasures. Most of it is eventually discarded in someone's back-yard. While there is certainly pleasure in having a small souvenir of a San Juan trip, please use restraint in the quantity you take.

Licenses and limits. Anglers, scuba divers, beach users, and boaters trapping crab and shrimp must observe all state regulations on the tak-ing of fish, shellfish, and any other food animal. A pamphlet, published by the state Department of Fish and Wildlife, is available in most sport-ing goods stores and lists bag limits and other restrictions. Recreational licenses required are:

- *Saltwater License* to fish for halibut, herring, lingcod, rockfish, perch, cod, shad, tuna, shark, salmon, and sturgeon, and related species. No license is required for smelt, carp, or albacore tuna.

- *Shellfish/Seaweed License* is required to harvest crab, clams, oysters, shrimp, sea cucumbers, sea urchins, squid, abalone, scallops, barnacles, cockles, mussels, octopus, crayfish, and seaweed. Dungeness crab require a sport fish catch record.

- *Freshwater License* is required for freshwater game fishing at such locations as Hummel Lake on Lopez Island, Sportsman and Egg lakes on San Juan Island, and the lakes of Moran State Park on Orcas Island.

- *Catch Record Cards* for salmon, sturgeon, halibut, steelhead, and Dungeness crab

If you dig for clams, state law requires that all holes be refilled. It may take several turns of the tide for displaced sand to be leveled; small marine animals brought to the surface by digging may die from exposure to the sun in that time.

Marine sanctuaries. All of the seashores and seabed of San Juan County and around Cypress Island in Skagit County are a marine bio-logical preserve. The taking or destruction of any living specimen, ex-cept for food use, is prohibited by state law. Special permission may be granted in the case of scientific research; such permission may be ob-tained by writing the Director of the Friday Harbor Laboratories, P.O. Box 459, Friday Harbor, WA 98250.

Paralytic Shellfish Poisoning (red tide). When the state Depart-ment of Health periodically issues a "red tide warning" and closes par-ticular beaches, the public usually reacts with confusion or skepticism. A clearer understanding of the phenomenon of red tide will lead to a greater respect for its dangers.

The name "red tide" itself contributes to some of the public's confusion, for it is not always visibly red, it has nothing at all to do with the tide, and not all red algae are harmful. Paralytic shellfish poisoning (PSP) is a serious illness caused by *Gonyaulax catanella*, a toxic, single-celled, amber-colored alga that is always present in the water in small numbers. During spring, summer, and fall, certain environmental conditions may combine to permit a rapid multiplication or accumulation of these microscopic organisms. Most shellfish toxicity occurs when the concentrations of *G. catanella* are too sparse to discolor the water; however the free-floating plants sometimes become so numerous that the water appears to have a reddish cast—thus the name red tide.

Bivalve shellfish such as clams, oysters, mussels, and scallops, which feed by filtering sea water, may ingest millions of the organisms and concentrate the toxin in their bodies. The poison is retained by most of these shellfish for several weeks after the occurrence of the red tide; butter clams can be poisonous for much longer. When the concentration of the toxin in mollusks reaches a certain level, it becomes hazardous to humans who eat them. The toxins cannot be destroyed by cooking and cannot be reliably detected by any means other than laboratory analysis. Symptoms of PSP, beginning with the tingling of the lips and tongue, may occur within a half-hour of ingestion. The illness attacks the nervous system, causing loss of control of arms and legs, difficulty in breathing, paralysis, and, in extreme cases, death.

Shellfish in all counties on Puget Sound are under regular surveillance by the state Department of Health. PSP (or red tide) warnings are issued and some beaches are posted when high levels of toxin are detected in tested mollusks. Warnings are usually publicized in the media; the state toll-free Marine Toxins/PSP Hotline listed in the back of this book has current information as to which beaches are closed to shellfish harvesting. Crabs, shrimp, and fin fish are not included in closures because there have been no recorded cases of PSP in the Northwest caused by eating any of these animals.

Walking, Hiking, and Bicycling

Roads in the San Juans are narrow, often without shoulders. Although traffic is usually light, take care not to endanger yourself and drivers. Walk on the left, facing oncoming traffic, but bike single file on the right, moving with traffic. Stop to rest only where there are turnouts, *not* on the narrow shoulder, on hills, curves, or in ditches. Wear light-colored and bright clothing so that you are easily seen. Flags are an excellent addition to bicycles.

Restrooms are often few and far between in the rural areas—plan ahead. "Taking to the woods" is often trespassing.

Camping

In addition to city, county, and state parks that have camping areas, a number of resorts also have campgrounds. Moran State Park and several commercial campgrounds take reservations in summer. Both Moran and Spencer Spit state parks post "Campground Full" signs at the Anacortes ferry terminal during summer months. *In summer, do not go to the San Juans unless you are sure of overnight lodging.* At other times of the year, if you have not made prior reservations, check for space as soon as you arrive at your destination, and go elsewhere if accommodations are not available. Campground managers will usually be helpful in suggesting alternatives.

PUBLIC LANDS

Public-owned lands in the San Juans are a calico quilt of city, county, state, and national parks, lands owned by the state Department of Natural Resources (DNR), Coast Guard-maintained lighthouses owned by the U.S. Bureau of Land Management, fishing lakes owned by the state Department of Fish and Wildlife, and wildlife refuges operated by the U.S. Fish and Wildlife Service.

Not including the wildlife refuges, this public property presently totals in excess of 12,000 acres, scattered about more than fifty separate locations. The wildlife refuges are an additional 353 acres on eighty-four individual sites. All of these lands—except the wildlife refuges (which have two exceptions that will be noted later) and the lighthouse reserves—are open to public recreation. In addition, The Nature Conservancy, a private conservation organization supported by memberships and donations, has purchased some environmentally important property in the islands, and holds it as nature preserves; some of this land is open to the public.

The public sites together offer a rich variety of recreation: boating, paddling, fishing, scuba diving, beachcombing, shellfish gathering, hiking, bicycling, birdwatching, camping, sightseeing, and many other activities. Facilities range from excellent parks with complete camping facilities to primitive patches of land with no improvements whatsoever.

Rules and regulations in the various areas are set up to preserve the natural environment and to maintain the safety and pleasure of all visitors. The observance of these regulations is especially important in San Juan County, where many local residents view public lands with an uneasy eye, fearing that public use of such lands will overflow onto neighboring private property. Additionally, many longtime islanders have a strong paternal feeling toward these areas, for they loved and cared for them long before any mainland tourist ever set foot on them.

Department of Natural Resources Beaches

Some 78 percent of the tidelands in the San Juan Islands are state owned and open for public use. For the most part these are only the lands lying below the mean high water level, even though upland property is privately owned. In some cases these shores are so steep and rocky that they are unapproachable. Some beaches, however, are suitable for recreation, but they should not be confused with privately owned property.

In the past the state Department of Natural Resources attempted to locate and identify all public beaches throughout the state utilizing an on-site marking system. Unfortunately, in the initial program such a large number of beach markers were destroyed by vandalism or natural causes that the marking project was abandoned. A booklet published by the DNR, *Your Public Beaches, San Juan Region*, has photos and maps of every one of these DNR beaches in the islands, so most are not described here.

At Obstruction Pass, Point Doughty, and Griffin Bay the DNR has upland areas that have been developed as parks and are described in this book. These parks are maintained by state parks personnel, by agreement between the two agencies. This arrangement provides more efficient servicing of the camp areas.

The Public Parks—Rules, Regulations, and Courtesy

The following comments apply specifically to the parks in the San Juans operated by the Washington State Parks and Recreation Commission. In general, these same rules, where relevant, also apply to city, county, and DNR parks. Many of the parks have specific rules and regulations prominently posted on a bulletin board, or have pamphlets available at park headquarters. Check local regulations when using any area.

Some activities listed here may not be specifically covered by park rules, but many do affect the aesthetics of the area and the enjoyment of others. While visiting, be courteous and considerate of other park users and treat the park itself with care. It is not our wish to set down a long, pedantic list of "don'ts" in order to restrict your freedom and pleasure, but in any public-use facility one must bend a little to the needs of others, perhaps sacrificing some individual freedom for the benefit of all.

Camping. Camp only in designated areas; camping is limited to 10 consecutive days at any one park. Do not dig ditches around tents, cut green boughs for beds, hammer nails into trees, or in any other way mutilate nature in the quest for a perfect campsite.

Garbage. Trash receptacles are provided at the larger state parks; please use them. Many of the smaller, more remote marine state parks have neither garbage cans nor garbage collection. With the increasing waste disposal problem in the San Juans, a sensitive visitor will take garbage back home whenever possible. In areas where garbage cans are not provided, all trash *must* be removed.

When on boats, do not "deep-six" debris, whether it is cans, bottles, orange peels, or chicken bones. It usually does not come to permanent rest six fathoms down, but will eventually wash up on some beach as ugly litter.

Campfires. Build fires only in designated fireplaces and fire rings. This park regulation is vitally important due to the extreme fire hazard during the summer months, and the difficulty of handling fires on the remote islands. Before leaving, be sure your campfire is out. Beach fires are prohibited in order to maintain the beaches in a nearly natural state. Report any out-of-control fire immediately. Emergency phone and radio contacts are listed in appendix A at the back of this book.

Some boaters cook on portable charcoal-burning barbecues or hibachis that they place on the float alongside their boat. Such cookers can badly char docks; when using any such stove on a dock be sure the wood is properly shielded from the heat of the cooker. Some places forbid the use of such stoves on docks.

Gathering fallen trees, branches, and driftwood for campfires is prohibited in all state parks. Decaying wood provides valuable nutrients to the forest ecology, and driftwood helps prevent beach erosion. Either bring firewood with you, or purchase it at campground registration booths or at island stores.

Living plants. Green wood may not be gathered from the forests for fires or any other purpose (it doesn't burn well, anyway). Plants may not be dug up, nor flowers picked.

Vehicles and bicycles. Motorized vehicles and bicycles are prohibited on service roads and trails (with certain exceptions for bicycles in Moran State Park, as noted in chapter 8). Observe posted speed limits on public roads within parks.

Boats. In the moorage area of marine state parks the boat speed limit is three mph (no-wake speed). In addition to being extremely annoying to other boaters, hot-rodding or racing, even in small outboard-powered dinghies, can create a wake that may swamp small craft, send hot food flying from a cruiser's galley range, or cause other damage. Boaters are legally responsible for any damage caused by their wakes.

Mooring and anchoring. Buoys and floats are on a first-come, first-served basis. The practice of individuals attempting to "reserve" space by tying a dinghy to a float or buoy is not legal in the state parks. Continuous moorage on floats or buoys is limited to three consecutive nights.

It is courteous to use the minimum moorage space possible on a float. Beach small boats whenever you can, instead of tying up to a float. Berth small cruisers or runabouts as far inboard as possible, leaving the end of the float for larger boats that require deeper water and more maneuvering space.

During the busy summer season, it is considerate (and often more fun) to raft together with a friend on a buoy, thus freeing a moorage for another boater. Because buoys can be displaced by having too heavy a load on them, there are restrictions on the number of boats that may be rafted together on a buoy, depending on boat size. For boats less than 24 feet long, three boats may be rafted

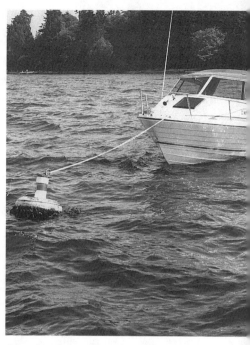

Mooring buoys provide safe spots to tie up in many of the marine state parks.

to the boat on the buoy; for boats from 25 to 36 feet long, two boats may be rafted; for boats from 37 to 45 feet long, one boat may be rafted; boats over 45 feet long may not have any others raft with them on buoys.

When anchoring, be sure your hook is properly set, that you are not drifting, and that the swing of your vessel will not permit you to collide with others. While artists may paint pretty pictures with boats all neatly swinging in unison, in real life it doesn't always work that way, as the shape of the hull greatly affects the way wind and tide push a boat, and the maximum northerly swing of one boat may coincide with the maximum southerly swing of another. Be sure your anchorage is secure before leaving your boat or retiring for the evening, or the "things that go bump in the night" may be you. In a tight anchorage it may be useful to set a second anchor, or row a line ashore and tie it to a tree in order to reduce swing.

Contrary to the rules proclaimed in some boating "bibles," an anchor scope of seven times the water depth is generally not necessary, and almost impossible to achieve in many of the small coves found in the San Juans. With a well-set anchor, in all but the most severe of weather, a three-to-one scope is quite adequate, and considerably more courteous for others who might wish to share a crowded anchorage.

Pets. Pets must be on a leash no longer than 8 feet and be under control at all times. Some boat-bound yachtsmen regard the land facilities of state parks merely as handy places to allow their dogs to relieve themselves. Even the most devout animal lovers find it hard to think kindly of these pets while trying to scrape doggy droppings from the grooves of their boat shoes. State park regulations state that pet owners must clean up after their pets. Violators are subject to fines.

Fees. There is a modest fee for use of campsites at any of the state parks. Fees are charged for moorage on the state park floats and buoys, whether you are tied directly to the float or buoy, or rafted alongside another boat. The fee schedule is published in newspapers and boating periodicals in the spring, and is posted on information kiosks in camping areas. Because some of the marine parks have a self-register system with fees deposited in a locked box, boaters should have the proper change on hand. You may pay by personal check.

Noise. Because sounds carry greater distances over water, use care that radios or boisterous noises do not penetrate to nearby boats or campsites.

Vandalism. It probably does little good to talk about intentional vandalism here. The damaging or removal of park property is, of course, illegal and when observed should be reported to the proper authorities.

Some acts of vandalism, however, are committed out of thoughtlessness or ignorance. Spray painting or scratching graffiti on rocks or other natural features may not be recognized by park visitors as vandalism until they are confronted with a lovely sandstone wall turned ugly with mindless scrawling. Such defacement is prohibited in all parks.

Digging into banks with shovels, picks, or any similar tool is also prohibited. Holes dug in beaches for clams or for any other purpose must be refilled.

Marine life and wildlife. Observe state Department of Fish and Wildlife regulations on the taking of fish and shellfish in saltwater areas and fish in freshwater lakes. All of the seabed of the San Juan Islands is a marine preserve. It is unlawful to remove from beaches any living animals such as starfish, sand dollars, or sea anemones, except those edible varieties defined and regulated by the state Department of Fish and Wildlife.

Hunting or harassing of wildlife and discharge of firearms is prohibited within the state parks.

SAFETY CONCERNS

Boating and beach travel entail unavoidable risks that every traveler assumes and must be aware of and respect. The fact that an area is described in this book is not a representation that it will be safe for you. The areas described herein vary greatly in the amount and kind of preparation needed to enjoy them safely. Some may have changed since this book was written, or conditions may have deteriorated. Weather conditions can change daily or even hourly, and tide levels will also vary considerably. An area that is safe in good weather at low or slack tide may be completely unsafe during inclement weather or at times of high tide or maximum tidal current. You can meet these and other risks safely by exercising your own independent judgment and common sense. Be aware of your own limitations, those of your vessel, and of conditions when and where you are traveling. If conditions are dangerous, or if you are not prepared to deal with them safely, change your plans. Each year many people enjoy safe trips in the waters and on the beaches of the San Juan Islands. With proper preparation and good judgment, you can too.

Emergency Assistance and Other Concerns

In parks where rangers or managers are not on duty, the proper authority can be reached by marine or citizens band (CB) radio if immediate action is necessary. In matters of less urgency, the rangers should be contacted by telephone or in writing. Some state parks have telephones on the grounds.

Overall legal authority in the San Juan Islands rests with the county sheriff. The emergency number is 911. Complaints or other business should be referred to the sheriff's office. A list of phone numbers and addresses for parks and legal agencies is included in appendix A.

The U.S. Coast Guard has primary responsibility for safety and law enforcement on the water. Marine VHF channel 16 is continuously monitored by the Coast Guard and should be the most reliable means of contact in case of emergencies on the water. The Coast Guard monitors CB channel 9 at some locations and times, but it has no commitment to full-time radio watch on this channel. Several volunteer groups do an excellent job of monitoring the CB emergency frequency and will assist as best they can with relaying emergency requests to the proper authorities. With the growing use of cellular telephones (at least one carrier claims to have complete coverage of the San Juans) the cellular providers in the Puget Sound area provide a quick-dial number, *CG, that immediately connects the caller to the Coast Guard Vessel Traffic Center in Seattle. The center coordinates all marine safety and rescue activities in the region.

A Washington State ferry in Harney Channel on the way to Thatcher Pass. Mount Baker in the distance

CHAPTER ✦ ONE ✦

THATCHER PASS

The "front door" to the San Juan Islands, Thatcher Pass is the main thoroughfare for much of the islands' pleasure boating and all of its ferry traffic.

Although the half-mile-wide channel has ample room for all the vessels that pass through it, it may seem snug quarters for sailboats trying to make way in a light wind when a monstrous green-and-white ferry is hard astern. The only navigational hazard in the pass is Lawson Rock, at the northeast side of the channel, which is marked with a daybeacon.

Thatcher Pass provides westbound ferry passengers with close-up views as the boat threads its way between Decatur and Blakely islands. Tourists get their first glimpse of the magic of the islands as the ferry passes little Armitage Island with its twin bays; they may sight a stately bald eagle perched atop a fir snag on the island, returning their stares.

At times, depending on tide and traffic conditions, the ferry comes seemingly within arm's reach of little Willow Island, on the southwest side of Blakely Island. This 9½-acre forested rock is one of the islands of the San Juan Islands National Wildlife Refuge. The broad streak of white guano visible on the south side of the island marks a nesting area for a small colony of pigeon guillemots. With its black body and white wing patches, this member of the auk family resembles a pigeon in coloring and size, and early settlers called it a sea pigeon. Although its beak is as sooty black as its body, the inside of its mouth (which it opens wide during mating rituals) and its legs are bright red, making it a very distinctive bird when sighted.

Blakely Island

Facilities (marina at Peavine Pass): Guest moorage with water and power, diesel, gas, groceries, marine supplies and repairs, laundry, restrooms, showers, picnic shelter, fireplace

Poised at either side of Thatcher Pass, Blakely and Decatur islands stand as guardians of the inner San Juan islands, their eastern shores bearing the brunt of storms that whip up Rosario Strait. Blakely Island,

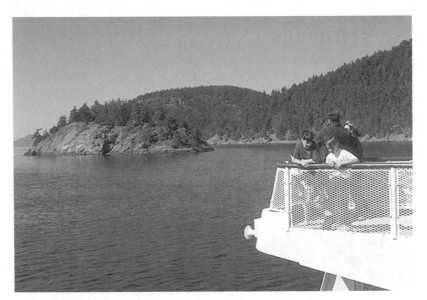

The ferry passes little Willow Island on the way through Thatcher Pass.

the larger, higher, and more imposing of the pair, lies to the north of the passage. Although the island covers only seven square miles, within that space its forested slopes rush sharply upward. Blakely Peak, at the north end of the island, tops it out at 1,042 feet. Underwater, the shores drop off just as dramatically, providing only a few skimpy beaches. The lovely island boasts two good-sized lakes: 84-acre Horseshoe Lake and 64-acre Spencer Lake. The stream that drains Spencer Lake forms a 100-foot-high waterfall that cascades into Thatcher Bay. The fall is prettiest in spring, when water is high.

On the far northern end of Blakely Island, facing on Peavine Pass, is a marina—the island's only commercial facility. Fuel and temporary moorage are available at the long float in the outer harbor, while a few additional overnight moorage slips are available in the inner harbor behind a rock breakwater. The entrance to the inner harbor is shallow but well marked; favor the breakwater side of the channel for the deepest water. The island's private airport is immediately southwest of the marina.

The marina store is well stocked—because it is the only store on the island, it provides groceries for residents. It also serves as the island's post office. A nearby picnic shelter with a nice view of Peavine Pass has tables, sinks, and a fireplace for use of visitors. Do not plan on extended shore leave here, for all island roads are private and are gated just beyond the marina.

Boaters can find nice anchorages behind beguiling little Armitage Island on the southeast end of Blakely Island, just east of Thatcher Pass. The center of the channel between the islands drops off to 7 fathoms, and numerous floats and buoys line the edges, but some suitable spots can be found. All buoys and floats in the bay are private, as is the shoreline. Tidelands of Armitage Island itself are public below mean high water level; however the shoreline drops off so steeply that the tidal shelf is very narrow. The bay has more than ample depth for boats of almost any draft.

Thatcher Bay, on the west side of Blakely, north of Willow Island, looks like an appealing spot for a boating stopover; however it is quite shallow, especially on its south side, and submerged pilings lurk under the water along the north shore. Safe anchorage can be had only well out from shore. Occasionally the bay is used for storing rafted logs.

Most of Blakely Island is owned by a small corporation that purchased the land from a logging company. It sells only a few home sites each year in order to ensure the island's orderly development. Such ex-

Pigeon guillemots nest on Willow Island and other islands of the San Juan Islands National Wildlife Refuge. (Photo: Bob and Ira Spring)

clusiveness stems not from snobbery or the desire for inflated real estate prices, but from a great love for this delicate island and concern for the welfare of the people who build their homes there. Boaters should respect their intent and admire the island from the water, but stay off private property.

Seattle Pacific University has been deeded several sections of the island, including beach lands and property bordering the two lakes, totaling about one-fourth of the island's acreage. The property was donated to the university to be used in its natural state for biological and environmental research and educational programs. The university has constructed a small library, laboratory, dining hall, and dormitory. In order to keep the island natural, only small groups of students use the facility.

Black Rock, Pointer Island, and Lawson Rock (all lying east of Blakely Island along Rosario Strait), along with Willow Island (on the west side), are part of the San Juan Islands National Wildlife Refuge, offering protection to nesting seabirds.

Decatur Island

Just half the size of its neighbor to the north, and with less dramatic contours, Decatur Island may not seem as exclusive as Blakely, but all property here also is privately owned, and there are no stores. The only public boating facility is a boat launch ramp on the north end of the island at the end of the county road that crosses the island. A short dock located on the southwest end of the island on Reads Bay at the community of Decatur is for use by residents only. Nearby is the island airplane landing strip.

Several good spots to drop an anchor can be found around the island. Brigantine Bay, a bit to the north behind Trump Island, has good anchorages quite close to shore; however, when southerlies blow the flat southern tip of Decatur offers no protection. Shrimp pots set here usually bring in enough of the tasty crustaceans to enhance a galley dinner.

Around a rocky headland is another fine anchorage at Sylvan Cove, sometimes known locally as Kan Kut Bay. The neat buildings and velvet grasslands at the head of the bay are an idyllic scene from the water. The largest of the buildings was a boat-in restaurant many years ago, but today all property surrounding the cove, including the dock and buoys, are part of a private real estate development.

On the east shore of Decatur Island is a large unnamed curving bight with a gentle, sandy beach punctuated by the dramatic round knob of Decatur Head. The south end of the bight offers some anchorages to overflow crowds from James Island Marine State Park, but there is precious little wind protection from any quarter. Use care anchoring here, as it is quite shallow, especially on the west side. The county boat launch ramp faces on this bay.

Decatur Head was once a separate little island, but the action of wind and waves over centuries of time built up the sand neck, a geological formation known as a tombolo, that now joins it to the larger island. Spencer Spit, on Lopez Island just to the west, is an example of a tombolo in the process of forming as it stretches out toward Frost Island.

James Island Marine State Park

Park area: 113 acres, 2⅓ miles of shoreline
Access: Boat
Facilities: 13 primitive campsites, picnic tables, picnic shelter, fire grates, composting toilets, pit toilets, dock with a 45-foot float, 5 mooring buoys, 1½ miles of hiking trails; *no water, no garbage collection.* (Designated Cascadia Marine Trail campsite)
Attractions: Camping, picnicking, hiking, fishing, boating, scuba diving

Lacking the broad beaches and sheltered harbors of other San Juan marine parks, James Island is often ignored by visitors in favor of more spacious and glamorous spots. Its coves are frequently used only as an overnight stop for southbound boaters awaiting the turn of the tide at Deception Pass. Nevertheless, the park offers pleasant camping and scenic hikes to those who linger awhile.

The park lies 4 nautical miles west of either Sunset Beach or Flounder Bay on Fidalgo Island, the nearest point where trailered boats can be launched. From Lopez Island, 4 nautical miles to the west, hand-carried boats can be launched at Spencer Spit. If heading from Lopez Island to James in a very small or paddle-powered boat, be aware that tidal currents can reach 2 knots in Thatcher Pass. Heavy boat traffic in the channel can add to the hazard.

James Island is one of the most rugged of the San Juan Island marine state parks, with high, steep bluffs broken by coves on opposing sides of the island. The eastern side of the island has two small adjacent coves holding two mooring buoys each. These anchorages are subject to weather and waves from Rosario Strait. A cove on the west side, sheltered by Decatur Island, contains a buoy and a dock with float large enough for three or four boats. Decatur Head lies west across the ¼-mile-wide channel, tethered to its parent island by a narrow spit of land.

Because moorage is so limited at James Island, be considerate by tying up boats to occupy the least amount of dock space, and do not take up dock space with dinghies. Dock space or buoys may not be reserved by tying a dinghy to them.

If you find the buoys and float occupied, the deep water of the island's coves and the strong current, especially on the west side, make anchoring a challenge. Small boats can be easily beached at either place. The western cove is a favorite scuba diving area; while fish are few, the invertebrate life is varied and colorful.

Scattered in the trees on the narrow neck of land between the coves, a picnic shelter and a dozen campsites provide picnic tables, fireplaces, and pit toilets. Campers must furnish their own fresh water.

From the camp area a broad, signed trail meanders into deep forest, arriving in ½ mile at a tiny beach on the far edge of the western cove. Three campsites, part of the Cascadia Marine Trail, lie in the forest above the beach. A secluded driftwood-strewn beach on the south flank of the island can be reached by boat or overland exploration.

Many trails lace the island. Most have recently been improved and

A classic sailboat hangs on a buoy on the east side of James Island.

are easy to follow; however, use care in following these paths along the high grassy bluffs as many of them dwindle away. Overzealous exploration can leave a hiker hung up on the cliffs; an unwary step can result in a bad fall into the rocks or water.

Persons planning to camp should be forewarned of a great horde of masked bandits that lie in wait onshore—raccoons. Although they may seem cute early in the evening as their bright eyes glimmer at the edge of your campfire, their charm palls when you wake at 2:00 A.M. to find them rattling cook pots and rifling groceries. To discourage these persistent pests, secure everything back on your boat or inside your tent.

CHAPTER TWO

LOPEZ ISLAND

Here's cow country—and sheep, and goats, and horses, too. A green patchwork quilt of fields and pastures, interrupted by sections of velvety forest rolling down to the edge of the sea; farmyards with chickens busily scratching around piles of fishing nets; arrow-straight roads edged by fences and hedgerows, disappearing into soupy San Juan mists. At the island's southern tip the level land tilts upward to form steep, craggy cliffs and deeply notched, rocky bays. As if to compensate for its meek, pastoral nature, here Lopez Island presents some of the most rugged shoreline to be found in any of the San Juans.

Lopez, the most level of the three largest San Juan islands, was once a major agricultural supplier for western Washington. Its dry climate favored crops of grain and orchards of fruit. Dams built on the Columbia River during the 1930s later brought irrigation to the arid lands of eastern Washington, converting them to bountiful farmland with which the San Juans could not compete. Agriculture, and with it the islands' economy, declined. Only a few farms are still in operation today. A vineyard near the north end of the island now produces quality wines.

Among an entire bevy of islands described as friendly and relaxed, Lopez is considered to be the friendliest and most laid-back of all. The common phrase here is "Wave, you're on Lopez." First-timers are surprised to find that drivers passing each other on the road offer a salutary wave, and wonder if they have been mistaken for someone else. Usually it dawns on the visitor that this is simply a charming practice unique to an island where the population is so small that everyone is known, and even "outlanders" are welcome.

Lopez Island does not display as much distinct marine flavor as Orcas and San Juan islands. Its shoreline does not attract the usual San Juan hordes of yachtsmen, because it lacks good harbors. Bays on the north are quite shallow, while southern ones are farther from the boating mainstream, and those facing on the Strait of Juan de Fuca are subject to bad weather and uncomfortable swells. Nevertheless, a few choice spots along its shores make fine stopovers for boaters, and the gently rolling heartland is a joy to hikers and bicyclists.

The island has an ever-growing reputation as the best of the San Juans for bicycling. A brief, steep uphill grade greets cyclists as they leave the ferry, but once this challenge is conquered, miles of quiet country roads reach out. Several cycle shops offer rentals and repairs. Public toilets are in Lopez Village and near the south end of the island, at Islandale.

The island is reached by ferry from Anacortes (about a 45-minute trip), or from Sidney, B.C., on Vancouver Island (slightly less than two hours away). The ferry landing is in a small cove at the tip of Upright Head, where the only tourist facility is a small coffee shop, generally open only around the time of arrival and departure of ferries. City folk visiting the San Juans for the first time have been known to unload their cars at Lopez, drive down the timber-bordered road of Upright Head, make a quick loop around the island, and scurry back to the next departing ferry, shocked at the lack of such amenities of "civilization" as shopping malls, fast-food chains, or movie theaters.

Lopez Island can also be reached by scheduled flights of West Isle Air and Horizon Airlines, which stop at the local airfield, and by seaplane service from Seattle via Kenmore Air. Charter airlines also provide service to the island.

Lopez Village, on the east shore of Fisherman Bay, is the island "center of commerce." The few dozen businesses you'll find here offer food,

The level roads of Lopez Island are favorites of bicycling families.

lodging, groceries, and basic necessities. Marinas on the bay have fuel, moorage, and repairs. On the south end of the island, the historic general store at Richardson that was a popular tourist attraction was destroyed by a fire in the fall of 1990. Boat fuel is still available at the Richardson dock; auto fuel is also available there, as well as at service stations at the intersection of Mud Bay and Mackaye Harbor roads and at Lopez Village.

An increase in campsites over the last few years at Odlin County Park and Spencer Spit State Park, the only two car campgrounds on the island, has raised the total number of available sites to 75. If these areas are all filled, it may be necessary to go elsewhere; check in early in the

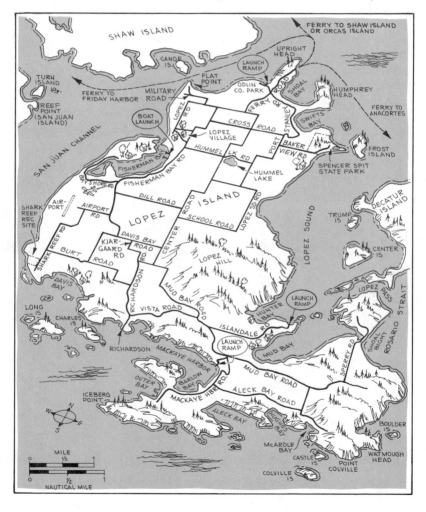

day to be sure you have a site. Camping along island roads is prohibited.

Although accommodations in campgrounds, resorts, and bed-and-breakfast inns may be filled in the summer, don't overlook off-season. The San Juans receive only half the amount of rain that falls on Seattle and other Puget Sound areas, so the dry climate can make spring and fall touring the most delightful of all. The crowds are gone, but the beauty remains—and is even enhanced. In spring, shores and pastures are filled with awakening life; by fall the scent and colors of autumn permeate the waysides, and bays host flotillas of migrating waterfowl.

Most businesses and facilities are open daily, year-round, although some drastically cut back their business hours at the end of the tourist season. Spencer Spit State Park closes from November 1 to March 1. Visitors are especially welcomed off-season; reservations are usually not needed, but check ahead to be sure.

THE NORTH END

Odlin County Park

Park area: 80 acres; 4,000 feet of shoreline
Access: Ferry to Lopez Island, boat
Facilities: 30 campsites, picnic tables, fireplaces, picnic shelters, group camp, drinking water, vault toilets, boat launch (ramp), dock with float, children's play equipment, ball field, hiking trails
Attractions: Camping, picnicking, beachcombing, fishing, boating, paddling, swimming, clam digging, hiking, scuba diving

Odlin is truly a family park, with a beached rowboat where youngsters can play at "going to sea" with driftwood oars, an old artillery gun to climb on, a softball diamond for family ball games, a volleyball net, and an open field for Frisbee matches. All this and an outstanding beach, too!

Odlin County Park is located within minutes of the ferry terminal at Upright Head. To reach it, follow Ferry Road south from the ferry landing for 1 mile; at the first two-way intersection turn right (west) and follow the road downhill for 300 yards to the campground.

The park, on a curving, sandy bay, makes a nice quick stop for lazing in the sun while waiting for the next ferry—you may even decide to linger awhile and catch a later one. Just offshore the ferry sails by in Upright Channel on the runs to Friday Harbor that bypass Wasp Passage.

A boat launch for trailered boats is straight ahead at the end of the park's main road; a narrow, unpaved road branching to the south leads past the ball field (complete with bleachers) to the camping area. The first of the park's 30 campsites is just above the beach, with elbow-to-elbow picnic tables and fireplaces.

Upright Channel as seen from Odlin County Park

The park road continues south into the trees to more private, sheltered sites and a small grassy clearing for group get-togethers. Bicycle and walk-in campsites are found beyond the road end, along the bank overlooking the bay. In summer the beachfront campsites are frequently more heavily used than those at Spencer Spit, where sites are some distance above the water.

By boat, Odlin County Park lies 3½ nautical miles southeast of Orcas, and 5½ nautical miles northeast of Friday Harbor. A dock with a float at the north end of the park is available for loading and unloading—no overnight moorage. The soft bottom of the shallow bay provides good anchoring. At the north side of the park, near the dock, the bottom begins to drop off quite steeply.

Scuba diving is excellent near the dock and along the sheer rock walls and submerged boulders on the west side of Upright Head. A rainbow assortment of sea stars cling to the rock, and schools of curious fish swim by. Tidal currents outside of the bay are quite strong. The sandy bottom of the bay is habitat for sea pens, sea cucumbers, and striped nudibranchs.

The fine sandy beach invites swimming, sand-castle building, and barefoot walks. At low tide dig clams—if those ahead of you haven't found them already. Uprising cliffs halt beach walks on the north side of the park. South, the gradual shoreline can be followed all the way to Flat Point, 1½ miles away.

Trails out of the campground circle around in a flatland of second-growth timber and brush. Although they make nice walking, none have particular destinations; some dead-end, others loop back on themselves. Good mushroom picking in season.

Do not attempt to walk the bank west of the park, as the bank is undercut and can be dangerous. In addition, walking the shoreline kills the vegetation needed to stabilize the embankment.

Upright Channel Picnic Area and Beach Access (DNR)

Access: Ferry to Lopez Island, boat
Facilities: Picnic tables, fireplaces, latrines, water, 3 mooring buoys (Closed October 1 to April 30)
Attractions: Picnicking, boating, beachcombing, clam digging

Upright Channel Picnic Area and Beach Access is a welcome addition to the day-use recreational facilities on Lopez Island. The park, developed by the Department of Natural Resources, has two picnic sites nestled in dense brush upland from the beach. Two other picnic sites with fire braziers and water sit in a grassy clearing on the bluff above the beach.

To reach the park by land, drive south on Ferry Road, and at a T intersection 2 miles from the ferry landing turn west on Fisherman Bay Road. In ½ mile this road heads south; continue straight ahead on Military Road. In ¼ mile Military Road heads north, then shortly turns west again. One-half mile west of this last corner is a parking lot, gated except during daylight hours. Park here and walk a short distance down the service road to reach the picnic areas and the path to the beach.

A gently sloping gravel beach with tide-line driftwood and beach grass looks out on Upright Channel. Over 1½ miles of shoreline can be enjoyed by walking east to Odlin Park or west around Flat Point to the end of the public beach 300 yards south from there. At the Flat Point residential area only the beach below mean high tide level is public. Three offshore mooring buoys are provided for visiting boaters.

Lopez Village

Access: Ferry or airplane to Lopez Island, boat (walk from Fisherman Bay)
Facilities: Groceries, restaurants, stores, lodging, public restrooms with showers, historical museum

The tiny hamlet of Lopez Village, at the entrance to Fisherman Bay, has restaurants and a number of stores, but no adjacent dock. A motel, a restaurant, and two marinas are ¾ mile to the south on Fisherman Bay Road. A pharmacy and a few additional businesses are found in a newer

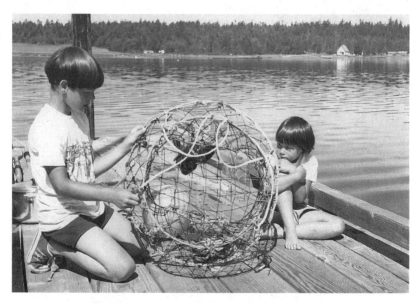

A crab pot on a Fisherman Bay dock fascinates youngsters.

section three blocks northeast of the heart of the village. A public restroom is across the road, north of the grocery store.

A block north of the village, the Lopez Historical Museum, open on weekend afternoons, houses a collection of island photographs and memorabilia. Old farm equipment recalls the days when fruit, grains, and vegetables grown on the island flowed to dining tables in cities throughout Puget Sound.

The only public beach in the vicinity is on the west side of Weeks Point Way, 2 blocks south of Lopez Village, across the road from the Weeks Wetland Trail.

To reach Lopez Village and Fisherman Bay by land from the ferry terminal, follow Ferry Road south for 2 miles. At a T intersection turn right (west), and in ½ mile head south on Fisherman Bay Road. In 2 miles the road to Lopez Village is on the right; turn here or continue on to Fisherman Bay, 5½ miles total distance from Upright Head.

Fisherman Bay

Access: Ferry or airplane to Lopez Island, boat
Facilities: Guest moorage with power and water, boat launch (sling, ramp)(fee), boat rental, marine supplies and repair, diesel, gas, restrooms, showers, laundromat, picnic area, restaurant, snack bar, stores, motel, swimming pool, hot tub, boat charters, dive shop, bicycle rentals, boat pumpout station
Attractions: Boating, paddling, bicycling, fishing, crabbing, clam digging

Fisherman Bay could more aptly be named Fisherman Lagoon; with its shallow bottom, stagnant water, and mud-flat barrier built up by wave action, it is more closely related to the small lagoons found throughout the San Juans than the clear, deep-water bays. But such a lagoon! Nearly a half-mile across and more than a mile in length, with shimmering, tranquil waters and evening sunsets that bring tears of joy to the eyes.

Many boaters bypass Fisherman Bay, feigning disinterest: actually they are apprehensive about the shallow entrance channel. Once this barrier is conquered, however, any skipper can lean back with the air of an experienced salt and play one-upsmanship with less accomplished pilots. It is claimed by businesses inside the bay that any boat that does not draw more than 4½ feet can enter the bay safely if the tide is not below zero. If that statement does not totally reassure you, enter on a rising tide to avoid the embarrassment of being stuck on a sand bar through a change of tide.

The accompanying map should be helpful when navigating the channel. The channel runs quite close to the shoreline after rounding the tip

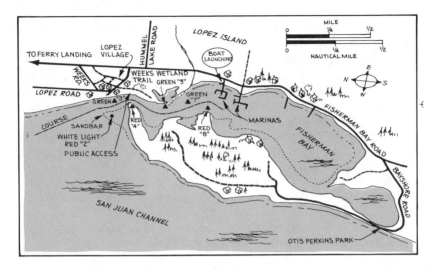

of a long shoal extending north from the peninsula on the west side of the bay. The end of the shoal is marked with a navigation light; do not cut south of it! Once into the channel keep red, even-numbered markers to starboard, green, odd-numbered to port when entering, the opposite when leaving.

If the anxious moments of the channel can be forgotten, the ½-mile journey is delightful, especially to large boats unaccustomed to such close quarters—cruising through the front yards of quaint little waterfront homes, with the banks almost within arm's reach.

Moorage, fuel, boat servicing, supplies, and launch and haul-out facilities are available at either of two marinas on the east shore. Picnic tables and bicycle service and rentals are also in the vicinity. Perhaps treat yourself to dinner at the restaurant or an inn farther down the bay. Good anchorages can be had anywhere once you're within the harbor.

The bay is superb for small boat paddling. Put in hand-carried boats at the marina and explore the channel and around the bay. Drop off a crab pot near the western shore and return in the morning to find it filled with Dungeness—perhaps.

Otis Perkins Park

Park area: 1 acre; 60 feet of shoreline on San Juan Channel, 600 feet on Fisherman Bay
Access: Ferry or airplane to Lopez Island
Facilities: Picnic tables, *no water*

A startling sight from the road at Fisherman Bay, especially at high tide, are cars virtually driving on water across the low sandspit at the head of the bay to reach a forested peninsula. This narrow neck of land is interesting to drive or bike, but spectacular to walk. To reach it, turn west at the south end of the bay on Bayshore Road and follow the road as it curves around the mud flat.

At the south end of the Fisherman Bay spit, facing on San Juan Channel, is tiny Otis Perkins Park. The park is named for a longtime Lopez Island resident who generously donated the land.

A pair of picnic tables and trash cans are the extent of the park's facilities, unless one counts the sweeping views up and down the length of San Juan Channel, across to San Juan Island, and back to the lagoon-like stretch of Fisherman Bay. Prevailing westerlies whipping off the Strait of Juan de Fuca over the "toe" of San Juan Island can make the site quite breezy.

Park cars here and walk along the narrow spit, either on the beach or at road's edge. Within a few feet of one another are two entirely different saltwater environments. Inside the bay is grassy saltwater marsh, where crabs, clams, tiny fish, and myriad other small critters live, pickleweed and marsh grass thrive, and where seabirds gather to feed and rest. Outside is smooth, clean beach with wave-swept sand and silvered driftwood, but little shore life. The constant movement of waves from San Juan Channel prevents the growth of marine life here.

The road continuing on to the forested peninsula dead-ends at private property, and offers no further public access or even views of either the bay or San Juan Channel.

Hummel Lake

Access: Ferry or airplane to Lopez Island
Facilities: Boat launch (ramp), vault toilet
Attractions: Fishing (freshwater), birdwatching, paddling

Here's a modest little pond that packs a lot of interest into its 36-plus acres of surface. It is a favorite for fishermen, a pleasant spot for wildlife watchers, and is large enough for boaters to take a brief paddle; boats with gasoline motors are not permitted. The lake is stocked with trout, bass, and bluegill.

Hummel Lake is located on the Hummel Lake Road, ¾ mile east of the village of Lopez. To reach it from the ferry landing, follow Ferry Road south for 2 miles to a T intersection. Turn left (east), then in ¼ mile turn right onto Center Road, which can be followed to the lake, about 4½ miles total distance from the start. The public boat launch ramp, parking area, and picnic tables, maintained by local volunteers, are on Center Road, just south of the Hummel Lake Road intersection. There's ample parking; a latrine is adjacent to the parking area.

Cattails and blackberry brambles edging the lake rustle with bird life, including marsh wrens and colorful red-winged blackbirds. Virginia rails nest among the reeds; their narrow bodies and strong toes are adaptations for living in the muck and tightly packed reeds of marshes. A quarter-mile to the south the Land Bank has developed 39 acres of lake frontage, which includes toilets, picnic tables, benches, a dock, and hiking trails.

Because the lake is only 12 feet deep at its maximum, the water warms early in the spring, and it soon blossoms with algae. Although the green growth is unappealing, it is harmless to swimmers.

Spencer Spit State Park

Park area: 129 acres; 1½ miles of shoreline
Access: Ferry to Lopez Island, boat
Facilities: 46 campsites, group camp, group day-use area, 3 primitive campsites, picnic tables, fireplaces, picnic shelters, beach fire rings, drinking water, restrooms, vault toilet, telephone, trailer dump, 16 mooring buoys; (closed November 1 to March 1) (Designated Cascadia Marine Trail campsite)
Attractions: Camping, picnicking, boating, paddling, fishing, beachcombing, clam digging, crabbing, shrimping, birdwatching, hiking

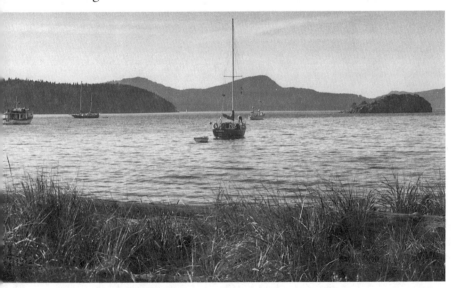

Visiting boaters tie to mooring buoys at Spencer Spit State Park. Flower Island is on the right, and Orcas Island in the distance.

Although Spencer Spit State Park does not receive the gushing accolades that Moran or the marine state parks do, its popularity grows with each new "discovery" by campers, bicyclists, and boaters. Visitors delight in the marine view and the many activities the beaches and waters offer. To the north, tiny Flower Island nestles against the imposing backdrop of Orcas Island. At sunset the channel is bathed in afterglow and the lights of ferries glimmer against Orcas's dark silhouette.

To reach the park from the ferry landing at Upright Head, drive 1 mile to the first road junction and turn left on Port Stanley Road. At 3¾ miles turn left onto Baker View Road, continuing straight ahead to the park at 5 miles. The route is well signed. The park is 8 nautical miles by boat west of Anacortes, the closest point on the mainland where boats can be launched.

Inside the park entrance a spur road leads to two loops of timbered campsites on the hillside above the beach. Almost half of the sites have space for RV trailers, although none have hookups. In the center of the northernmost loop is a walk-in group camp with two large Adirondack shelters equipped with bunks. Fifteen more walk-in campsites for cyclists and boaters are strung along the beach. Three Cascadia Marine Trail sites for the use of campers in kayaks or other hand-powered boats are located just above the beach southwest of the lagoon.

Vehicles are permitted to drive on the service road from the park office to the beach only for loading and unloading. A group picnic area

Spencer Spit State Park

is located at the top of the bluff next to a parking lot; trails from there lead to the beach. Restrooms (no showers) are located at the camping and parking areas, while lower sites along the beach make do with a vault toilet. Fire rings, stoves, and picnic tables located on the beach invite daytime picnicking and evening bonfires. Build fires only in designated areas.

Scattered on either side of the spit, 16 mooring buoys accommodate boaters, with plenty of space for additional boats to drop anchor. There is no trailered boat launching at the park; however small boats can easily be hand carried the short distance to the beach from the loading area.

Winter storms toss up driftwood and shells for beachcombers on the mile-long sandy beach. Butter, horse, and littleneck clams can be dug during summer low tides, and the waters yield crab, shrimp, and bottom-fish. During warm summer days the broad beaches heat the usually frigid water to bearable swimming temperatures.

Spencer Spit is an excellent example of a sandspit enclosing a saltchuck lagoon, commonly found in the San Juans. These lagoons are formed over a long period of time by the action of wind and tide on sandy beaches. In many cases lagoons of this type eventually fill with sediment and over time progress from marsh to meadow. The perimeter of the lagoon displays a rainbow of colors from various algae and saltwater plants. A wide variety of birds pause at the lagoon during migration, including several kinds of gulls, a dozen types of ducks, great blue herons, kingfishers, black brant, and Canada geese. A billboard display near the parking lot explains the geology and ecology of this unique lagoon.

Rabbits tunnel in the sandy hillside behind the beach and at dusk the long-eared residents appear. Raccoons, too, roam the beaches at night, scavenging for tasty sea creatures. These animals, as well as the local black-tailed deer, can usually be seen during a quiet evening stroll along the beach or park roads.

A log cabin on the end of the spit has been reconstructed in the original style and on the site of a beach cabin that was built here more than fifty years ago. Some of the logs are from the original cabin, others were scavenged from the beach. The historic old structure now serves as a picnic shelter, although heavy use by birds that roost in its rafters can make it unappealing. A second picnic shelter, built in the remnants of the old Spencer family home, is at the base of the hill above the spit.

Frost Island lies just a stone's throw off the east end of the spit. Although all of its shores below the mean high water level are a public DNR beach, the rocky shoreline drops off so steeply that it is not walkable except at very low water. Do not trespass on property above the tideland, as it is all privately owned. When boating around the island in small craft navigate with care, as the tidal current can be strong in the channel.

Trails beginning at the lower campground road climb up the hill to the other camp areas and beyond into the thick timber of the hillside. There are no views, due to the heavy growth, but it is still a lovely, cool hike on a warm summer day. These trails are primarily firebreaks terminating at the park boundary.

Flower Island and Leo Reef

Flower Island, less than ½ mile offshore, north of Spencer Spit State Park, is part of the San Juan Islands National Wildlife Refuge. While the shores are interesting to explore by kayak or dinghy, do not go ashore, for such intrusion by man disturbs nesting birds. Harbor seals and sea lions are often seen sunning on rocks or peering curiously from the nearby water.

Leo Reef, ½ nautical mile farther north, is also a favorite haul-out spot for these mammals. State ferry passengers with binoculars are almost assured of seeing them on the rocks or in the water as the boat passes by. The highest of the rocks has a lighted navigation mark. Boats should give the reef a wide berth, as there are a number of submerged rocks in the vicinity.

LOPEZ SOUND

This is one of the prettiest little cruising corners of the San Juans, with rockbound islets trimmed with ragged fringes of "bonsai" evergreens, secluded bays, and a narrow pass with a bit of a navigational challenge—just to keep things interesting. Squeezed between long Lopez Island and the comma-shaped Decatur, Lopez Sound is just enough off the beaten path that it does not suit the boater hurriedly headed for somewhere else. Instead it attracts cruisers willing to leisurely putt by, inspecting the shoreline, or sailboats looking for some wind.

The west shore of Decatur Island is punctuated by two smaller islands, Trump and Center. The passage beween Decatur and Center is quite shallow, and a rock lies in the center of the channel.

Small Island, on the west side of Lopez Sound opposite the north end of Center Island, is a bird sanctuary of the San Juan Islands National Wildlife Refuge. Other refuge islands in the sound are Fortress, Crab, and Skull islands, between Hunter and Mud bays. In addition to seabirds, seals can sometimes be seen basking on their sunny rocks.

Sperry Peninsula, a rounded bit of land south of Lopez Pass joined to the island by a slim tombolo, was once the site of a summer youth camp. It is now privately owned.

At the head of the sound, the Lopez Pass exit is guarded by the protruding reef of Rim, Rum, and Ram islands. Here skippers heading out through the pass must continue south 200 feet beyond Ram Island to avoid kelp-flagged rocks tagged by a red daymark, R"4," then make a hairpin turn to the left to run the tight little pass into Rosario Strait.

Some recent charts show Rum Island renamed as Cayou Island—evidently the State Board of Geographic Names gave it that title, not realizing it already had a dandy one. Rum it will always remain, however, to anyone who has a shred of whimsy in their heart.

Rim and Rum (or Cayou, if you will), the middle island, are part of the San Juan Islands National Wildlife Refuge. Ram, the larger wooded island on the south, is privately owned but has been designated as open space, and the public is permitted to go ashore. Approach only with small boats, and even then use care, as the surrounding water is fouled with submerged rocks.

Hunter and Mud Bays

For boaters waiting to cross Rosario Strait and catch a favorable tidal current at Deception Pass, Hunter Bay offers peaceful anchorages in 20 feet of water. A short county dock with a float and a launch ramp on the southeast side of the bay provide land-to-water access. The tideland on the tip of the peninsula separating Hunter and Mud bays is a public DNR beach, although the shores drop off so steeply that there is little space for walking. Uplands are private.

To reach the county dock by land, follow Mud Bay Road south from the Center Road intersection for about 2 miles, then turn left (east) on Islandale Road. Follow this road for 1½ miles, avoiding private drives, as it winds downhill to the boat ramp and dock. There is parking for cars and boat trailers alongside the short spur road to the dock and ramp. There are no stores or other facilities nearby.

Mud Bay, at the extreme south end of Lopez Sound, is too shallow for dropping an overnight anchor, but it has more extensive stretches of public tidelands. The obvious solution is to anchor in Hunter Bay and dinghy around to Mud Bay for beach walking, clam digging, and exploration.

Two upland accesses on Mud Bay provide a place for land-bound visitors to reach the beaches. A public access near the head of the bay is reached by taking Mud Bay Dock Road, the first road east of the end of Mud Bay, heading north on it along the shore; it is marked "dead end." Pass beach homes on a single-track dirt road that ends in ½ mile at a fence and parking space for a couple of cars. An easy scramble leads down to a beautiful flat beach. Most of the beach to mean high tide on Mud Bay is undeveloped state parks land. Avoid any posted beaches and all upland property.

Another access is on the northeast edge of Mud Bay; to find it continue on Mud Bay Road past the head of the bay and turn left on Sperry Road, heading north. When the main road curves right, a single-lane dirt road continues straight ahead for 300 feet to a turnaround at the road's end. Here boats can be hand carried the short distance to the water. The nearby lagoon and pebbled beach provide interesting exploration by boat or foot.

Islandale Bicycle Rest

A bit of land adjacent to the Lopez Island fire station was once a welcome stop for bicyclers journeying down the island. The site was converted to a gravel pit, with no public facilities available. However, a service station/cafe across the road does have water, groceries, beverages, and sandwiches. The service station also offers bicycle repairs and air for tires.

The rest area is at the intersection of Mud Bay and Mackaye Harbor roads, about 11½ miles south of the ferry landing, depending on the route taken.

THE SOUTHWEST SHORE

Shark Reef Recreation Area

Park area: 39 acres
Access: Ferry to Lopez Island
Facilities: Latrines, *no water*

State land at Shark Reef, the legacy of a former military reservation intended to guard the entrance to San Juan Channel, now guards precious marine mammal and bird life, and climax forest. The land, which was held by the Department of Natural Resources, was scheduled to be logged in 1980 to provide money for funding state schools. At the behest of local groups it was wisely decided that the educational interests would be better served by preserving this unique forest as a wildlife sanctuary. In 1986 the state gave the county a 50-year lease on the property, to be used as a minimum-facility park.

To reach the recreation site turn west on Davis Bay Road 1 mile north of Richardson, and in 1¼ miles, when Davis Bay Road turns north, continue west on Burt Road for ¾ mile to Shark Reef Road. Turn south, and in 200 yards reach the parking area at the trailhead to the beach; pit

Boats round Deadman Island near Shark Reef Recreation Area as they head into San Juan Channel.

toilets are near the beginning of the trail. No garbage cans are provided; please pack out all your trash.

A level, 10-minute hike through forest leads to the rock and grass bluffs above the turbulent tidal currents of San Juan Channel. Shark Reef itself actually lies nearly a mile north of the park, and the view of it is blocked by Kings Point. The jumble of islets lying only 400 feet off-shore from the park is a reef that is unnamed except for Deadman Island, the largest and highest of the rocks. With binoculars, harbor seals and sea lions can be seen ponderously heaving themselves along the rocks to favored sunny sites, or slipping into the water with the grace of dancers. Harbor seals breed here, and glaucous-winged gulls and oystercatchers nest in rocky crevices.

The forest is one of the few remaining old-growth and late-successional second-growth forests on Lopez Island. Cavities in the trees provide nesting sites for screech owls and saw-whet owls; insects in rotting wood sustain a variety of woodpeckers. Four bald eagle nests are known to be in old trees in the vicinity.

With binoculars, sea birds and seals can be observed on rocks offshore from Shark Reef Recreation Area.

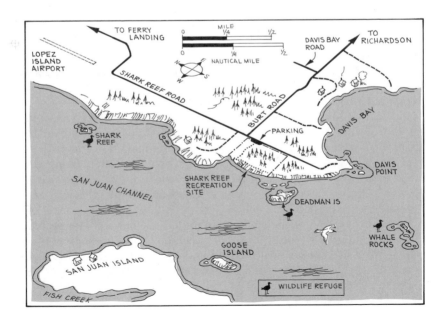

Vague trails wind along cliffs above the water south for another ¼ mile, with views of nearby rocks and across the channel to the end of San Juan Island. The gull cacophony from across the channel at Goose Island serves as atonal background music for the rugged scenery. Above, Cattle Point Light serves its lonely mission. A place to rest, observe, and meditate.

Boaters should stay well away from Shark Reef, Deadman Island, and all adjacent rocks; numerous rocks lie under the kelp-filled water, and currents are strong and tricky. Only experienced kayakers should attempt negotiating the narrow slot between the rocks and the island. These islets are also a part of the San Juan Islands National Wildlife Refuge.

Richardson

Access: Ferry to Lopez Island, boat
Facilities: Diesel, gas, dock (no float)

Richardson, which looks directly into the Strait of Juan de Fuca from behind the limited protection of Iceberg Point and offshore islands, is the southern outpost of the San Juans. At the turn of the century it was one of the major ports of the islands, shipping produce from the farms and orchards of Lopez Island via steamship to Puget Sound markets. A large fishing fleet, comprised of nearly fifty outfits, was based here, unloading their catches at the wharf or taking them directly to mainland canneries.

During this time, it is told, San Juan Channel ran thick with salmon, and at times nets were so full they could not be lifted into boats. Today the great runs of fish are depleted and fishermen are fewer and must go farther afield for their catches. Gillnetters and purse seiners still raft together in the harbor during fishing season, but the activity does not nearly approximate the days when the harbor burst with commerce.

The historic general store at Richardson, built on pilings over the water, was tragically consumed by fire in the fall of 1990. The fuel tanks and dock were saved, so the only facilities remaining are the fuel dock for boats and two gas pumps for autos. There are no current plans to rebuild the store.

When approaching Richardson by boat, be wary of numerous rocks around Charles Island and be forewarned there is no float, only a stationary pier; crew members may be needed on hand to fend off shiny fiberglass from creosoted pilings. If the strait is kicking up a bit, strong surges can make docking difficult. Richardson lies 12 nautical miles across Rosario Strait, west of Deception Pass, and 9 nautical miles southwest of Friday Harbor, via San Juan Channel.

To reach Richardson by land, follow Ferry Road, then Center Road south from the ferry landing. In about 8½ miles, where Center Road ends at a T intersection, turn right, then in ¼ mile, left on Richardson Road; total distance is about 10½ miles.

The tour down-island is a pleasure for bicyclists, with gently rolling blacktopped roads passing neat farms and cattle-filled pastures. Birds call from hedgerow and marsh, and the San Juan rabbits dash across the road—perhaps just a breath ahead of a hawk. Watch for eagles soaring above the range of low hills to the south.

Mackaye Harbor

Facilities: Launch ramp

Mackaye Harbor, lying east of Richardson, offers some good anchorages at the east end of the harbor and in its southern extension, Barlow Bay. Two old fishing docks, previously used by commercial fishing fleets, occupy the south shore of Barlow Bay; the dock on the point to the northwest is privately owned.

A launch ramp at the northeast corner of the harbor offers access for

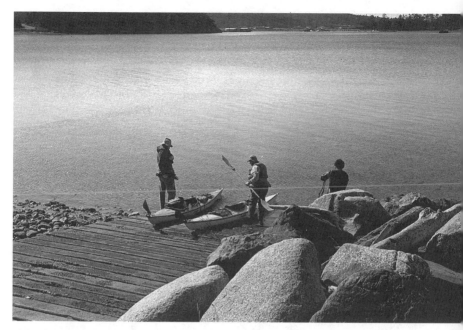

Kayakers prepare to launch at Mackaye Harbor.

trailered and hand-carried boats. To reach it, at Islandale turn south from Mud Bay Road onto Mackaye Harbor Road, and in a few hundred feet turn right on a single-lane dirt road, signed "Boat Ramp." The narrow road swings downhill to meet the corner of Mackaye Harbor at the single-lane concrete launch ramp. An adjacent parking lot can accommodate a dozen cars and trailers. A rib of submerging rocks on the north side of the ramp is marked with a pole at its outer end.

Boats put in here can explore the multitude of bays and niches along the south shore of Lopez Island. Remember to stay well away from the offshore islets and rocks of the San Juan Islands National Wildlife Refuge to avoid disturbing protected birds.

Agate Beach Picnic Area

Park area: 2 acres, 600 feet of shoreline
Access: Ferry to Lopez Island, boat
Facilities: Picnic tables, pit toilets, *no water*
Attractions: Beachcombing, scuba diving

Nothing pretentious, but a welcome resting spot and a lovely beach to walk. To reach the park, turn east onto Vista Road ¼ mile north of

Richardson and follow it for 1½ miles to its intersection with Mud Bay Road. Turn right (south) onto Mud Bay Road, then leave it in 1 mile, turning right again onto Mackaye Harbor Road, which circles the shore of the harbor, crosses a neck of land, then contours Outer Bay. In 2 miles reach the small grassy picnic area located near the middle of the beach, on the east side of the road.

Across from the picnic area a stairway descends to the pebbled beach on Outer Bay, facing the "toe" of distant San Juan Island. Lying just offshore, a distinctive smooth rock shaped like a shark's fin beckons to kayak explorers. Perhaps it can be reached by foot at low tide. What else does low tide bring? Agates? Crabs? Stop and find out. Farther offshore is tiny Iceberg Island, an undeveloped state park property.

Outer Bay is a favorite with scuba divers, who explore the sand and cobblestone beach and offshore rocks. Sea urchins grow in particular abundance here. Strong currents can present a problem in the outer portions of the bay, and in summer kelp growth is heavy in some areas.

A wooden stairway leads down the steep bank to Hughes Bay County Park.

Hughes Bay County Park

Access: Ferry to Lopez Island, boat
Facilities: None
Attractions: Beachcombing, picnicking

A small, enchanting sand and gravel pocket beach on the east shore of Hughes Bay was acquired by the county in 1989 as a park. A steep wooden staircase drops down the high clay bank to a narrow, 75-foot-wide strip of cobble beach that grades to sand at minus tide. A towering rock cliff bounds the southeast side of the beach.

To reach the park, turn south from Mud Bay Road onto Watmough Head Road, and in ¼ mile continue straight ahead on Huggins Road. Take the next dirt lane heading right, which leads to the parking area above the beach.

Iceberg Point and Point Colville

Two stretches of land on the far recesses of Lopez Island are held by the Bureau of Land Management as lighthouse reservations. Iceberg Point houses a navigational beacon, Point Colville does not. The two areas can be reached only by boat; land access is closed.

The shores beneath the points are extremely rugged. The difficulty of landing boats varies with the tide level and the turbulence of the water. Between these rocky "toes" of the island are lodged a succession of intimate bays. The looming rock shorelines make these the most spectacular to be found in the San Juans.

The most easterly is Watmough Bay, facing east on Rosario Strait. It is sometimes used as an overnight stop for boaters headed for Deception Pass. Although the narrow slot is well protected from weather, its rocky bottom may present some difficulty in getting anchors to hold.

Farther west, around Watmough Head and Point Colville, are McArdle and Hughes bays. These two south-facing harbors are open to weather off the strait and are only marginal holding ground, especially in winds and waves one may encounter.

Aleck Bay, which tends northwesterly for nearly ¾ mile, is the jewel among these bays, with good protection and a muddy bottom for holding anchors. Clear days reveal a glorious sight—views all the way down Puget Sound to the crystal mass of Mount Rainier.

Rocky walls along this end of the island plunge as dramatically under water as they rise above. Undersea gardens that cloak these walls with a colorful tapestry are a favorite of scuba divers who visit dive sites at Iceberg Point, Davidson Rock, and Colville Island. Marine life runs the gamut from red and green sea urchins, pecten scallops, bass, and rockfish, to wolfeels and octopuses. Strong winds, kelp, and the presence of commercial and sport fishing boats make this an area for alert, experienced divers.

OFFSHORE ISLANDS

More than two dozen barren rocks and islets lifting out of the sea off the tip of Lopez Island have been set aside for wildlife management.

What's a Wildlife Refuge Doing in the Middle of a Tourist Paradise?

Cormorants drying on offshore rocks in the San Juan Islands

It is well established that the numbers of sea birds have dramatically diminished throughout the world in the last century; civilization is almost totally responsible. Before the coming of man, birds nested throughout the San Juans and raised their young here, while migratory birds used the islands as resting stops. Seals and sea lions hauled out on rocks and foraged the waters. Early Native Americans looted rookeries for eggs and killed birds for food and for their decorative value. The parrotlike beaks of tufted puffins were valued for ceremonial rattles and as adornment, and large numbers were killed just for that purpose. Despite this predation, the great flocks of birds survived.

Today man threatens their existence with subtler methods: he preempts their habitat, depletes their food sources, and poisons their environment. Aside from the moral and aesthetic issues raised by the loss of huge numbers of birds, this tinkering with one of the important links of the food chain must ultimately affect man, too.

Anticipating man's insatiable demands for home and recreation

These bits of rock are part of the San Juan Islands National Wildlife Refuge, administered by the U.S. Fish and Wildlife Service.

Islands holding this status in the vicinity of Lopez Island are Shark Reef, located on the west of Lopez near San Juan Island's Cattle Point; Buck Island and Mummy Rocks near Davis Bay; several small islets on the south side of Long Island; Secar Rock, Round Rock, and Hall Island south of Richardson; small unnamed islets southeast of Iceberg

sites, a number of these islands have been set aside as the San Juan Islands National Wildlife Refuge, providing sanctuaries for pelagic birds and animals. To offer further protection, most of these refuge islands have also been designated as wilderness areas. The U.S. Fish and Wildlife Service, which administers these sanctuaries, recognizes that safeguarding of such lands enhances the human benefits associated with wildlife and its environment.

The wilderness area dates back to 1914, when Smith and Minor islands, located in the Strait of Juan de Fuca, were first designated as wildlife refuges. Jones and Matia islands became refuges in 1937, and in 1960 Turn Island, Bird Rocks (in Rosario Strait), Williamson Rocks (west of Fidalgo Island), Colville Island (south of Lopez Island) and Bare Island (north of Waldron Island) were established as a collective San Juan Islands National Wildlife Refuge, with a total of 52 acres of land.

Since that time other islands have been added as refuges, and in the 1970s 81 of them (excluding Turn, Jones, Smith and Minor islands, and five acres of Matia Island), achieved wilderness status. Turn and the Matia area remain as national wildlife refuges, permitting some recreational use. These protected islands today total 353 acres at 84 distinct locations, and range in character from barren reefs, which at high tide are little more than inhospitable offshore rocks, to wooded islets that support deer, raccoons, foxes, river otters, weasels, and other small mammals, as well as birds and seals.

Going ashore on any of the islands of the wilderness area at any time is prohibited in order to protect the wildlife there. Special permission may be granted in the case of scientific research. Such permission must be obtained from the Refuge Manager, San Juan National Wildlife Refuge, 100 Brown Farm Road, Olympia, WA 98506. Boaters and anglers are urged to stay at least 300 feet away from the islands to avoid disturbing the seals and nesting birds. Going ashore is prohibited, and discharge of firearms is, of course, also prohibited, and is subject to a stiff fine.

Looking across Hughes Bay to islands at the south end of Lopez Island

Point; four unnamed islands on Flint Beach; Aleck Rocks and Swirl Island south of Aleck Bay; Blind Island and nearby unnamed rocks; 9-acre Castle Island and 11-acre Colville Island (largest of the bird refuges in the vicinity), off Point Colville; Davidson Rock; Boulder Island east of Watmough Head; and numerous other small, unnamed rocks.

The sanctuaries were established primarily to protect nesting birds. They are also important as resting areas for seals and sea lions; these pelagic mammals, as well as dolphins and whales, forage in surrounding waters. Glaucous-winged gulls, cormorants, murres, pigeon guillemots, and black oystercatchers nest in large numbers on the islands, while nearly 50 other species of seabirds are known to stop here during their migration on the Pacific Flyway.

These scattered, inhospitable rocks, swept by heavy seas from the Strait of Juan de Fuca, rarely attract recreational boaters; however, the area is growing in popularity with scuba divers. At this time their numbers are small enough so they do not constitute a serious problem; increased activity could seriously disrupt the rookeries. The presence of humans also prevents seals and sea lions from hauling out on the rocks to rest and warm themselves, a necessary function for these animals.

CHAPTER THREE

THE CENTRAL CHANNEL

Splitting the San Juans from east to west, a central waterway comprised of Harney Channel and Wasp Passage forms a saltwater freeway used by many boats traveling in the islands. Broad and deep throughout most of its length, the channel is constricted only at its western end, where the capricious architect of the sea dumped a load of rocks known as the Wasp Islands.

On this sheltered waterway the Washington State ferry makes three of its four island stops to discharge passengers. When the route that continues west through Wasp Passage is used, tourists look down from the heights of the ferry onto everyone's dream of a vacation retreat—private little islands and points and bays, each decorated with a summer cabin or retirement home, a bit of a dock, and a bobbing sailboat.

SHAW ISLAND

With a total of only 4,937 acres, Shaw Island is the smallest of the islands served by the ferries. The paucity of water on these rocky acres has limited the real estate development, and most Shaw islanders prefer it that way. Its population of around a hundred permanent residents swells to about three times that in the summer, and that is about all these shores can support.

Most Shaw Island roads are inland, with few views of San Juan waters and no access to bays. Instead, the roads roll gently through heavy timber and past small fields edged by bird-filled hedgerows. Here are not the wide agricultural expanses of Lopez Island, but instead small acreages with a few cattle and crops. Hike or bike the byways and enjoy the catharsis of rural island life. The most scenic road on the island is the one following the west shore of Blind Bay, with views across the bay to Orcas Island; it dead-ends at private property.

Arrive on the morning ferry and spend the day on the island, but

Ferry passengers are fascinated by cars loading at Shaw Landing.

plan to leave on the evening boat unless you are fortunate enough to claim one of the 12 campsites in the county park or have a good friend on the island. There is no other place to park a camper or pitch a tent, and there are no motels or cabins.

Shaw Landing

Access: Ferry to Shaw Island, boat
Facilities: Guest moorage by prior arrangement, restrooms, laundromat, groceries, bait, fishing tackle, hardware, gift items

The island's sole "commercial" development is the combination general store/post office/ferry terminal/marina at the ferry landing. Since 1976 the store has been operated by a small group of Franciscan nuns. The Little Portion store was named by the nuns after an Italian church named Portuncula, meaning "little portion of earth"; the small stone church was the favorite spot of Saint Francis of Assisi. The store is closed Sundays.

The U-shaped docks of the small marina lie east of the ferry landing, in a basin protected by the pilings of the ferry landing and a jutting rocky headland. Overnight moorage requires advanced arrangements with the store. It formerly offered fuel; however, that facility is now closed.

The forested headland east of the ferry landing and marina hosts a large heron rookery. Watchful ferry passengers may at times spot up to a dozen birds perched in trees.

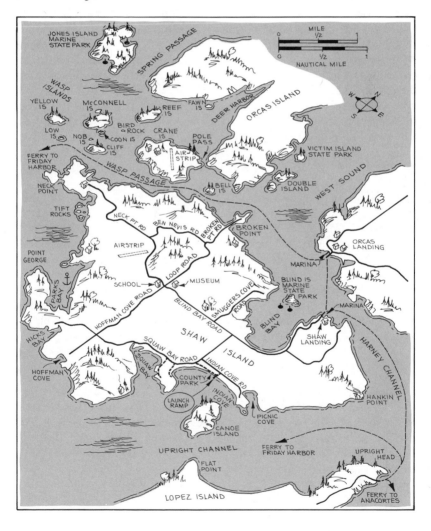

Blind Island Marine State Park

Park area: 3 acres; 1,280 feet of shoreline on Harney Channel and Blind Bay

Access: Boat

Facilities: 4 primitive campsites, picnic tables, fire grates, pit toilet, 4 mooring buoys; *no water, no garbage collection* (Designated Cascadia Marine Trail campsite)

Attractions: Primitive camping, picnicking, beachcombing, fishing, shrimping, scuba diving, birdwatching

This 3-acre rock stuck in the entrance to Blind Bay boasts only limited public facilities, a couple of tenacious trees, four sparse campsites—and an unparalleled nighttime spectacle! After sunset, ferries ablaze with lights ply Harney Channel, stopping at times at Shaw and Orcas. Small craft cruise by, resembling nautical fireflies, their reflections glimmering in the darkened sea.

On the southwest side of the rocky island, four buoys give moorage to boaters, although in rough weather better anchorages can be found farther into the bay. Rocks around the island are a navigational hazard; a large one that has claimed a number of boat hulls lies southeast of the island, midway in the channel. It is marked with a locally maintained caution sign on a pole. Boaters approaching the mooring buoys should enter the bay on the east side of Blind Island, but favor the Blind Island side of the channel. Reefs west of Blind Island make entry via that route even more hazardous.

Low tide exposes rocky beaches all around the island; at that time the best landing site for small boats is on the northeast side. Hand-carried boats may be put in at the marina next to the ferry landing at Shaw Island, ¼ nautical mile away, or at Orcas Landing ¾ nautical mile across Harney Channel. Boating traffic is usually heavy in the channel and can present a danger to small boats. Bring a sleeping bag and stay overnight to watch the evening show. The island's campsites are favored by kayakers.

"The Little Red Schoolhouse"

The main "point of interest" on Shaw Island is near the center of the island at the intersection of Blind Bay Road and Hoffman Cove Road, where a classic one-room schoolhouse stands. Known as "The Little Red Schoolhouse," the building is on the National Register of Historic Places. Instead of sending their children by boat to larger schools on Orcas or San Juan islands, as residents on most of the other small islands do, Shaw Islanders prefer to operate this school for their small population of elementary-age students.

The Little Red Schoolhouse on Shaw Island is on the National Register of Historic Places.

Across the road is the island's library and historical society. A reef-netting boat is displayed on the lawn. The library and an adjacent one-room log cabin that houses a historical collection are open to the public in the afternoon on Tuesdays and Saturdays, and in the morning on Thursdays.

South Beach County Park

Park area: 65 acres; 3,249 feet of shoreline
Access: Ferry to Shaw Island, boat
Facilities: Campsites, pit toilets, picnic tables, fireplaces, picnic shelter, drinking water, boat launch (ramp)
Attractions: Camping, picnicking, beachcombing, hiking, clam digging, crabbing, swimming, fishing, birdwatching

Facing on Indian Cove, South Beach County Park encompasses 65 acres of prime Shaw Island real estate and one of the grandest sandy beaches on any of the San Juans. The land, once a military reservation, was purchased by Shaw Islanders for public use. Express your gratitude to these farsighted residents by observing posted regulations and respecting private property bounding the park.

To reach the park from the ferry landing, follow Blind Bay Road, which heads south and then curves westward, to an intersection with Squaw Bay Road in 1¼ miles, signed to South Beach Park. Turn left (south); in ½ mile more, an inconspicuous sign points left to the South Beach Park camping area. There is another entrance from Indian Cove Road ¼ mile east of its intersection with Squaw Bay Road.

The day-use picnic area is located on a slight embankment above the shore of Indian Cove. A planked ramp at the end of the entrance road on the east side of the park provides launching for trailered boats; however, due to the shallow beach it is usable only at high tide.

Up the road, away from the beach, the campground contains 12 sites for the fortunate few. Some overflow camping is permitted in the grassy playground area, but don't expect more; the fragile ecology of the area cannot tolerate the intrusion of hordes of tourists.

Indian Cove lies just 3½ nautical miles east of Friday Harbor, where boats can be rented. Small boats are easily beached on the shore; deep-keeled vessels will have to anchor well out in the bay as it is extremely shallow.

Canoe Island, a lovely, 45-acre forested enclave on the southeast side of the bay, is the site of a unique summer camp for teenagers. Although the camp has the usual summer activities of swimming, sailing, tennis, and archery, the focus is on lessons in the French language, along with related subjects such as French cooking and French folk dancing.

The protected, sandy beach of the county park slopes gradually outward for several hundred feet. Sand dollars and heart cockles lie near the surface; dig deeper to find more tender clams, and perhaps even the mighty geoduck. On hot summer days the water of the bay warms enough for wading and swimming.

A forested thumb of land on the west that separates Indian Cove

A beachcomber checks out the tidelands of South Beach County Park. Canoe Island is in the distance.

from Squaw Bay is also part of the park. Tides permitting, circumnavigate the peninsula on sandy beaches that turn to rock as they round the point. On the east side of the peninsula, a dirt road goes through forest to reach the privately owned tip of the island, where a summer home is located. There is no parking and only minimal turn-around space; do not trespass. The road is pleasant enough as it leads through second-growth cedar and Douglas-fir, but has few water views and no beach access.

A single-track road on the west side of the peninsula is more attractive. Although it is driveable and has parking at its end for half a dozen cars, it is more interesting to park at the road junction and walk, enjoying the gentle murmur of the forest and views of Squaw Bay. At road's end a trail continues less than 50 feet beyond to two tiny coves, embraced by overhanging madronas. They are accessible by an easy rock scramble down to the beach.

No overnight camping is allowed here, and no fires; just peaceful forest, beach, and water to enjoy by day.

Squaw Bay, which nearly empties at low tide, is a favorite feeding and resting area for numerous species of birds; others nest in nearby rushes. The lagoon and sandspit at the head of the bay are privately owned, but birds can easily be seen from the road. A roadside sign at the head of the

Reef Netters

The unique, colorful fishing method of reef netting was originated long ago by Native Americans in the San Juans who used dugout canoes and nets fashioned from thin strips of willow or cedar bark. Pioneers adopted the method and added high, ladderlike lookout towers in the bows of the boats.

Reef-netting boats on a Shaw Island beach

Reef netting, which is most commonly utilized for sockeye and humpback salmon, employs the use of two boats anchored about 50 feet apart in shallow water or around reefs, with a square net stretched between them and weighted at the bottom. In early times, the salmon chief, wearing a broad-brimmed hat that shaded his eyes and enabled him to see into the water, served as lookout. A cedar pole was suspended horizontally a few feet under the water surface just ahead of the net, causing fish approaching the net to swim over the pole and break the surface of the water, making them easier to see.

Lookouts today wear polarized sunglasses to aid their underwater view. When a school of fish is spotted swimming into the net, it is quickly pulled up and the catch dumped into holding nets. Very clear water and long, shallow reefs, such as are found in the San Juans, are necessary for this fishing method. This is the only place in the world it is used.

Reef netting has continued to the present time, only being modernized by the use of skiffs or barges with large outboard motors, modern nets of synthetic materials, and powered winches to haul in the catch. Diminished salmon runs have made reef netting less effective than other more high-tech methods, however it is still practiced by some fishermen.

bay tells that herons, kingfishers, cormorants, mergansers, scaups, and eagles are but a few of the many birds frequently spotted here.

Commercial reef-netting fishing boats working in Upright Channel between Shaw and Lopez islands can often be seen from the county park. Boats are sometimes anchored at the entrance to Squaw Bay.

Parks Bay

On the southern end of the island, land surrounding Parks Bay and all of Point George is held by the University of Washington's Friday Harbor Laboratories as a biological preserve. Property here has been donated, purchased, or leased in order to maintain the shores and uplands in a nearly natural condition for research and educational purposes. Parks Bay is an excellent boat anchorage in 15 to 30 feet of water; however, going ashore is not permitted, due to its status as a nature preserve.

Tift Rocks

On the northeast side of Shaw Island, just north of Parks Bay, lie Tift Rocks. These grass-covered rocks, snuggled close to the shore of the island, usually go unnoticed by passing boaters. The northernmost and largest of the islands holds the deteriorating stone walls of a cabin that was built by a recluse who once lived here.

The rocks are part of the San Juan Islands National Wildlife Refuge and now host nesting seabirds and a number of seals that haul out to warm themselves in the sun. Going ashore is prohibited, but the animals and the rock walls of the cabin can easily be seen from the water.

THE WASP ISLANDS

Ferry passengers may be treated to a close-up view of the Wasp Islands if the inter-island ferry squeezes through narrow Wasp Passage. Choice of the route through Wasp Passage, or the less scenic route south of Shaw Island through Upright Channel, depends on the destinations scheduled. Hope for the intimate and beautiful Wasp Passage route.

The group of assorted islets and rocks at the west end of Wasp Passage, known locally as "the Rock Pile," received its name not from the pernicious insect, but from the American warship *Wasp*, which distinguished itself during the War of 1812. Jones Island to the north was named for the *Wasp*'s commander, Jacob Jones.

Early pioneers frequently rowed sheep to these small islands for summer grazing, and because most are dry, it was also necessary to regularly haul over barrels of drinking water for the flocks.

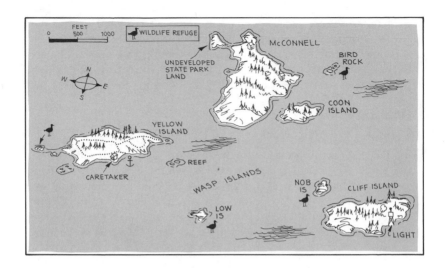

Smuggling

In the late 1880s, the United States closed its doors to Chinese immigrants eager for jobs in this bountiful nation. Smuggling these aliens, who had made their way from their homeland to Canada, became a lucrative profession. Along with them came cargoes of opium (which was legal but heavily taxed at the time), silk, and other commodities. A few years later when imported wool was slapped with a stiff duty, enterprising boats slipped north to Canada to purchase cheap fleece that could be mixed with the San Juan product and innocently resold at a tidy profit, causing revenuers to wonder at the productivity of island sheep.

When Washington went "dry" in 1916, four years before the Volstead Act decreed nationwide Prohibition, the smuggling flotilla heeded the cry of the thirsty and dutifully swung into action, importing everything from fine bonded Canadian whiskey to watered-down rotgut from the willing northern neighbors.

The San Juan archipelago is ideally suited to such clandestine activities, with its maze of channels spotted with rocky hiding places and soupy fogs clinging about the shoulders of the islands. Local sailors in small fast-moving craft knew every inch of the waterways and every trick of the trade. One favorite ploy was to slip on the

Much of the colorful history of the San Juans, when pirates and smugglers frequented these waters, centers around the Wasp Islands. McConnell Island was the family home of Victor McConnell, one of these early-day racketeers—until his relatives discovered his activities and requested his absence.

Crane Island, with many private residences on its 222 wooded acres, is the largest and most developed of the Wasp group. Planes that land on the airstrip in the center of the island provide transportation and bring supplies to residents. The only public lands on the island are two sections of narrow, unappealing rock beach on the north and west sides.

Smaller Bell Island to the east and Cliff, Coon, McConnell, and Reef islands scattered to the west are all singly owned, with one or two summer hideaways on each. All of Coon Island's tidelands, which include a few small pocket beaches, are public. McConnell Island has 2,000 feet of public tidelands along its southern half. The public lands are only those below the mean high water level. Do not trespass onto private property.

lee side of a ferry and sneak by under the very noses of the watchful revenue boats.

Romantic as it may sound, smuggling was not an innocent pastime, for those were the days of undercover agents, hijackings, bloody shoot-outs, mysterious disappearances of crews and boats, and blatant murders. Frequently cargoes—even human ones—were hurriedly "deep-sixed" by smugglers fearing apprehension. At least one instance is reported of Chinese aliens being forced overboard; their bodies, with hands and feet bound, later washed up on nearby shores.

Charged with enforcement of Prohibition, the Coast Guard, with its larger, slow-moving boats, was hard-pressed to apprehend the elusive rumrunners. However, the government boats knew a few tricks too. One skipper in particular, Lorenz A. Lonsdale, captain of the tug *Arcata*, gave such a good account of himself that he was in constant danger of being relieved of command and "kicked upstairs" by pressure exerted by corrupt politicians dismayed by his successes.

Life today is much more sedate along this central channel. Instead of woolly flocks the islands are dotted with summer homes—although it is still necessary to import water to many of their occupants. On foggy mornings it is easy to imagine ghosts of early smugglers slipping furtively past mist-cloaked shores.

A tiny rock on the northeast side of McConnell Island, which at low tide is joined to the larger island by a sandy spit, is owned by the state, although it is undeveloped. It is an excellent spot to beach small boats or kayaks for a brief rest.

Down the scale of "ownership," the barren, inhospitable rocks that cannot even support a shack are given over to seabirds and seals. Bird Rock east of McConnell Island, the Nob Island group, Low Island west of Cliff Island, and an unmarked low-tide rock west of Yellow Island are all part of the San Juan Islands National Wildlife Refuge.

Boaters enjoy exploring the watery nooks and crannies of the Wasp Islands, but extreme care must be used, for there are many submerged rocks and reefs. Kelp marks many of these danger spots, but a slow speed and vigilant eye on the navigational chart are the pilot's best allies. Smaller, unpowered boats should also be wary of wakes from other boating traffic.

Yellow Island Preserve

Island area: 11 acres
Access: Boat
Facilities: Hiking trails, *eating and drinking prohibited (no restrooms)*

Yellow Island, the most westerly of the Wasp group, was purchased in 1980 by the Nature Conservancy as a nature preserve. The island's woodlands, open meadows, and rocky shoreline support more than 150 varieties of wildflowers—nearly every natural species to be found in the San Juan Islands. Plants include prickly pear cactus, the only cactus species native to western Washington. At the peak of the blooming season, from late March through early June, the island becomes a riot of color. Meadows brim with blossoms of green chocolate lilies, buttercup, camas, harvest brodiaea, and sea blush. Later in the season the dainty lilac-pink blossoms of nodding onion and white swaths of yarrow grace the island slopes.

A tenuous anchorage can be had in a small rocky cove on the south side of the island near the caretaker's cabin; the buoys here are for use only by the residents. The beach near the caretaker's cabin is the only spot where visitors may come ashore; landing at the ends of the island is prohibited.

Going ashore is permitted, subject to restrictions necessary to maintain this as a nature preserve: remain on designated trails; no pets, picnicking, camping, or fires; no collection of plants or animals; prior written permission must be obtained for groups of more than six. Contact the Nature Conservancy at (206) 343-4344 to arrange for group access or for information on guided tours.

Two cabins on the island, one on the south shore and another above the western point, were built by Lew and Elizabeth ("Tib") Dodd from driftwood gathered from the beaches and rocks, and other native materials from the island. The Dodds bought the island in 1947 and lived here in contented solitude for 14 years. The Nature Conservancy purchased Yellow Island from the Dodds' children, and the cabins are now used by the resident caretakers.

Lew Dodd was a reader of Thoreau, and Yellow Island became his Walden. The Dodds' sensitive care of Yellow Island is evident in the bounty of native plants that grow here, in spite of the heavy impact of civilization on neighboring islands. A bronze plaque beside the trail in the eastern meadow memorializes Lew Dodd with a poem that he loved that expressed his unending joy of life in this, his personal paradise.

Two trail loops have been carefully laid out to provide maximum appreciation of the island vistas and flora. Due to the fragile nature of the land, hikers *must* stay on trails.

One loop leaves the south shore cabin for the west point and the western meadow, with views across Spieden Channel and north to Spieden, James, Flattop, and Waldron islands and Spring Passage. As this loop meanders back to its starting point through old-growth Douglas-fir and madrona, a second trail heads east to reach the east point and circle the eastern meadow. Occasional faint side trails signed "Otters Only" are for the use of four-legged residents exempt from staying on the main trails.

Purple-blossomed harvest brodiaea are found on Yellow Island.

Jones Island Marine State Park

Park area: 188 acres, 4¾ miles of shoreline on San Juan Channel
Access: Boat
Facilities: Dock and float, 7 mooring buoys, 21 primitive campsites, picnic tables, reservation group camp, fire grates, composting toilets, pit toilets, drinking water (well may go dry by midsummer) (Designated Cascadia Marine Trail campsite)
Attractions: Camping, picnicking, beachcombing, paddling, clamming, crabbing, fishing, hiking, scuba diving

A choice little island with welcoming bays and bountiful shores, located so near the main highways of Wasp Passage and San Juan Channel that most passing tourists drop in for a brief visit—and many fall in love and linger awhile.

Jones Island is located less than ½ mile off the southwest tip of Orcas Island, and 2 nautical miles from Deer Harbor Marina. Boaters approaching Jones Island through Spring Passage should be cautious of several rocky shoals just off the east shore.

A cove deeply notching the north side of the island holds a dock with float and 4 mooring buoys. On nice summer weekends this bay is always filled with small boats drawn up on the beach and larger ones tied to the float, rafted on buoys, or bobbing on a hook.

Anchoring in this bay can be tricky, especially with a bit of wind or a strong tidal current to complicate matters. The bottom is rocky and steeply sloping, making it difficult to set a hook solidly. Savvy seamen will often drop a second anchor or will row a stern line ashore and tie up to a tree to keep their craft in position. If unsure about the security of your anchor or that of nearby boats, do not leave your boat unattended. A favorite pastime among those familiar with the bay is sitting on deck with an air of an "old salt" (one whose boat is solidly nailed down), and watching the embarrassment of the uninitiated as they drift on their anchors.

On the south side of the island is a wider, shallower bay, split by a rocky headland. The three additional buoys placed here are more open to tossing by wind and waves.

The park attracts many visitors in small boats who overnight ashore in the campgrounds overlooking the two bays. At the north cove 10 campsites with picnic tables and fireplaces were once clustered in cool timber. A devastating storm, with winds in excess of 100 mph, hit the island in the winter of 1990 and toppled hundreds of trees, many in the vicinity of this campground. Negotiations on the ecological impact of removal of downed trees and restoration of the campground rambled on for nearly two years before the present camping facilities were finally restored. A large area of downed forest just south of the campground is an impressive reminder of the havoc wreaked by the storm.

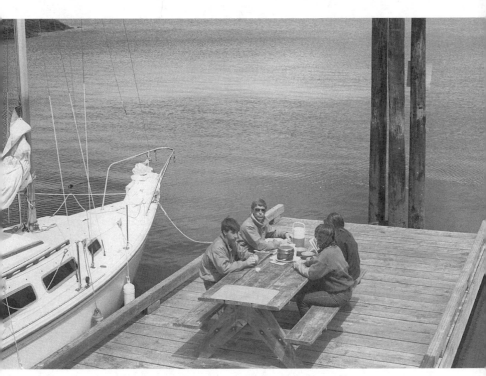

Boaters enjoy a picnic on the dock at Jones Island.

A ½-mile trail from the north cove campground leads across the island to the two small bays on the south side of the island below a large grassy meadow fringed with the remains of an ancient apple orchard. Here is the island's group campsite. There are two sunny sites closer to the beach with views of the Wasp Islands and passing ferry traffic. One additional campsite is found on each of the headlands defining the two bays; the westernmost of these headlands has been designated a Cascadia Marine Trail campsite.

At the approach of low tide, boaters traipse southward along the cross-island path, armed with shovels and buckets, headed for clam beds on the far shore. Even without the incentive of clams, visitors will enjoy the forest walk through the deep green of the island's interior. Cedar, hemlock, sword fern, and salal suddenly give way to the warm, golden meadow on the south bay. Halfway along the trail, just north of the two water tanks, is a magnificent example of a cedar nurse log. The downed giant, several hundred feet long, has two 200- to 300-foot offspring growing from its base root.

An unmarked spur just above the north campground heads west to a small cove on the west-side beach. Here there is one primitive campsite in open timber above a small rocky head framing the gravel-beach cove.

A small herd of black-tailed deer that inhabits the island often grazes in the meadow. Many are now so accustomed to the crowds of visitors that they will venture to be hand-fed. Although they are appealing, they should not be fed "people food"—to do so may actually harm them. Inbreeding and poor diet have caused the deer to be quite undersized. Raccoons, weasels, and martens, which are occasionally spotted at dusk, swim across Spring Passage to raid the nests of seabirds; some of the bolder raccoons also check out the garbage cans by the campground.

Several sketchy trails circle eastward on low bluffs looking down into little one-boat bays facing on Spring Passage. Use care scrambling about the rocky embankment, as footing can be insecure; hikers have been injured here.

The west shore, at the edge of San Juan Channel, is a favorite spot for salmon fishermen. Dungeness crab, which migrate around the island at some primitive whim, can sometimes be trapped in the south bay.

Until 1982, Jones Island was owned by the federal government as a part of the San Juan Islands National Wildlife Refuge, and leased to the state as a marine park. Because the throngs of people using the island were not particularly compatible with its wildlife status, the U.S. Fish and Wildlife Service relinquished its claim and turned it over to the state in return for several smaller, more remote, state-owned islands.

Jones Island, in a microcosm, reflects many of the problems besetting the San Juans as a whole. With its many attractions and convenient location, it may ultimately be "loved to death" by squadrons of boaters

One of Jones Island's friendly deer

who arrive on its shores in greater numbers each year.

Today ignorant visitors scar campgrounds by "ditching" their tents, injure trees with nails driven to support tent ropes, strip branches from anything green to fuel their campfires, pockmark the beach and shore with randomly built bonfires (and also risk setting the entire island ablaze), trample undergrowth by careless hiking, frighten wildlife, and kill or cart away even inedible living beach creatures. Even the well-intentioned camper who treats the land with care, simply by his or her presence has a negative impact on the environment. The space requirements and waste disposal logistics of tens of thousands of visitors create problems that must be dealt with.

As with all of the San Juans, Jones Island simply cannot tolerate the pressure of unlimited use and abuse by demanding recreationists. Without careful development and management, and sensitive, responsible use, the future may well see its beaches stripped naked, its meadows ground to dust, its forest destroyed, and its wildlife departed.

Touring bicycles crowd the racks at Friday Harbor.

CHAPTER FOUR

SAN JUAN ISLAND

Verdant, pastoral country punctuated by forested mountains. The most populated of the San Juan islands. Home of the county seat and its largest (and only incorporated) town. The islands' center of commerce and industry. Home port for the local fishing fleet. Crossroads of these boundary waters, with a steady flow of international traffic through two customs offices. In short, the archipelago's busiest island.

Yet "busy" is a relative term in this slow-paced paradise. Even in summer, when tourists stream from crammed-full ferries, and harbors and bays swarm with boats, the customary tempo only slightly quickens. Many visitors, understanding the ambiance of the island, arrive on bicycle or on foot with a backpack, prepared to enjoy the country at a leisurely rate.

The early Spanish explorer Lopez Gonzales de Haro, who sailed through here in 1791, noted the important strategic location of the island facing on two major waterways and its outstanding physical features, and named it San Juan, principal landfall of this archipelago. Arriving later, British settlers claimed it for the queen and changed its name to Bellevue Island; eventually the original Spanish designation was restored.

Pioneers recognized San Juan as prime real estate, with its gently rolling farmland ideal for cattle and crops, its thick forests ripe to be turned into cabins, fences, and firewood, and its fine harbors providing sheltered access to the shores. Generation after generation they sank their family roots into the island soil.

Today's San Juan settlers are retirees, artists, authors, and dropouts from the rat race who prefer their air without smog, their beaches without pollution slicks and beer cans, their highways without traffic jams, and their starry skies without obliterating city lights.

Friday Harbor on San Juan Island can be reached by Washington State ferry from Anacortes or Sidney, B.C., about a 1½-hour trip either way. During the summer months San Juan Shuttle Express offers scheduled passenger ferry service from Bellingham to Friday Harbor. For quicker access, both West Isle Air and Harbor Airlines have regularly scheduled flights from Bellingham, Anacortes, and Seattle to the airport at Friday Harbor. Kenmore Air also offers regularly scheduled floatplane service to Friday Harbor and Roche Harbor. Other air services offer charter flights.

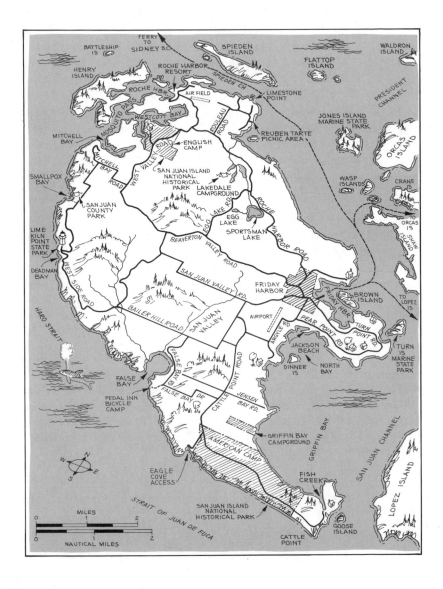

Private boats visiting the island will find guest moorage and supplies at Friday Harbor and at resorts on Roche Harbor and Mitchell Bay. Numerous fine anchorages are found around the island.

Hikers, cyclists, and moped riders will enjoy the gently rolling roads edged by pastures and forests, sometimes dropping down to round a salty bay, at other times skirting the edge of a bluff, offering marine panoramas. Nearly all roads are two-lane blacktop with very little shoulder, but traffic moves at a relaxed pace, and traveling the roads is quite safe if simple precautions are observed. There are a few short sections of county road on the southwest side of the island that are teeth-jarring gravel washboards.

Virtually all facilities and services found on San Juan Island are located at Friday Harbor. Small stores at Roche Harbor and Mitchell Bay pump fuel and carry supplies for campers, boaters, and anglers, but the selection is limited.

A handful of resorts, hotels, and motels at Friday Harbor and a few other locations on the island provide overnight accommodations by day or week, ranging from modern motels to rustic beach cabins. A number

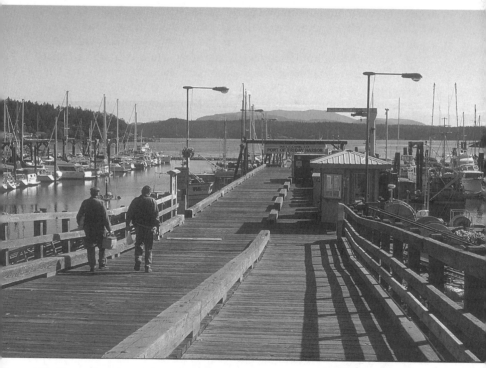

The Port of Friday Harbor dock hosts both pleasure and commercial vessels.

of homes that have been converted to bed-and-breakfast inns offer over-night lodging in a gracious, homey atmosphere. A local real estate agency carries listings of private homes that can be rented for a week or longer. Advance reservations are essential in summer for all lodging.

In addition to the county campground at Smallpox Bay, commercial camping facilities are available at a trailer park in Friday Harbor, at Lakedale near Sportsman Lake, and at the marina at Mitchell Bay. There is also a bicycle campground about a mile west of False Bay. Some camp-grounds will accept reservations; call for current information. Parking or tenting overnight along the road is not permitted.

The only public saltwater boat launch ramps on the island are at Jack-son Beach and San Juan County Park. Commercial ramps, which may be used by the public for a fee, are located at Shipyard Cove Marina on Turn Point Road ½ mile east of Friday Harbor; at Roche Harbor Re-sort; and at Snug Harbor Resort on Mitchell Bay. Numerous parks and road ends provide put-ins for kayaks and other hand-carried boats.

FRIDAY HARBOR

Access: Ferry or airplane to San Juan Island, boat
Facilities: Groceries, stores, gas, diesel, marine repair, boat launch (sling, ramp) (fee), boat rentals and charters, guest moorage, dock with water and electrical hookups, restrooms, showers, laundry, fishing tackle and bait, hotels, restaurants, movie theater, bicycle and moped rentals, car rentals, tour buses, U.S. Customs
Attractions: Boating, paddling, fishing, shopping, sightseeing, several annual festivals, marine laboratories, museums

An enchanting mix of old and new establishments, some "shopping-center modern," some elderly but beautifully renovated, still others nostalgically decrepit—all with a dash of salt thrown in. Shopping facilities are within easy walking distance of the ferry landing and public boat moorages. Several grocery stores provide delivery service to the Port of Friday Harbor dock, fine restaurants cater to tourists with offerings ranging from ethnic to gourmet seafood, galleries offer quality work by local artists and craftspeople, while other shops have selections of souvenirs, books, and gifts for the folks back home.

Ferries from Anacortes, Sidney, and the other ferry-served islands arrive regularly during the day to disgorge their passengers. Sometimes two of the green-and-white behemoths are in the harbor, one patiently treading water in the outer bay, awaiting its turn at the slip.

Friday Harbor is virtually a nautical Times Square of the Northwest—stand there long enough and eventually every cruising boat that you know will pass by. The public dock plays host to around 12,000 overnight transient boats in June, July, and August, and an equal number stop briefly to refuel, shop, or clear customs.

The marina has a total of 463 slips, 151 of which are available for transient moorage; 21 of these may be reserved. Guest slips are on both sides of G dock and the inside of H dock, the first two docks encountered upon entering the moorage area. In addition, both sides of the A breakwater, the inside of B breakwater, and both sides of C breakwater provide another 1,500 feet of guest moorage. If unable to find overnight moorage space in the visitors' floats, check with the dock office for available space in the permanent moorages. Do not tie up to a permanent moorage without permission from the dock office. Make slip reservations by calling the port office on VHF channel 66A, or by telephone at the number listed in appendix A.

If unable to secure a space, the area southeast of the ferry landing or near the University of Washington Laboratories provides some anchorages within dinghy range of the floats. Use care to anchor well out of the path of the ferries. Spring Street Landing, just west of the ferry slips, is reserved for commercial moorage and charter vessels.

The building at the head of the Port of Friday Harbor dock complex houses the harbormaster's office and restrooms with showers for visiting mariners. U.S. Customs is located in the yacht club building half a block to the west. During summer daytime hours customs officers can also be found at a shed on the outer breakwater. Booths at the end of A breakwater, at the head of G dock, and at the head of the main dock, may be staffed by the port to facilitate registration for moorage in the summer.

Even nonsailors will enjoy a stroll down the floats to admire, and perhaps envy, the many boats, some from exotic hailing ports. The commercial fishing fleet ties up on the larger docks—gillnetters and purse seiners with huge stern-mounted metal spools rolled fat with nets.

At low tide, dock pilings reveal underwater coatings of fluffy sea anemones, feather duster worms, opalescent nudibranchs, and spidery decorator crabs who glue bits of seaweed to their bodies as protective camouflage. Youngsters also enjoy dipping nets for shrimp from along the edges of the floats.

If interest in the nautical scene of Friday Harbor palls, the rest of the island awaits. For persons arriving by boat or on foot via the ferry, various forms of transportation are available—some of them quite unique. Cars, bicycles, or mopeds are available for rent, tour buses make regular guided circuits of the island in summer (one is an old-fashioned double-decker bus), at times a horse-drawn carriage offers rides, or planes can be chartered at the airport for aerial sightseeing.

Whale Museum

Where can you go to get a fish's-eye view of the 20-foot underbelly of an orca, stare into the jaws of a minke whale, or listen to whales singing? In Friday Harbor, where the country's only museum devoted exclusively to the study of whales is located!

This outstanding facility features interesting displays on these great mammals. Models (some of them life-size) and actual whale skeletons fill the rooms, while murals, videos, and other exhibits give further information on the evolution of whales, kinds of whales and their anatomical differences, how whales communicate, and how to identify local whales. One room has related activities especially designed for children. A gift shop stocks a broad selection of books on whales and marine ecology, as well a variety of whale-decorated souvenirs.

The Whale Museum is not an attic for storing old bones, but a vital, ongoing research and educational facility dedicated to the living whale, as well as other aspects of marine ecology. Volunteers from the museum staff whale observation posts at various sites on the island. Kayak cruises, workshops, and classes, are offered regularly. The museum's publications include a newsletter, an elementary school teaching curriculum about whales, a guide to Puget Sound marine mammals, and a video.

A "Whale Hotline," maintained here, catalogs calls of sightings to better understand the habits and movements of local pods of orcas.

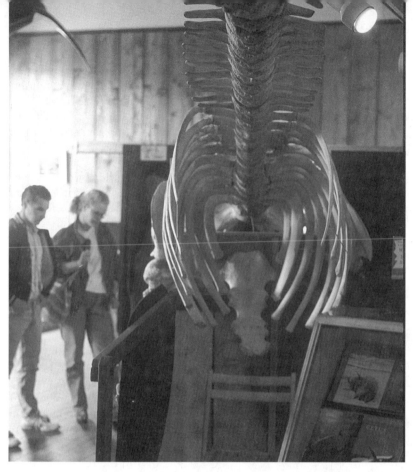

Exhibits at the Whale Museum in Friday Harbor fascinate visitors.

Researchers have identified over a hundred different orcas by means of their size, sex, distinctive fin shapes, and scars. Each individual identified is given a number and, in some cases, an affectionate name. Some are known as Jelly Roll, Ewok, Victoria, Chinook, Squirty, and Granny.

The Orca Adoption program is a unique service that was instituted by the Whale Museum. Persons who contribute $25 or more receive an adoption certificate, photo, and biography of the whale of their choice, along with a quarterly newsletter and membership benefits in the museum. Money raised by this program is used for research to help protect the future of the Puget Sound orca.

The Whale Museum is located in Friday Harbor at 62 First Street North, at the intersection of First and Court streets, three blocks from the ferry terminal. To find it, go south on Spring Street to First, then right two blocks to Court. From the port dock it can be reached via a short trail that leaves Front Street across from the road leading to the dock.

The facility, which is housed in the conspicuous two-story building with a whale painting on it, is easily recognized from the harbor. It is open daily from 10:00 A.M. to 5:00 P.M. June through September, and 11:00 A.M. to 4:00 P.M. October through May. Group tours are available with advance notice. Some commercial wildlife cruises include a tour of the Whale Museum as part of their package.

Once you've absorbed all you can about whales, head for Lime Kiln Point State Park, on the west shore of the island. Here visitors have a good chance of seeing whales as they pass by in Haro Strait. The park is described later in this chapter.

San Juan Island Historical Museum

It has been claimed that San Juan County has more museums per capita than any other county in the United States. Whether this is true or not, there's no disputing their quality. The fine San Juan Island Historical Museum is housed in a two-story white clapboard farmhouse in Friday Harbor, at 405 Price Street, just north of the intersection of Price and Spring streets, about ½ mile from the ferry dock. Park in the lot shared by the Saint Francis Catholic Church.

The house, which was once the home of pioneer James King, is furnished in the style of a gracious home during the turn of the century. It also contains memorabilia from pioneer times and the Pig War. Outbuildings hold antique farm equipment. The museum is open May through September on Wednesday through Saturday, 1:00 P.M. to 4:30 P.M., but during the winter only on Thursday and Friday, or by appointment.

An antique fire bell graces the lawn outside the San Juan Island Historical Museum.

The Pig War Museum

One of the most famous historical incidents in the San Juan Islands is the "almost" Pig War with Great Britain in the late 1800s. In 1958 longtime San Juan resident Emelia

Bave was invited to produce a play commemorating the Pig War at a pageant. Although she was able to cajole local citizens to serve as actors in the initial presentation, few were bitten by the stage bug enough to put in the required time on produce the pageant annually.

The "San Juan Saga" continued for a time using a minimal group of actors, substituting mannequins and tableaus for the missing cast. When Bave's health no longer permitted her to present the show, the various tableaus that had built up over time were assembled and housed in a museum, where they can be seen today. Each scene depicts a significant event in San Juan Island's history between 1850 and 1870, and placards explain the history depicted.

The museum, which is located at the corner of Guard and Tucker, about ½ mile from the ferry landing, is open Memorial Day to Labor Day from noon to 6:00 P.M., or by special appointment.

University of Washington Friday Harbor Laboratories

With shorelines ranging from quiet bays and saltwater lagoons to rocky shelves swept by swift-flowing tides, the San Juan archipelago provides an exceptional opportunity for marine research. Tidal fluctuations of nearly 12 feet expose vast tidelands harboring specimens of many diverse marine plant and invertebrate species.

Recognizing the unique character of the archipelago, the University of Washington established a marine biology research center on San Juan Island in 1904. When land from a former military reserve at Point Caution just north of Friday Harbor became available, the laboratories moved onto the 484-acre tract, there growing to become a fine educational and research facility, attracting visiting scientists from all over the world.

Ferries arriving at Friday Harbor pass the attractive campus on the north shore of the outer harbor. A modern-day aqueduct can be seen snaking along the bank; fashioned of polyethylene, the pipe delivers contaminant-free sea water to the laboratory aquaria.

In the past the laboratories offered guided tours to visitors. Unfortunately, funding constraints made it necessary to discontinue these popular tours. At present the labs are open only to those involved in research.

The University of Washington also administers biological preserves at several areas in the San Juans. These lands have been donated, purchased, or leased to protect them in a nearly natural state for research and educational purposes. The largest of these holdings is on Shaw Island, and includes most of the land and shoreline extending from Point George to Squaw Bay; others are at Argyle Lagoon and False Bay on San Juan Island and Iceberg Point and Point Colville on the southern end of Lopez Island.

Intertidal Life

Intertidal lands in the San Juan Islands are vast displays of marine life, where the competition and predation of these animals and their peculiar adaptations for survival can be seen. Delicate interrelationships are easily disrupted by public misuse, and overcollecting of any particular species, even natural predators such as starfish, can have far-reaching effects on the overall marine balance (in addition to being unlawful).

Especially sensitive are very slow-growing species that must not be harvested in quantity due to their long replacement cycle. While the edible mussel is fast-growing and readily replaces itself, the California mussel— larger, with a rougher ribbed shell—is much slower to replace itself in chilly Northwest waters. Goose barnacles, which sometimes are gathered for food, are also slow-growing in the San Juans. Abalone were once rare here, then became quite abundant; overharvesting of this popular food item in recent years has depleted their numbers. Harvesting of abalone is now closed until the population recovers.

Scuba divers and anglers often take rockfish on rocky bottoms near pilings. A rockfish two feet long needs thirty years to grow that large, compared to a salmon, which will grow to an equal size in three to four years. It makes a lot of sense to protect large rockfish, because they contribute relatively enormous numbers of young fish to the population annually, in addition to taking a long time to achieve their large size. Taking smaller individuals, e.g., one to three pounds, has a lesser impact on future generations.

With an increasing scarcity of choice butter clams, oysters, and Dungeness crabs, human beach-foragers are displaying a greater interest in adding to their gastronomic fare the more bizarre marine

Turn Island Marine State Park

Park area: 35 acres; 3 miles of shoreline on San Juan Channel
Access: Boat
Facilities: 10 campsites, picnic tables, stoves, composting toilet, pit toilets, 3 mooring buoys, 3 miles of trail, *no water*
Attractions: Camping, picnicking, beachcombing, hiking, fishing, clams, crabs, mussels, tidepools, scuba diving, paddling

Just around the corner from Friday Harbor is a gem of a little island. For those who do not make it to the more highly touted marine state forms: leathery chitons, limpets and moon snails, grotesque sea cucumbers and goose barnacles, and a variety of edible seaweed.

The taking for food use of nearly every form of marine life in Washington is controlled by state law. The Department of Fish and Wildlife sport-fishing guide, available at most sporting goods stores, lists bag limits and other restrictions. The gathering of seaweed is also regulated.

Even the removal of non-living things such as driftwood or empty shells from the beaches can have negative effects on marine life. For example, at Lime Kiln Lighthouse hermit crabs have severe competition for shells. People removing

Anemones in a San Juan tidepool

shells that could serve as shelters can cause these invertebrates to become exposed to predators or the environment.

In order to protect marine lands, all of the seashores and sea-bed of San Juan County and around Cypress Island in Skagit County are designated a marine biological preserve. Areas with this status are open for public recreation, but Washington State law prohibits the taking or destruction of any living specimen, except for food use, without written permission of the Director of the Friday Harbor Laboratories.

parks lying at the fringes of the San Juans, Turn Island gives them a tasty sampling. The island is under joint jurisdiction; it is owned by the federal government as a part of the San Juan Islands National Wildlife Refuge, and is managed cooperatively by the state for public recreational use as a marine state park.

The best anchorages are found on the west side of the island, where there are three buoys (the southernmost of these is within about 30 to 35 feet of the rocky shore at minus tides). Moorages here are only slightly sheltered by the landmasses and can be quite uncomfortable in a stiff northerly or with the slosh of heavy boat traffic on San Juan

Channel; at other times they promise a pleasant night's stay.

At low tide the southwest end of the island becomes a big tideflat, with clams and mussels awaiting harvesting. Tidepools are exposed at low, low water, or they can be observed by floating in a dinghy just offshore and gazing down into the water at the dazzling undersea world of marine life: brilliant purples, oranges, and reds; pastel pinks, greens, and lavenders—the color range is limitless. Polarized sunglasses reduce glare on the water and make viewing easier. The shallow water is excellent for snorkeling.

Camping and picnicking is concentrated on the southwest end of the island; the balance of the land is a wildlife refuge. Five campsites and pit toilets are sequestered in the open timber at the main campsite above the west beach, another four sites and toilets are found above the gravel beach of the next cove to the south, and two more sites are found on the east side of the low south point of the island. In summer the few campsites are frequently full, although the lack of drinking water precludes an extended stay.

A 300-yard path cuts across the middle of the island, connecting the main camping area with a pretty, 500-foot-long gravel beach on the far side. Encircling the island, another connecting trail invites a pleasant 1-mile tramp through light timber, looking out over busy San Juan Channel. At points on the southeast side of the island, the trail hangs very

A Turn Island campsite

close to an eroding bluff about 100 feet above the beach—not the place for unattended children!

Near the northeast end, Turn Rock, with its navigational beacon, can be seen just offshore. The island and rock are so named because they mark the point where vessels must turn in the channel. The rock is another of the bird sanctuaries of the San Juan Islands National Wildlife Refuge, and is usually covered with chattering, busybody gulls.

The northeast side of the island is precipitous, with only a few tenuous trails dropping to beaches that disappear at high tide. Beaches around the rest of the island are easily reached from the trail above. Near the east end of the island the trail passes an enormous 10-foot-high rock erratic, silent testimony to the geological forces that shaped this region.

Rabbits, raccoons, and other small mammals inhabit the forest, along with black-tailed deer. These deer, which can be found throughout the San Juans, swim from island to island, sometimes across extremely broad and swift-flowing channels.

Turn Island at one time held a huge bald eagle nest; however, the tree supporting it broke in a storm, destroying it. Reported to have been in continuous use by several generations of eagles for over seventy years, the nest had been abandoned at the time of its destruction. Frequent disturbances by humans can cause the birds to abandon a nesting site, or they may be driven out by infestations of vermin brought to the nest on captured rodents. There are other eagle nesting sites in the vicinity.

Situated so near the boating throngs at Friday Harbor, Turn Island receives considerable use, especially by boaters with small craft that can be beached on the island's inviting shores. In good weather even rowboats can manage an excursion through Friday Harbor and along the shores of San Juan Island to the park. En route, view the many gracious homes lining the shores on San Juan and Brown islands. Total distance is less than 2 nautical miles, all of it near land. Boats can be launched at Shipyard Cove Marina on Turn Point Road, for a fee.

Turn Point Road Access

Put in hand-carried boats at a public access area on San Juan Island just spitting distance from Turn Island. To reach it by car, follow Harrison, a one-way street heading east along the shore of Friday Harbor. In a few blocks Harrison joins Warbuss Way and then becomes Turn Point Road. The road winds around Turn Point, and about 2 miles from Friday Harbor, arrives at a gravel parking lot where a path leads to picnic tables on nice grassy patches above the beach. Turn Island can be seen ¼ mile across the channel.

Jackson Beach

Park area: 10 acres
Access: Ferry to San Juan Island, boat
Facilities: Boat launch (ramp), portable toilets
Attractions: Picnicking, volleyball, boating, paddling, beachcombing

A public launch ramp for trailered boats in the vicinity of Friday Harbor is found at Jackson Beach. To reach it drive south out of Friday Harbor on Argyle Avenue. In ¾ mile turn east on Pear Point Road. Just after a large former sand and gravel operation is reached, Jackson Beach Road branches south and heads downhill to the launch ramp.

The road along the spit enclosing Argyle Lagoon ends at a fish cannery. With the exception of this commercial property and the lagoon itself, the spit is a public day-use area. On the inside of the spit, between the lagoon and the cannery, a two-lane concrete ramp with adjacent float drops into a small, protected cove.

More than just a boat launch, this narrow strand also includes one of the nicest beaches on this end of the island, sloping and with a jumble of driftwood logs at the high-tide level. Three pullouts above the beach provide ample parking. The north end of the beach is wide, flat sand, with a volleyball court and ample space for kite flying, Frisbee™ games, or other beach pastimes.

Argyle Lagoon, on the inside of the spit, is a research area for the Friday Harbor Laboratories; one condition for public use of the beach is

Jackson Beach occupies a long sandspit.

that the lagoon will be protected and restricted from any public access. The lagoon is used primarily for short-term research projects, as it functions as a "mini-ocean." In such a controlled environment distinct populations can be followed, or small plots can be manipulated in order to observe the effects.

THE NORTH END

Sportsman and Egg Lakes

Area: Sportsman Lake—87 acres; Egg Lake—6½ acres
Access: Ferry to San Juan Island
Facilities: Sportsman Lake—boat launch (ramp); Egg Lake—float
Attractions: Fishing, birdwatching, paddling

Bird heaven! Cattails and bogs edge the open water of two lakes only a few minutes' drive from Friday Harbor. Red-winged blackbirds perch sidesaddle on cattails; an array of wild migratory waterfowl coexists with plump domestic ducks and geese from neighboring farms. During spring mating season, marsh birds loudly advertise their territorial

Sportsman Lake

boundaries. All this and fish too!

Sportsman Lake lies to the left of the Roche Harbor Road, 4 miles northwest of Friday Harbor. A short spur road on the northeast side of the lake leads to a gravel boat ramp.

Open to fishing year-round, the shallow, 87-acre lake contains largemouth bass and spiny ray. All surrounding lands are private, but no matter, for the beauty lies in the bogs and the birds and the tranquil water. Drop in a boat for fishing, birdwatching, or just paddling around the lake.

Sportsman's tiny counterpart, Egg Lake, lies just 300 yards to the west. To reach the lake, continue west on the Roche Harbor Road for less than ½ mile to the intersection with Egg Lake Road. Turn left and follow the road for ¾ mile; through the trees on the left the lake and a small float can be seen. This is the only public access.

Egg Lake is regularly stocked with rainbow trout. Fishing is permitted year-round; gasoline motors are not legal. Aside from the public dock, all bordering lands are private.

Lakedale Campground

Area: 82 acres
Access: Ferry to San Juan Island
Facilities: 88 standard campsites, 10 bicycle campsites, 19 RV sites, 6 group campsites, 3 tent cabins, 6 2-bedrooms cabins, picnic tables, restrooms, showers, drinking water, fireplaces, boat and fishing-gear rental, fishing docks, groceries, camping equipment
Attractions: Camping, fishing, swimming, birdwatching, paddling

The overburdened little county campground at Smallpox Bay is the only public facility for campers on San Juan Island; however, a 200-acre commercial campground and recreation area located just north of Egg and Sportsman lakes offers everything a camper might wish—and then some. Here, former marshes have been dammed to form a network of three private lakes for fishing, swimming, rowing, and canoeing, and the shorelands are available for camping or daytime picnics.

Nearly a hundred campsites are scattered along the shores of the lakes, some in timber, others in open grassy areas. Because the lakes are private, fishing licenses are not required, but a fee is charged.

The entrance to the campground is on Roche Harbor Road, ¼ mile north of the Egg Lake Road intersection.

Reuben Tarte Picnic Area

Park area: 6 acres; 600 feet of shoreline on Spieden Channel
Facilities: Portable toilet during summer months
Attractions: Scuba diving, birdwatching, picnicking

This out-of-the-way corner offers no facilities other than a portable toilet and garbage containers, but it is an interesting little nook that has a certain appeal.

Reuben Tarte Picnic Area is located on a rocky prominence southwest of Limestone Point, on the north side of San Juan Island. To reach it, follow Roche Harbor Road for 8 miles from Friday Harbor, and turn right (north) onto Rouleau Road. In 1 mile turn right again (east) at the intersection with Limestone Point Road. At a T intersection in 1 mile, turn right, now heading south, on San Juan Drive.

In about ¼ mile a road, which may be unmarked, goes left down to the beach. For a year or so, the steep, rutted, slippery road was gated, but after much controversy and threats of lawsuits by the handicapped, the county finally agreed to pave the road to the beach and install a gate to limit use to sunrise to sunset. Parking at the road end is restricted to 15 minutes for unloading and loading only. Additional parking is provided at the top of the hill. Trailers, motorcycles, and ORVs are not permitted on the road.

A grassy rock knoll pokes into San Juan Channel, between two tiny coves. The underwater rock formations of the point and offshore reefs are home for copious amounts of marine life, making the area a favorite with scuba divers, who explore along the channel and northwest to Limestone Point.

Colonies of coral and other sedentary marine animals, growing in the warm waters of an ancient sea, created the typical beds of white limestone that distinctively mark the 80-foot-high knob of Limestone Point.

ROCHE HARBOR

Access: Ferry to San Juan Island, airplane, floatplane, boat
Facilities: Guest moorage, dock with water and electrical hookups,
mooring buoys (fee), boat launch (ramp)(fee), boat rental, gas, diesel,

restrooms, showers, laundry, groceries, hotel, restaurant, swimming pool, tennis courts, moped rental, U.S. Customs

Attractions: Boating, paddling, fishing, hiking, scuba diving, sightseeing, historic landmarks

Relics of an earlier, much different era mingle easily with the trappings of a modern-day vacation resort. A 100-year-old log cabin stands within a few feet of busy tennis courts and an Olympic-size swimming pool. Skeletons of a tug and a ferry, reminders of the industrial heyday of the town, molder on the beach overlooking the posh fiberglass cruisers bobbing at their moorings. Visitors register at the hotel, which in the 1850s saw duty as a Hudson's Bay trading post and which later hosted Presidents Teddy Roosevelt and William Howard Taft.

To reach Roche Harbor from the Friday Harbor ferry landing, drive west on Spring Street, turning right on Second Street. In 3 blocks turn left on Guard and after one more block, right on Tucker. At a Y in the road, bear left on Roche Harbor Road, which continues to the resort, 10¼ miles from the ferry landing.

The harbor is 11 nautical miles by boat from Friday Harbor and 22 nautical miles from Victoria Harbor on Vancouver Island. In summer the bustling docks are a happy mingling of Canadian and Yankee boaters checking in at Customs and stocking up on provisions and fuel before moving on to more remote islands. Rows of buoys in the harbor are filled by early evening, and courtesy boats from the resort, like large

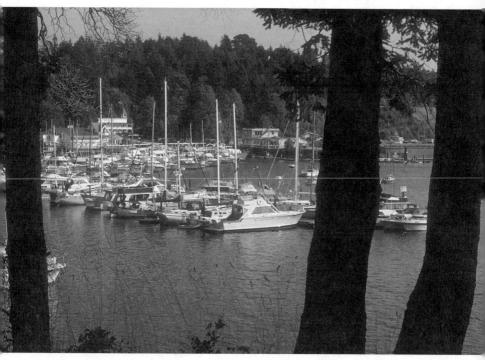

Roche Harbor Resort has moorage space for boats on floats and buoys.

water bugs, ferry boaters from their buoys to the shore and back. Old friends are met, new ones are made, and sea stories are swapped.

On the week of Dominion Day (July 1) and the Fourth of July, the harbor is jammed with upwards of 500 boats and is even more festive, with fireworks and special events. The evening flag-lowering ceremony, which takes place throughout the summer months, holds special meaning at this time when Canadians and Americans join together in friendship to honor their countries.

Trailered boats may be launched for a fee at a surfaced ramp just south of the resort parking area. Boat trailer parking is on the hill south of the quarries. The resort can also be reached by private plane at an airfield near the resort.

The historic old hotel and restaurant, graced with a prize-winning formal flower garden, are the center of harbor activity. A display in the lobby of the Hotel de Haro tells of Roche Harbor's history. A young Indiana lawyer, John S. McMillin, built the largest lime-producing company west of the Mississippi, and for fifty years "ruled" the town. He

Visitors enjoy a stroll in the formal garden at Roche Harbor Resort.

became one of the richest and most influential men in the state, ran (unsuccessfully) for the U.S. Senate, and even entertained hopes of becoming governor of Washington.

After McMillin's death in 1936, his son operated the family business until the lime deposits began to play out. In 1956 the town was sold; the lime kilns were shut down shortly thereafter. Subsequent owners have restored the deteriorated buildings and developed the property into a modern resort that offers fine vacation and boating facilities to visitors.

Afterglow Vista Mausoleum

Forsake the activity of Roche Harbor for a stroll through quiet woods to rub elbows with the McMillin family ghosts. From the Hotel de Haro follow the path northwest past the church toward the swimming pool. On the left is a one-room log cabin, believed to have been the home of the Scurr brothers, who lived here in the mid-1880s and who sold the property to John McMillin.

Continue on the path until it joins Roche Harbor Road in 1½ mile. Turn left (north) and follow the blacktopped road past a small cemetery that sits just above the road, and in ¼ mile find a dirt side road on the right. This side road is barred to vehicles, although it is often used by horseback riders and bicyclists. In 200 yards the path reaches the gateway arch of the mausoleum.

Several tiers of stairs lead to a platform encircled with Doric columns. In the center is a round stone table surrounded by six stone chairs. The encroaching forest adds to the eerie calm of the spot. It is a privilege to be permitted to visit this unique shrine; please treat it with respect.

John McMillin chose this spot for his final resting place because he enjoyed the splendid sunset afterglow on Spieden Channel; however today second-growth timber obscures the view he so prized. The significance of the construction of the tomb is based on the family history and on the Masonic Order, of which McMillin was a member. The intentionally broken column represents life broken by death, while the ring supporting the remaining columns represents the eternal life after death.

The table and chairs are placed just as they were in the family dining room, with McMillin at the head of the table and an open space at the foot facing westward, so that all could enjoy the sunset. The bases of the chairs hold the ashes of the deceased members of the family, who rest here for eternity, their spirits watching the sunset just as they did in life.

Beyond the road to the mausoleum, the main road drops downhill to end at private drives. Near the swimming pool/tennis court complex are more antique log cabins, still in use as storage sheds, and the debris of two boats wrecked long ago. From here walk the beach back to Roche Harbor; total distance of the loop hike is 1 mile.

Lime Quarry

A row of abandoned lime kilns overlooks the waters of Roche Harbor. For a closer inspection of the kilns and the quarries that were the lifeblood of the town, take a loop hike along the road, pausing to inspect the rusted railroad tracks and machinery, visualizing the quarries at the height of their productivity, when 15,000 barrels of lime per day were turned out.

From the grocery store walk southwest along the road at the water's edge. Immediately to the left are the lime kilns, with their gracefully arching brickwork still intact. Continue uphill, following the road left when it turns sharply at the first intersection. Pass gaping quarries where undergrowth is creeping back to gentle the harsh outlines. A short, marked trail wanders through the forest that now grows in the quarries, reaching a hilltop viewing platform.

Near the top of the hill, stop and enjoy a sweeping view of Roche Harbor, Spieden Channel, Mosquito Pass, and Henry Island before the road ducks into the timber, losing sight of the harbor. Turn left at the intersection with a blacktopped road, then left again at a driveway that drops steeply downhill past some private homes, headed back to the bay. The driveway dead-ends at a path that brings the hiker back to the plaza between the hotel and the restaurant, a short distance from the grocery store. Total round-trip distance is 1¾ miles.

Posey Island Marine State Park

Park area: 1 acre, 1,000 feet of shoreline on Spieden Channel
Access: Boat
Facilities: 2 campsites (maximum 16 persons), picnic tables, pit toilet (Designated Cascadia Marine Trail campsite)
Attractions: Camping, picnicking, beachcombing, fishing, paddling, scuba diving, snorkeling, tidepools

A dot of an island just outside Roche Harbor provides a lovely afternoon picnic spot, or in fair weather a campsite with a superb sunset. The accommodations at Posey Island are meager, with a couple of scruffy picnic tables and space for a few tents, but its proximity to Roche Harbor makes this a popular site.

The island lies less than a nautical mile northeast of Roche Harbor, the nearest place where boats can be launched. Boaters in small craft can take a shorter route through the channel at the east end of Pearl Island, while deeper draft vessels are better advised to stay in the main channel at the west end of Pearl and anchor well out, as the water surrounding Posey Island is quite shallow and reefs extend out on the north and east. The protected, shallow water makes this an ideal voyage for a canoe or kayak, and the island is designated as a Cascadia Marine Trail campsite.

Because the sun goes down in the rainy district of Vancouver Island, the San Juans have exceptionally vivid sunsets. The crimson and gold colors, intensified by the black masses of the islands, linger in the sky and sea long after the sun has disappeared. Posey Island, with its open views of Haro Strait and Canadian islands, is a prime spot for savoring the afterglow.

THE WEST SIDE

Mosquito Pass

Mosquito Pass, a skinny, 1½-mile-long waterway separating Henry and San Juan islands, connects Roche Harbor and Westcott, Garrison, and Mitchell bays. The pass and the three shallow bays are ideal for small-boat exploration, although tidal currents can be strong and unpredictable in Mosquito Pass itself, where unpowered boats should use great care.

Deep-keeled vessels should not attempt the channel without the aid of charts, as there are many rocks and shoals where the unwary can find themselves embarrassingly aground. A phalanx of reefs and shoals marks the south end of the channel. Pay close attention to navigational markers and observe the 7-mph, no-wake zone in the pass.

Henry Island

Resembling a letter H crudely scrawled in the water to the west of Mosquito Pass, Henry Island shelters the San Juan bays from waves off Haro Strait. The island rests on the protruding edge of an underwater shelf, and bluffs on the west side plunge steeply downward to a depth of 120 fathoms. The edges of this shelf, especially areas off Kellett Bluff on the south and McCracken Point on the north, provide fine fishing and scuba diving. At Kellett Bluff, deep caves that harbor enormous lingcod are a major attraction for divers.

Open Bay, indenting the bottom of the H, and a small bight north of Nelson Bay, at its top, give anchorage to boaters escaping the summertime bustle of Roche Harbor. Do not go ashore, for the entire island is privately owned. Approximately 80 acres at Kellett Bluff on the tip of the southwest lobe of the island are a lighthouse reservation; however, the steepness of the shore makes landing there impractical.

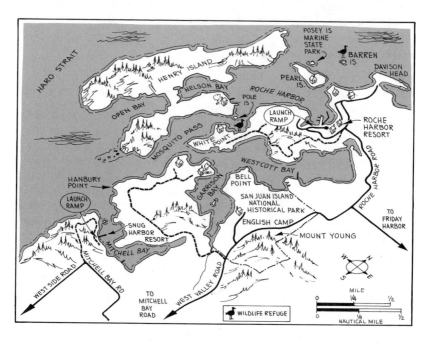

Battleship Island

One mile due north of Henry Island, chunky Battleship Island, with "smokestacks" of three trees, surely does resemble its namesake in both size and shape. Battleship Island, Barren Island (lying to the east of the entrance to Roche Harbor near Davidson Head), and Pole Island (in the north entrance of Mosquito Pass) are all part of the San Juan Islands National Wildlife Refuge.

Underwater rocks host abundant sea life. Sea urchins, encrusting sponges, and anemones create a colorful fantasyland that attracts scuba divers.

Westcott Bay

Although most boaters visiting the English Camp portion of San Juan Island National Historical Park drop anchor in Garrison Bay, some choose to stop in Westcott Bay and walk the short trail along Bell Point. For descriptions of adjacent Garrison Bay and English Camp, see the following chapter.

Two protruding points on either shore divide Westcott Bay into two areas. The best anchorage is in the southwest portion of the bay; the northeast end becomes quite shallow. An extensive aquaculture operation on the southeast shore raises oysters, mussels, and clams for sale to restaurants. Give the underwater pens a wide berth. The sea farm has oysters for sale to visitors.

Mitchell Bay

Access: Ferry to San Juan Island, boat
Facilities: (at Snug Harbor) Guest moorage, gas, outboard mix, boat launch (ramp) (fee), cabins, campground, restrooms, groceries, boat rental and charter, marine repair and supplies, fishing tackle, scuba air
Attractions: Camping, boating, fishing, scuba diving, crabbing

The small marina on the south shore of Mitchell Bay is well named, as the entrance to the harbor is, indeed, very snug. However, once inside this cozy little haven the water is adequately deep for most small craft in all but extremely low tides. At the entrance a shoal marked by a small island extends from the south side of the bay; stay well to the north of this rock. All beaches and docks are private, except for the marina on the south shore.

To reach Mitchell Bay by land, head south from Roche Harbor Road on West Valley Road, and in 3¾ miles turn west on Mitchell Bay Road. The road winds downhill to the marina and resort in 2 miles. On the hillside behind the resort 11 campsites are laid out on a series of graded

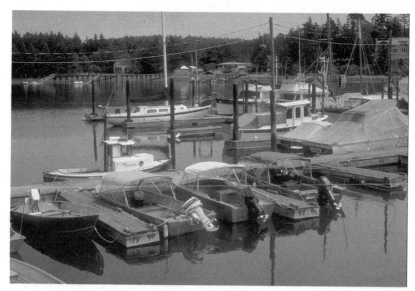

Snug Harbor Marina in Mitchell Bay

platforms in the woods above the bay; a few RV campsites can be found just above the beach and resort gate.

HARO STRAIT

San Juan County Park

Park area: 15 acres
Access: Ferry to San Juan Island, boat
Facilities: 11 campsites (restricted commercial use), picnic tables, fireplaces, restrooms, groceries, boat launch (ramp), group camp, *no water*
Attractions: Boating, scuba diving, snorkeling, beachcombing, tidepools

The story is told that long ago a number of Indians stricken with smallpox plunged into the icy San Juan waters to rid themselves of their burning fever; as a result they died of pneumonia. The tiny bay on the west side of San Juan Island where the tragedy occurred has since that time been called Smallpox Bay.

Despite its unfortunate history, today the bay is of more pleasant significance, for it is the site of popular San Juan County Park. Located on West Side Road, 3 miles southwest of the intersection of West Valley and Mitchell Bay roads, the park occupies land at the head of the bay and an abandoned orchard on a bluff. Although the park officially has only 11 campsites, and a group camp near the office/store, nearly a hundred people may be crammed into its 12 acres on summer weekends. To be assured of a site during busy times, make reservations well ahead. Campers must bring their own water or purchase it in jugs at the campground store.

The pressure of such numbers is beginning to show in the pollution of the water system, the deterioration of the flora, and the irascibility of local residents who are unable to find a place to camp in their own park. To better enjoy the area and be appreciated by the San Juan Islanders, visit off-season.

In winter, when it is uncrowded, it is a relaxing spot with exquisite nighttime views across Haro Strait to the lights of Vancouver Island. Explore the shores of the bay or saunter through twisted madronas to the top of the bluff, but even the healthy risk pneumonia by attempting to swim in the bay.

With dive spots within walking distance of campsites, the park is a favorite among scuba divers. Easy snorkeling is found in the bay, while the rocky bottom that plunges steeply to 80 feet just offshore is a challenge to more experienced divers. In addition to the usual bright palette of anemone, urchins, and starfish, look for abalone clinging to rocks and octopuses hiding in crevices.

Gulls, and sometimes seals, congregate on Low Island, 100 yards offshore—another of the bird refuges of the San Juan Islands National Wildlife Refuge.

The tiny log cabin in the campground was built at the turn of the century as a home for a widowed homesteader and his daughter. While the building was under construction, the pair lived in a cave that he dug in the side of a nearby hill. The cabin once had an outside stairway to provide access to the daughter's bedroom on the second floor.

Lime Kiln Point State Park

Park area: 36 acres; 2,550 feet of shoreline on Haro Strait
Access: Ferry to San Juan Island
Facilities: Composting toilets, picnic tables, interpretive displays, drinking water
Attractions: Whale watching, birdwatching, picnicking, lighthouse, interpretive programs

Passing San Juan County Park, West Side Road continues southward through thick second-growth timber. In 3 miles it curves around a hill and bursts suddenly into open marine views. To the right, at the bend of the hairpin curve, a single-lane dirt road leads to Lime Kiln State Park.

Recognizing the unique location of the park on a rocky point overlooking Haro Strait, the state has developed it as a whale-watching site, complete with interpretive signs. Volunteers from the Whale Museum are usually on duty to answer questions daily between June 1 and August 10, and on weekends from May to September.

A hundred feet down the road are two parking areas. A modern restroom with composting toilets is by the lower lot. The trail leading to the whalewatching viewpoint is disabled accessible; other trails follow the rocky shoreline north to additional viewpoints and the lighthouse.

From the parking lot a short trail leads to grass-covered rocks above Haro Strait, dotted with picnic tables for resting while awaiting the arrival of whales. A set of interpretive signs here explains identification of minke whales, orcas, Dall's porpoises, and harbor porpoises, and describes characteristics of their behavior.

June through September is prime whale-watching season as these mammals search Haro Strait for runs of salmon returning to Fraser River spawning grounds. There's no guarantee that whales will appear on cue; come armed with binoculars and a lot of patience; in summer whales may pass by here several times during the day, usually within ¾ mile of the shore, and at times much closer. While waiting for the whales to appear, focus binoculars on the variety of waterfowl that gather to feed in offshore tide rips, explore tidepools along the shore, or have a picnic.

Beyond the parking area for the park the road is gated, but it continues as a footpath past ranger residences to Lime Kiln Lighthouse. Poised on a rocky outcropping where it balefully hoots its presence to passing

Spotting Whales

Whale sightings are certainly one of the most thrilling experiences of the San Juans, and one that is not reserved for boaters alone. Family groups (called pods) have been seen from land at many places in addition to Lime Kiln Point State Park, and even from the ferry. At such times ferry captains have been known to slow their engines and alert passengers who want to take in the sight.

A spotting may consist of only a momentary revelation—a fish flinging itself out of the grayness of the sea, twisting frantically, then dropping back into the water, to be followed by a pursuing boat-sized curving back, displaying a 5-foot-high triangular fin that is gone as quickly as the small fish.

At other times you may notice a ruffling on the surface of the water; then suddenly the water is filled with several great black bodies slashed with white, surfacing and blowing for several minutes, which may then disappear and reappear a quarter of a mile away. Porpoises have been known to playfully escort passing boats, swimming alongside or even diving back and forth beneath the keel for minutes at a time.

At the turn of the century, settlers reported regular sightings of great pods of whales containing more than a hundred individuals. Although these reports may have been exaggerated, there is no doubt that there once were far more whales than there are today. It is believed that three pods, totaling about eighty individuals, now are seasonal residents of the inland waters. Other pods of itinerant whales pass through here regularly.

While whale sightings are not commonplace in the San Juans, neither are they rare. The Whale Museum catalogs all whale sightings in the islands, Strait of Juan de Fuca, and Puget Sound, in order to attempt to identify them and chart their movements. Any whale sightings should be reported to the Orca Survey at 1-800-562-8832. Information on sightings should include the time and location, direction of movement of the whales, the number sighted, and, if possible, the type of whale and any identifying characteristics of the individuals, such as scarred or bent fins.

Most commonly seen in the San Juan Islands are the "killer whale," *Orcinus orca* or orca as it is more correctly called, and the minke (*mink-ee*) whale. Northwest Indians considered the orca, a toothed whale, to be the "wolf of the sea" because, working in highly organized packs or "pods" of up to 30 individuals, they are swift, efficient predators of schools of fish, dolphins, and even larger

Orcas in the San Juan Islands

whales. Bad press to the contrary, however, authenticated reports of attacks by orcas on humans are quite rare, and when captured by man they display gentle, friendly, intelligent behavior.

Unlike orcas, minke whales usually travel alone or in pairs. They are baleen whales, having comblike structures in their jaws that are used to strain food from sea water. Minkes, the smallest of the baleen whales, are similar in size to orcas, but have lower dorsal fins and slimmer bodies. Gray whales (also baleen whales) are sometimes seen in Puget Sound, but are more rare.

Smaller harbor porpoises and Dall's porpoises (both of which, like orcas, are toothed whales) are also frequently spotted in the San Juan Islands. Dall's porpoises are black with white markings, but only orcas display the striking white underbelly reaching from the jaw to near the tail, the great fin ranging from 3 to 5 feet tall, and the awesome 20- to 30-foot-long body.

There is a valid concern that continued heavy traffic by whale-watching tours, harassment by inconsiderate boaters, and diminishing salmon supplies may lead these orca pods to abandon the San Juans for more hospitable surroundings. Be considerate, follow regulations, and hope that this will not come to pass. It is illegal to harass or pursue with a boat any marine mammal. If whales are sighted, they should be observed at a slow speed. Federal law prohibits approaching whales closer than 100 yards or deliberately positioning boats in their path. Boaters are far more likely to be able to observe a pod for a length of time if they stay at a distance. Frequently whales will come quite close to boats if they do not perceive them as a threat; they seem totally aware of even small boats, and there has been no incident reported in the San Juans of even a canoe being overturned by a whale surfacing under it.

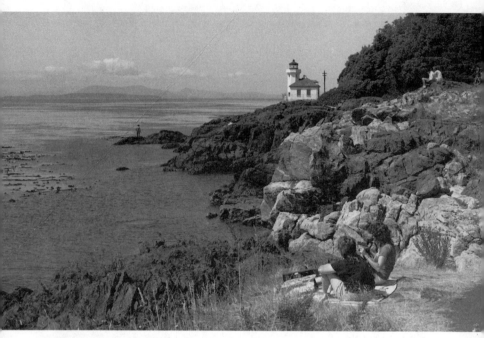

Whale watchers at Lime Kiln Point State Park

ships, it is one of the most scenic in the state. Built in 1919, the light-house, now automated, has been in continuous operation since that time, and is listed on the National Register of Historic Places. In 1984 the State Parks Commission took over maintenance of the surrounding property for public use.

At this site was one of the earliest lime kiln operations in the San Juans; excavations and remnants of some of the old structures can still be seen north of the lighthouse.

Deadman Bay, just south of the Lime Kiln Road intersection, is a popular scuba diving spot. It is said to be named for a sensational murder that occurred here in the late 1800s. Despite its macabre name, the tiny cove is a delight. Surrounding cliffs plunge 100 feet from the road to the sheltered beach, and a tiny stream trickles down the gully.

The land surrounding Deadman Bay and stretching north to Lime Kiln State Park was acquired by the Trust for Public Lands in early 1994, with the intent that it would be sold to the State Parks and Recreation Commission for an expansion of Lime Kiln State Park. For a variety of reasons San Juan residents were opposed to camping at the site. In late 1994 State Parks dropped the project. The San Juan Land Bank has

acquired 31.5 acres of the Deadman Bay property, including 1600
feet of shoreline and 174 adjacent
acres, and permits public use of it.

West Side Road

South of Lime Kiln Lighthouse
the 2-mile stretch of West Side
Road is one of the most spectacular in the islands, well worth the
drive in itself. Twisting high on
rocky bluffs, it offers views across
the glittering expanse of Haro
Strait and downward to waves beating against the rugged toes of San
Juan Island. In spring, masses of
California poppies flame between
rocky outcrops. The outstanding
view and paved road make the
route appealing for bicyclers.

False Bay

Shallow, nearly circular False
Bay is located on the southern end
of San Juan Island, with its narrow
mouth opening onto Haro Strait.
Quite a number of unfortunate
boaters, seeking shelter from
weather, have discovered what the
significance of its name is when
they've found themselves hung up

*Bicyclers enjoy the view of Haro
Strait from West Side Road.*

on a tideflat, for the entire bay holds less than a fathom of water at mean
low water.

The shores provide a pleasant beach walk at moderate-to-high tides,
but the real fun comes at low water, when the entire bay nearly dries. Don
rubber boots and wander through the muck to observe seashore life.
Investigate more than 200 acres of strange creatures: skittery purple
shore crabs; two-foot, flame-colored ribbon worms; shoe-shaped chitons; prehistoric-appearing clingfish; barnacles and rock oysters (jingle
shells) fated to spend life fastened to one rock, with never a change of
scenery.

To reach False Bay by land from Friday Harbor, drive west out of town on Spring Street. At an intersection 1½ miles from town turn left (south) onto False Bay Road, which can be followed 3½ more miles to the bay. Small pullouts for parking are adjacent to the road at both the south and north ends. Overnight camping and beach fires are not permitted.

The bay is owned and carefully monitored as a biological study area for the University of Washington. Several scientific theses have been written on the ecological systems found here. The contained environment, sheltered from the disturbing action of large waves, allows the study of discrete marine populations. Do not disturb rods, sticks, tubes, or anything that looks peculiar; these usually mark a research project in progress. Avoid any such staked-out areas, and do not dig in the vicinity. Look all you wish, but *do not kill or collect any specimens anywhere in the bay.* Walk carefully to avoid damaging any of the marine life.

A good seashore guide, such as one of those listed in the reading list in appendix C, helps immeasurably in the identification and understanding of these invertebrates. A magnifying glass is also useful. A clear glass jar filled with fresh seawater aids in studying the delicate animals; slip the specimen carefully into the jar to observe it, then quickly return it to its home. If the water becomes too warm it may die. Handle shell-less creatures with damp hands to avoid damaging their protective slime coating.

When walking this or any beach, avoid dislocating stones harboring marine life. Certain marine specimens live only on the exposed tops of rocks, while others seek protection of the bottom; eggs are often attached to the undersides of beach rocks. If a stone is lifted and then replaced upside down, the invertebrates formerly on the top will suffocate on the bottom, while the others die of exposure on top.

Study a single rock to see the many kinds of life it supports. Pick up a piece of seaweed and check it out for hitchhikers. Pools hold tiny fish waiting to be released by the next incoming tide.

Pedal Inn Bicycle Camp

Access: Ferry to San Juan Island
Facilities: Campsites, toilets, showers, laundromat, groceries (limited)

The only campground on the south end of San Juan Island, a commercial facility restricted to bicycles, offers a pleasant respite after a long pedal down-island. To reach the Pedal Inn, turn west off Cattle Point Road onto False Bay Drive just a mile north of the American Camp boundary. In about 1 mile the road takes two sharp turns, first to the south, then to the west. A sign at the second corner points down a lane to the campground. The camp can also be reached from the West Side Road via Bailer Hill and False Bay roads.

Pedal Inn's 25 campsites lie in trees along the shores of a serene little pond edged with lily pads and cattails. A resident bald eagle that nests on the property dines regularly on waterfowl frequenting the pond.

Eagle Cove Public Access

Park area: ¼ acre; 100 feet of shoreline
Attractions: Beachcombing, picnicking, swimming, scuba diving

Just outside San Juan Island National Historical Park's American Camp is a small public cove fronting on the Strait of Juan de Fuca. This rock-rimmed cove is surrounded by a high bank that protects its beautiful sandy beach from much of the wind that whips the shoreline to the east.

In addition to being popular with San Juan residents for beachcombing, swimming, and sunbathing, the cove is also a favorite scuba diving area, with underwater forests of kelp hiding rockfish, lingcod, abalone, and other marine life. Walls plunging steeply downward have ledges that hold octopuses and wolfeels. The nearest launch ramp is at Smallpox Bay, 8½ nautical miles to the north, or Roche Harbor, 5 nautical miles beyond.

To reach the Eagle Cove access, turn south on Eagle Cove Road, just west of the American Camp boundary. In ½ mile there is a blacktopped parking area for a few cars with a sign stating "Public Access. No Overnight Camping." A 100-yard-long path descends through a tall, cool arch of underbrush alongside a creek drainage; the trail is muddy and slippery when wet.

At low tide one can walk the shore south to American Camp and all the way to Cattle Point, 3½ miles distant. Be careful not to get forced up onto the bluffs by incoming tides.

SAN JUAN CHANNEL

Griffin Bay Campground

Park area: 15 acres; 330 feet of shoreline
Access: Boat
Facilities: Campsites, picnic tables, fireplaces, pit toilets, mooring buoy, drinking water (Designated Cascadia Marine Trail campsite)
Attractions: Camping, picnicking, beachcombing, boating

One of the beauties of this remote little park is that few people stop here, so one is almost assured of getting away from the hordes. For a number of years the Department of Natural Resources tried to establish a park at this location. After some resistance from nearby property owners

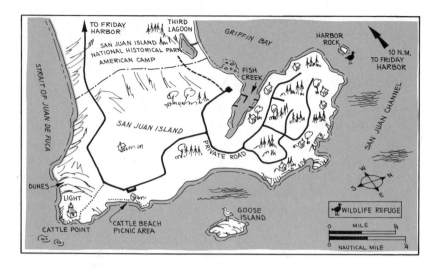

who feared the hazard of untended campfires at such a remote spot, the park was finally opened in 1984, but was limited to a boat-in site with no upland public access.

The park lies about ½ nautical mile south of Low Point, due west of Halftide Rocks. Avoid rotting pilings and a submerging rock on the west side of Halftide Rocks. Stay at least 200 yards off the north or south sides of Halftide Rock until close to shore and the buoy, which rests in about 9 feet of water at mean lower low water. Skippers of deep-keeled boats may find the vicinity of the park a bit scary, as the depth sounder begins to drop off some distance from shore. At low tide the buoy may be in water too shallow for some boats.

Halftide Rocks is one of the sanctuaries of the San Juan Island National Wildlife Refuge. You may spot seals basking on the sunny rocks.

Picnic tables are on the low bank above the water, but campsites and fireplaces are 400 yards back from the shore. Water is available from a hand pump that will delight the kids.

Fish Creek

Why it holds this name is a puzzle, for it's not a creek at all, but a slotlike saltwater cove at the extreme end of San Juan Island. The "fish" part of the name is more understandable: during the 1850s the Hudson's Bay Company had a fish-packing station here.

All the shoreland around Fish Creek is private, so there is no way to reach the water by land. For boaters, however, it is an enchanting little corner and a handy little anchorage for waiting out fog or bad weather in the straits. All docks and floats are private.

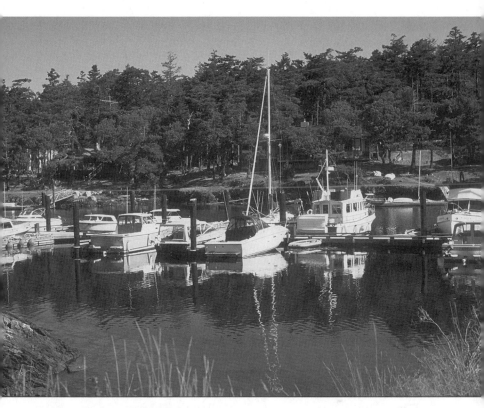

Private docks at Fish Creek

Cattle Beach Picnic Area

Access: Ferry to San Juan Island, boat
Facilities: Picnic tables, pit toilets, *no water*
Attractions: Picnicking, beachcombing, hiking

Two small gravel and driftwood beaches, separated by a glacier-scoured rock promontory, face on the entrance to San Juan Channel. Beach life is scarce here, but water-smoothed agates are often turned up among the pebbles.

This Department of Natural Resources picnic area is located ¾ mile east of the American Camp boundary, along Cattle Point Road. Several picnic tables on top of the bluff provide sweeping views of the channel and Lopez Island. A nearby concrete building, built in 1927 as a Coast Guard radio station, has been converted to a picnic shelter complete with fireplace, well protected from the prevailing winds.

Interpretive signs near the picnic area tell of the geological history of the point, the centuries of use by Salish Indians, British and American settlers, and the history of the Coast Guard radiocompass facility that was located here. A steep trail descends earthen steps in the bank to the small southern bay; the northern bay requires steeper slippery scrambles down from bluff top to beach.

Small boats may be landed on either beach, but there is no offshore anchorage. Use great care in small boats on this end of the island; tide rips can be quite strong.

Goose Island

Just 400 yards off Cattle Beach is Goose Island, which is owned by The Nature Conservancy and administered by the Friday Harbor Laboratories as a biological preserve. It is one of few such islands in the San Juans to have nearly natural vegetation—Yellow Island is another.

During pioneer times it was the practice to row sheep to grassy islands for summer grazing. (It was also necessary to frequently row barrels of fresh water to the flocks.) As a result of the grazing, some plant species were completely wiped out on the islands, and tougher species took over. For some reason Goose Island escaped this fate, making it a unique botanical study area today. Its only current inhabitants are the hordes of squawking gulls and harbor seals and sea lions that sun here.

Cattle Point

The white concrete tower of Cattle Point Light has long been a welcome sight to boaters emerging from fog banks of the Strait of Juan de Fuca. Perched on sand dunes 80 feet above the beach, it can be reached by a 300-yard trail southwest of the Cattle Beach Picnic Area parking lot at the "toe" of San Juan Island, or by walking the beach at low tide east from South Beach for 2 miles. Vehicles of any type are prohibited beyond the parking lot, as the dune area is quite fragile.

The dunes are a rarity in the San Juans. Winds sweeping off the strait pile the sand in great, smooth mounds that are inviting to walk on and explore. Farther back from the beach, the sand has been stabilized by tough grass and bramble bushes. Here the ubiquitous San Juan rabbit digs burrows and peers insolently at visitors from the safety of the thicket; in summer and fall a myriad of yellow-and-black American goldfinches flit and forage among the Canada thistles along the trail.

CHAPTER FIVE

SAN JUAN ISLAND NATIONAL HISTORICAL PARK

Perhaps it was the kindly hand of fate that determined that the United States and Great Britain be brought to the brink of war over a pig. With tempers as testy as they were, the deceased party could easily have been a man instead of a recalcitrant porker. As it was, the military authorities felt foolish at being at loggerheads over a pig, and this permitted more rational minds to prevail and avert a serious war.

The Treaty of 1846 caused it all. When British and American negotiators signed a document establishing the Oregon Territory boundary, they overlooked the vague language defining the boundary through a cluster of "worthless islands" lying between the mainland and Vancouver Island. Hudson's Bay Company, however, was well aware of the value of the timber, fur, fish, and grazing lands of the San Juan Islands. They claimed the territory for Queen Victoria by establishing an outpost overlooking the Strait of Juan de Fuca on the southern end of "Bellevue" Island, as San Juan Island was then called. Meanwhile the American westward expansion brought to this paradise Yankee set-

A park interpreter sports a period costume at American Camp.

tlers who scraped out homesteads, disregarding the property claims and, perhaps more important, the tax collectors of the British.

Lyman Cutlar chose as his farm site a few acres in the middle of a Hudson's Bay sheep pasture. There he built a shack and planted potatoes. Cutlar was mighty attached to his crop, for that spring of 1859 he had rowed 40 miles round trip across the Strait of Juan de Fuca to purchase the seed potatoes. Thus, when a Hudson's Bay pig proceeded to willfully and regularly trespass into his potato patch, he violently objected. After registering a complaint with the unsympathetic Hudson's Bay agent, Cutlar solved the problem by dispatching the offending pig with his rifle.

Tempers flared and Cutlar was threatened with arrest. In somewhat pithy language he questioned the jurisdiction of the Crown and appealed to American authorities. James Douglas, the governor of British Columbia, who had long been rankled by the incursion of American settlers, saw an opportunity to settle the matter of British sovereignty in the islands and ordered a ship to San Juan Island to support the Hudson's Bay position.

American and British militarists who scouted the waters in the years following the Treaty of 1846 had noted that San Juan Island strategically guarded the Strait of Juan de Fuca, Haro Strait, and the mouth of the Fraser River. They were determined the territory should not fall into the hands of a potential foe. Soon both sides were massing ships, men, and armaments. At times they were only a bullet away from all-out war. The superior British flotilla could easily have leveled American fortifications with their heavy guns. However, if a battle had actually begun, all American settlers in the area would have entered into the fracas and the British would have been outnumbered. Moreover, the fight was sure to spread to Vancouver Island, where there were nearly four American "for-eigners" to every British subject. Leaders on both sides realized that any serious war would bathe the islands in the blood of hundreds of American and British citizens.

Lt. Gen. Winfield Scott was dispatched by President James Buchanan to take command of American matters in the San Juan archipelago. Arriving in October of 1859 and finding the battle had fortunately not yet begun, he proposed to Douglas that the island be jointly occupied by equal forces of the two factions until arbitration could settle the boundary dispute.

The British eventually accepted this plan, and American Camp was established on the southern tip of the island on barren slopes near the Hudson's Bay trading post. Meanwhile British marines landed on the shores of a protected harbor on the northwest side of the island, which they named Garrison Bay.

Once the threat of all-out war in the San Juans was assuaged, the

U.S. government turned its attentions to more urgent internal problems in the southern states. With the beginning of the Civil War in April of 1861, the San Juan dispute was relegated to a diplomatic back burner. Britain, too, was embroiled in domestic problems and did not press for settlement of the dispute. Time wore on and the hastily erected tents at British and American Camps were replaced by permanent barracks, hospitals, and social halls. Timber was cleared for parade grounds and gardens. Duty was good, although boring, on San Juan Island.

Finally, with the boundary commission at an impasse, the question was submitted to an impartial arbitrator, Kaiser Wilhelm I of Germany, who in October of 1872 decided in favor of the United States. The dispute was finally settled—13 years after a British boar filled his jowls with American potatoes and thus waddled into history.

Several excellent books on the complete history of the war are available. Keith Murray's *The Pig War* and James McCabe's *The San Juan Water Boundary Question* are both quite authoritative.

Following the withdrawal of armed forces, the lands of American Camp and English Camp were privately owned. In 1966 Congress commemorated the almost-war by designating the two areas as San Juan Island National Historical Park, and parcels of land on Griffin and Gar-

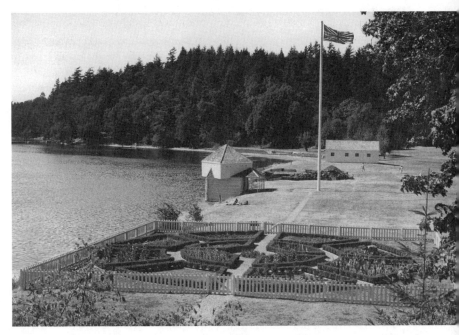

The British flag flies over the formal garden and guardhouse at English Camp.

rison bays were purchased. This is the only park in the United States that honors the peaceful settlement of a dispute. Numerous interpretive displays and signs have been installed to help visitors understand the historical significance of the park. The park's primary function is historical, not recreational, but in such a beautiful setting, with beaches, forests, and grasslands, even those who have only a limited interest in our heritage cannot help but love the park.

The park grounds are open during daylight hours year-round, although buildings at English Camp are closed off-season. The park headquarters is at American Camp. Information is also available at the park's office on Spring Street in Friday Harbor, which is open during business hours. On summer weekends historical programs are presented at American Camp by park rangers and volunteers wearing dashing replicas of British and American military uniforms or other costumes appropriate to the time. Tours are available to groups, by advance arrangement.

Archaeological Finds

Archaeological digs completed by park personnel in 1977 searched for Native American and pioneer artifacts. Additional annual digs, sponsored by the University of Washington, have been conducted since 1983 to explore Native American use of the area over the past 4,000 to 7,000 years. Finds have included fascinating items from the time of the Pig War and pioneer settlement. These include coins, a pocket watch, jewelry, and a cribbage board. A number of the items found by archaeologists are on display at British and American camps.

Visitors walking over the grounds of either camp may occasionally discover artifacts. It is imperative that these discoveries are not disturbed, and are left exactly where found, as the location and surrounding soil are of as much archaeological importance as the artifact itself. Note the location and report it to a ranger, who will contact a trained archaeologist to ensure proper examination and removal of the find.

ENGLISH CAMP

Park area: 529 acres; 1½ miles of shoreline
Access: Ferry to San Juan Island, boat
Facilities: Dinghy dock, picnic tables, pit toilets, hiking trails, *no water, no overnight camping*
Attractions: Historical displays, hiking, boating, paddling, clam digging *(observe posted regulations for clam digging)*

Most of the buildings that still exist, along with other relics of the Pig War, are found at English Camp. Three of the original buildings from the old garrison have been restored; one houses artifacts, an interpretive display, and a self-operated slide show on the history of the park. A fourth building, believed to have been the hospital or surgeon's quarters, was sold and moved to another location on the island after the British left. When found it was returned to its original site and restored.

The blockhouse near the beach was built to protect the marines from marauding Indians, rather than from warring Yankees, and also served as a guard house. A white picket fence encloses a traditional formal garden that is typical of those planted during the time. Near the barracks grows a spreading big-leaf maple tree; once it was the largest of its kind in the world, but it is now slightly outranked by one in Oregon.

An interpretive trail leads a few hundred feet uphill from the formal garden to a grassy bench overlooking the bay where the officers' quarters were located. On a second, higher flat quarters were built for the commanding officer of the Royal Marines and his family. The small stone obelisk found here was erected on October 12, 1904 to commemorate the thirty-second anniversary of the resolution of the boundary dispute.

To reach English Camp from Friday Harbor, follow Roche Harbor Road, which curves around the north end of San Juan Island. At a major intersection 8½ miles from Friday Harbor, turn left (south) from Roche Harbor Road onto West Valley Road. Entrance to English Camp is on the right in 1½ miles. From the parking area a 200-yard path, edged by a picturesque split-rail fence, leads to the military site on Garrison Bay.

The 1½ mile boat excursion from Roche Harbor to English Camp winds through lovely Mosquito Pass and the narrow entrance to Westcott Bay. Consult a good chart for the location of numerous shoals along the way; Garrison Bay is quite shallow throughout and deep-keeled vessels should enter with care. The two protected bays are ideal for kayak or dinghy exploration.

Tiny, wooded Guss Island, which lies only 300 yards offshore in Garrison Bay, was named during British occupation for a San Juan storekeeper. Although it is also part of the park, it has been designated as an archaeological preserve and is closed to the public.

Vague remnants of one of the old docks are still visible near the blockhouse. A small dock with space for a few dinghies is now located farther north along the beach. In summer the bay is often filled with boats anchored and rafted together. Skippers may also anchor at Westcott Bay, then dinghy to Bell Point and walk the trail to English Camp.

Bell Point

A level, ½-mile hike through madrona and fir leads to pretty Bell Cove on Westcott Bay. Rusted spikes and planks still scarring old trees along the way give evidence of pioneer use of the area. The signed trail

Hikers on the Bell Point Trail

starts on the north side of the English Camp clearing near the shore. Tides permitting, Bell Cove can also be reached by walking the beach.

For an alternative return to English Camp, follow the old wagon track heading east from Bell Point, skirting Westcott Bay. In about ¼ mile the route reaches a clearing. Turn right (south), following the grassy track between the old-growth timber of Bell Point and a thick stand of recent-growth firs. Listen here for the distinctive trilling song of the chipping sparrow, which nests in the area. The track eventually emerges at the north corner of the English Camp clearing. Total distance of the loop trail is about 1 mile.

A larger, more distinctive bird that sometimes startles visitors by its presence at English Camp is the wild turkey. These nearly domestic fowl were introduced on San Juan Island almost a decade ago, and have become well established. Even occasional poaching by Thanksgiving-minded hunters has failed to make a dent in the population.

The beaches of Bell Point may be closed to clam digging during certain seasons, although Bell Cove is normally open year-round. Observe posted signs. Dig clams only if you intend to use them, and observe limits; heavy public use of the clam beds could exhaust them, causing the beaches to be closed in order to let them reestablish.

British Military Cemetery

A small plot on the slopes of Mount Young holds the graves of seven marines who died during the British occupation of San Juan Island. Locate the trailhead to the cemetery at the picnic area that is at the northeast corner of the parking lot at English Camp. The signed trail wends steadily uphill along an old overgrown wagon track.

Sun filters through second-growth alder, fir, and madrona. Walk quietly and perhaps you will be rewarded with glimpses of black-tailed deer, or occasionally great horned owls blinking sleepily in the trees. An owl's favorite perching spot can sometimes be located by watching for piles of droppings beneath the tree. The owls take large numbers of rodents, and are responsible, even more than eagles and hawks, for controlling the island's rabbit population. The winter wren nests here; listen for its lovely sustained warbling song as you hike.

Although the route crosses the West Valley Road in ¼ mile, hikers must begin the trip at the parking lot, as there is no parking space along the road. Above the highway the trail continues.

The cemetery, in a grassy clearing, is reached in another ¼ mile, just beyond the Mount Young trailhead. A neat white picket fence encloses four tombstones for servicemen who died in accidents while serving at English Camp. The stones tell the story of each mishap; note that one commemorates two marines who drowned at sea. Two other graves are

One of the gravestones in the English Camp cemetery

unmarked. Gravestone inscriptions have been duplicated on interpretive signs along the fence to prevent people from going inside the fence to read them.

Total distance from the English Camp parking lot is less than ½ mile; elevation gain is 250 feet. A short spur trail leaving the northeast corner of the cemetery clearing shortly joins the trail that goes to the top of Mount Young.

Several of the trees in the clearing were killed or badly scarred by a 1972 fire. Even more than 20 years later the damage can be seen. Take heed of the havoc a cigarette ash accidentally dropped in dry grass can cause.

Mount Young

Probably the most spectacular viewpoint on San Juan Island is reached by hiking a little more than ½ mile beyond the British Military Cemetery. The trip is well worth the effort on a clear day. From a trail branch just before reaching the cemetery the path heads north, circling the west side of Mount Young.

The trail climbs steadily to round a north-facing rib of Mount Young, then heads south on a path cut through high arching brush. At a bench 100 feet below the summit, the trail forks. Switchbacks to the left lead to the top of the mountain; at the end of the path to the right is an interpretive display on an open, grassy rock platform. The British marines maintained an observation post on the summit of the mountain during the Pig War.

Views, views, views. Henry Island, White Point, Bazelgette Point, Mosquito Pass, Westcott Bay, and Garrison Bay all merge in a mosaic of land and water. Mitchell Bay, its entrance obscured by land, looks like a small lake—but with a fleet of large pleasure boats bobbing on it! Southward can be seen the snowy peaks of the Olympic Mountains, while to the north are the Canadian Gulf Islands, marked by the imposing profile of Saltspring Island. Across Haro Strait lies Vancouver Island, where, over 100 years ago, British frigates sailed forth to uphold the sovereignty of the Crown. The display at the lower viewpoint identifies all major landmarks.

An aged madrona frames the view of Mitchell Bay and Haro Strait from Mount Young.

Stroll to the east side of the hill for views through timber of Mount Baker. Looking southeast from the summit, immediately above the silhouette of Mount Erie on Fidalgo Island, on a very clear day Sloan Peak can be seen. Ranging southward are the misty outlines of Mount Baring, Mount Index, and other Stevens Pass peaks more than 90 miles distant.

Elevation gain from the parking area is 590 feet; from the cemetery trailhead, 370 feet. Round trip from the parking lot to the top and back is 2½ miles.

AMERICAN CAMP

Park area: 1,223 acres; 4¼ miles of shoreline
Access: Ferry to San Juan Island, boat
Facilities: Picnic tables, restrooms, drinking water, fire pits, *no open beach fires, no overnight camping*
Attractions: Historical display, hiking, boating, paddling, fishing, beachcombing, birdwatching, nature trail

American Camp is a marked contrast to English Camp. Instead of the protected harbor and wooded enclave, here are vast marine panoramas and miles of surf-swept beach. First-time visitors may be struck by the austerity of the park, but those who linger discover its diversity, ranging from the subtle beauty of rippling grass on the slopes of Mount Finlayson to the exhilarating rage of winter storms pounding on South Beach.

To reach American Camp from English Camp, continue south on West Beach Road and in 3¾ miles turn right (south) onto Boyce Road. In 1 mile turn left (east) on San Juan Road and in 2¾ miles right (south) on Douglass Road. In 1½ miles turn left (east) on Little Road, which ends shortly at a T intersection with Cattle Point Road. Here head right (south) and in 2¾ miles reach the American Camp entrance. Total distance from English Camp is 12 miles. The small building that houses the park headquarters and some historical displays is just inside the entrance.

To travel directly to American Camp from Friday Harbor, at the Y intersection on the south side of town, bear left (south) on Argyle Avenue. Follow the arterial south and then west to its intersection with Cattle Point Road. The route is well signed. Total distance to the park is 5 miles. Bicyclers making the long, dry trek from Friday Harbor should note that the only drinking water in the park is at the headquarters just inside the park entrance. There are restrooms here as well; other locations have pit toilets.

For visitors traveling by boat, there are no docking facilities at American Camp; however, in calm weather small boats can be beached on the gentle shores on either side of the park. Griffin Bay provides the only

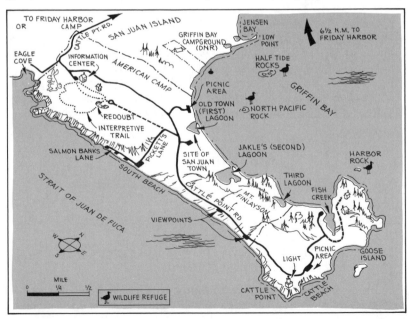

semi-protected anchorage; when entering the bay, carefully check nautical charts and depth finders for the location of numerous submerged rocks. The north beach of the park is about 6½ nautical miles from either Friday Harbor or Fisherman Bay.

Kayaking or canoeing around the park is interesting, especially along the southern shore; however it is recommended only for experienced paddlers. Great care must be used in small boats as the wind and current can be extremely strong; attempting to maneuver an underpowered boat under such conditions can be a frightening experience. Shark Reef, lying to the east immediately across San Juan Channel along the shore of Lopez Island, is an inviting destination for those skilled enough to attempt it.

Park History Programs

On summer weekends and holidays at American Camp, the national park presents an outstanding series of programs and special events that attract both tourists and local residents. The programs are designed to make history come alive; in some presentations parks personnel and volunteers wearing period costumes re-create the daily lives of the sol-

A park interpreter dressed as a laundress leads a tour at American Camp.

diers, laundresses, and settlers during the time of the Pig War. Authentic props such as a Sibley tent and laundry tubs fashioned from whiskey barrels complete the scene. For other programs employees and visitors take part in songfests, square dances, and games reminiscent of the 1860s.

At American Camp, volunteer-guided tours are held daily throughout the summer. These walks, which begin at 11:00 A.M., leave from the park headquarters and information center and cover the areas of Pickett's Redoubt and the Hudson's Bay farm. Large groups planning to visit the park can request a tour with a guide in costume.

Interpretive Trail

For those who miss the excellent guided tour, or who would rather walk at their own pace, a ¾-mile-long self-guided interpretive trail covers the historical section of the park. The starting point for the tour is at the picnic area east of the park information center. Signs at numerous points along the way narrate Pig War history and interesting features of the park. At the top of the ridge, Pickett's Redoubt commands views of American Camp and waters stretching to Victoria. Still in evidence are the earthworks (redoubt) thrown up by the American troops, where five cannons were mounted.

South Shore Walk

Leave the interpretive trail and wander open slopes above the ocean to enjoy the austere beauty of the park. There are no formal trails. In late summer the inland section of the slope is covered with patches of stinging nettles and Canadian thistles, so long pants are advised.

Near the edge of the cliff the harsh environment causes the vegetation to be miniaturized. Many of the species of plants are so tiny that novice botanists can identify them only when they bloom. Collinsia grow less than an inch tall, showing quarter-inch blue-purple blossoms in late May. Lupine, whose distinctive leaf whorls grow over four inches across on the alpine slopes of Mount Rainier, here have ground-hugging leaves smaller than a thumbnail.

Bays along this section of the island are unlike those found anywhere else in the San Juans. The soft glacial till, scooped out by winds from the Strait of Juan de Fuca, form perfect, grassy amphitheaters dropping steeply to beaches jammed with huge driftwood logs. Explore the small coves if you wish, but bear in mind the difficult, 50-foot scramble back to the top.

The rounded bay to the west was the site of the original Hudson's Bay Company settlement. Artifacts can sometimes be found in the vicinity; rabbits dig them out occasionally and toss them aside with total disregard for their historical significance. Unauthorized digging for ar-

South Beach at American Camp

Rabbits

A San Juan rabbit

The long arm of San Juan Island is largely covered by soft glacial till deposited centuries ago by retreating ice. The loose mixture of sand, stone, and boulders, ideal for tunneling, made American Camp a "Watership Down West" for San Juan rabbits. The rabbits are believed to be descendants of domestic animals brought here during the 1880s by settlers. They either escaped from captivity or were turned loose and, finding local conditions to their liking, multiplied—and multiplied—and multiplied!

By the late 1970s, an estimated 250,000 bunnies (give or take a few) populated San Juan Island. Their evidence was everywhere at American Camp at this time: droppings covered the ground to the extent that in places more dung than dirt was visible, and park rangers swept the walks daily to enable visitors to walk. Tunnel entrances made the ground look like a bombed battlefield.

In the mid 1980s, for reasons not entirely understood, the rabbit population decreased dramatically. One plausible theory is that plants such as vetches, when subjected to overgrazing by large numbers of rabbits, produce a chemical that acts as a birth-control agent. When grazing returns to normal, this chemical is no longer produced. Another theory credits an increase in the population of animals that prey on young rabbits. Whatever the reason, the rabbits seem to be making a slight comeback in recent years. Hunting or trapping has not been permitted since 1966, when the park was established. This allows useful data to be gathered on population cycles.

The rabbits are a major food source for eagles, great horned owls, and other predatory birds living on the island. Fluctuations in the rabbit population can also be reflected in the natural balance established between the predators and their food supply.

tifacts (by humans) is prohibited, and any that are on the surface must be left where they are found and their location reported to a park ranger.

If hiking legs need further exercise, traverse the bank eastward, staying well above the shore. Do not walk near the edge, as the earth is soft on the high bank, and footing may be insecure. When the slope gentles, drop down to South Beach near the parking lot. Return to the information center via the road. Total distance of the loop hike is about 3 miles.

South Beach

For road access to 2 miles of unbroken beach edging on the Strait of Juan de Fuca, turn right off American Camp Road onto Pickett's Lane. In ½ mile is the first parking lot, where there are picnic tables, fire pits, and pit toilets; Salmon Banks Lane leads west to three more parking areas and more picnic tables. Fires are permitted only in fire pits. Lightweight boats may be carried the short distance from the parking areas for launching, surf permitting.

When storms kick up in the straits, heavy wave action along the beach is exciting to watch. Drift logs are dangerous at these times; stay well away from moving logs. Such storms toss flotsam and jetsam onto the beach, making this the prime area on the island for finding beach treasures.

With calm weather and favorable tides the beach can be walked all the way east to Cattle Point, 2 miles from the parking lot. Very little marine life is found on the gravel beach; constant movement of the surf-tumbled sand and gravel lets nothing survive for long. Low tide exposes rocky shelves to the west and tidepools holding fascinating critters. During the summer and fall salmon runs, numbers of commercial fishing trawlers are frequently seen tending their nets just offshore.

San Juan Town

When American troops built their stronghold on San Juan Island, a shanty town sprang up nearby just outside the military camp boundary on the shore of Griffin Bay. Shopkeepers in San Juan Town sold a few supplies to the soldiers, settlers, and Indians, but it was soon apparent that liquor was the commodity in greatest demand. Other enterprising merchants brought in Native American women for "nefarious purposes." Robberies, assaults, and sometimes murders took place, with open defiance of civil and military officers. Authorities were able to tame the town a bit, but it always remained a center for booze, brothels, and brawls.

In 1873, when San Juan County was established, the new commissioners felt that San Juan Town, with its rowdy reputation, was unsuitable for a county seat. Instead they selected a few acres at Friday Harbor on the north end of the island. In time businesses drifted away from Old

San Juan Town (especially when Friday Harbor also acquired a saloon), and by the late 1800s the once thriving village was a ghost town. The deserted buildings were accidentally burned to the ground in 1890, bringing to a close the career of the colorful, if somewhat tarnished, village.

The saltwater lagoon visible on the north side of American Camp Road is just west of the old town site. A few footings of the original buildings have been excavated and can be found by searching the grassy fields. Halfway down the hill the track of an old road is faintly visible.

Griffin Bay

Early sailing ships hove to in Griffin Bay waiting out westerlies whipping the Strait of Juan de Fuca. Today fast-moving powerboats whiz by in San Juan Channel, rarely stopping to enjoy the languid pleasures of the bay.

Harbors of Refuge

During the late 1800s, the U.S. naval strategy was to develop "harbors of refuge" that were safely out of range of the capabilities of naval bombardment at the time and that could be protected by land-based weaponry. Griffin Bay was designated as such a harbor of refuge, and land was set aside for military reservations on Lopez Island at Shark Reef and Upright Head, Shaw Island, and San Juan Island at Cattle Point and Point Caution near Friday Harbor. Other such harbors of refuge were planned at sites such as Neah Bay, Sequim Bay, Discovery Bay, and Port Townsend Bay.

It was intended that the Griffin Bay would serve as a safe haven for both commercial and military vessels if adjoining waterways were blockaded by an enemy's superior naval forces. Ships coming in or going out of the Strait of Juan de Fuca could hide here until it was possible for them to make a run for their destination or the next "harbor of refuge."

About this time the strategy of naval combat changed, with the U.S. Navy no longer taking a passive defensive role of protecting home shores, but assuming an aggressive stance and taking the battle to the enemy. The military reservation land in the San Juans was no longer needed; over the years some of it was transferred to the DNR or other government agencies, and some was sold off to private interests. The parks at Shark Reef on Lopez Island, and the DNR picnic area at Cattle Point are a result of these land holdings.

Even though the water of the bay is inviting when seas are calm, boaters should be aware that a number of rocks are scattered at or near the water's surface. Consult a good, large-scale chart and approach with care. Barren Halftide Rocks lie northeast of the park boundary, near a row of rotting pilings. About ½ nautical mile south of these rocks is North Pacific Rock; it is unnamed on most charts but is shown as a rock baring at tides of minus 2 feet or less. Harbor Rock lies farther east, just off the tip of Cape San Juan. These three groups of rocks, nesting grounds for marine birds, are part of the San Juan Islands National Wildlife Refuge.

Between North Pacific Rock and Harbor Rock the approach to the beach is clear, except for rocks lying quite close to shore. Some good anchorages can be found in this section of the bay, although those to the west are exposed when winds are stiff—which is most of the time. The best spot to drop an anchor is to the east, in or near Fish Creek.

The gentle shore of Fourth of July Beach, which extends west for ½ mile from the San Juan Town Lagoon (First Lagoon) to the park boundary, holds driftwood and some interesting marine life. Here is a parking lot with a picnic area, picnic tables, and a large grassy field for kite flying or tossing Frisbees. The path leads past pit toilets to the beach. Carry a small boat or kayak the short distance to the beach and you will be rewarded with a leisurely paddle the length of the park.

To reach Fourth of July Beach, turn north off Cattle Point Road at a signed intersection 1 mile east of the park entrance.

Jakle's Lagoon

While American Camp is impressive, it can at times seem bleak. Jakle's Lagoon, a secluded nook of the park, offers a delightful contrast, with ferns, rich moss carpet, and tall firs. At the urging of The Nature Conservancy, the road to the lagoon is closed to vehicles to protect eagle nesting areas as well as the delicate lagoon habitat.

The lagoon itself has been set aside as an environmental study area. It is used by the University of Washington as a collecting site for marine specimens and has been the subject of several studies and PhD theses.

The trailhead to the lagoon is located a few hundred feet east of the Pickett's Lane intersection on Cattle Point Road, where a side road branches north, ending in a short distance at a gate. There is parking space for a few cars; use care not to block the gate in case of emergency. Hike the abandoned road downhill, dipping into the forest.

This is also the start of the Jakle's Farm Nature Trail, which is a fine destination in itself for those not wanting to hike all the way to the lagoon. The nature loop, which is marked, follows an uphill fork for ¼ mile, then wanders over very gentle terrain; total distance is slightly less

Jakle's Lagoon

than 1 mile. A brochure available at the park office describes the flora found at numbered stakes along the trail. This, the first such guided nature trail on San Juan Island, was developed jointly by the park and the San Juan Horticultural Society.

The land was originally farmed by Frank Bryant, an American soldier stationed at Garrison Bay. After Bryant accidentally died in a drowning mishap, his widow married another U.S. soldier, George Jakle. The site is known to have been actively farmed by them at least as late at 1927.

Hikers continuing on to Jakle's Lagoon will find a confusing network of old roads crisscrossing the hillside; keep bearing downhill and eastward to reach the lagoon. When the only four-way intersection is reached, turn left; the lagoon is about 200 feet farther. A grassy point protruding into the southwest side of the lagoon is a fit spot for a hobbit home. In winter, when the forest drips with San Juan mist and fog lies heavily over the lagoon, one can easily imagine magical creatures scurrying in the undergrowth.

Signs posted along the trail warn hikers not to smoke while on the trail. Campfires are also forbidden in the forest and on the beaches. In the dry summer the fire hazard here is extreme and a spark could start a blaze that would destroy the entire wooded area, bringing death to the birds and animals living here.

With moderate-to-low tides, the Griffin Bay beach can be walked between the site of San Juan Town and Jakle's Lagoon for a loop trip with an opportunity to beach-comb. Round trip is 1½ miles.

Third Lagoon

Another smaller lagoon lies ½ mile east of Jakle's Lagoon. San Juan Town Lagoon is first, Jakle's is second, and this, appropriately, is known simply as Third Lagoon. It can be reached one of several ways; the easiest route, tide permitting, is to walk the gravel beach east from Jakle's Lagoon.

For an inland route, return to the abandoned road from Jakle's Lagoon and continue east. The beauty of the forest makes this route worthwhile. In spring, find calypso, twinflower, and bleeding heart popping through the carpet of rich moss.

The road climbs to the top of a ridge, then descends again. Where it levels off at the bottom, watch for a faint road on the left leading to the lagoon. If you miss the side road, continue until the lagoon is clearly in sight through open timber and head cross-country. A hundred yards east of this side road, a trail heads right (south) next to a marsh. This path climbs uphill through thick timber, emerges at a meadow, and joins the Mount Finlayson Trail.

Just beyond the lagoon the road is gated at the eastern park boundary; from here it crosses state and Department of Natural Resources property to Fish Creek. Round trip from the parking lot is about 2½ miles. Elevation gain (on return), 130 feet.

Mount Finlayson

The rolling hill of Mount Finlayson is the highest point on this end of the island. A trail that follows a mowed firebreak leaves the Jakle's Lagoon parking area and wends through the meadow near the edge of the forest. Magnificent examples of wind-shredded Douglas-fir tower beside the track. Along the way two faint trails head north into the forest; the westernmost one is the return loop of the nature trail, the farthest east leads down to Third Lagoon.

From the mountaintop look north to Griffin Bay, east to Lopez Island and the Cascades, and south across the Strait of Juan de Fuca to white Olympic peaks. Ocean freighters ply the strait, bearing cargoes from exotic lands headed for Puget Sound ports. Once they carried silk, tea, and spices; today they are laden with plywood and Hondas. Distance from the upper parking lot to the summit is 1 mile; elevation gain is 200 feet.

From the top of Mount Finlayson the trail continues east out of the park and onto state-owned land, then drops steeply down the eastern

Eurasian Skylark

The vicinity of American Camp is the only known nesting area in the continental United States of the Eurasian skylark, although the bird has been sighted recently on Whidbey Island and the Olympic Peninsula. Introduced to Vancouver Island by the British, who brought several pairs from Europe in 1903, some individual birds winged their way to San Juan Island, where they took up residence.

Skylarks frequent open grassy fields where they forage for seeds and insects and build their nests. Its drab brown-streaked plumage appears similar to that of a female house sparrow; however, it can be distinguished from the sparrow by its larger size (7 to 7½ inches) and its distinctively marked white stomach, wing tips, and outer tail feathers.

The Eurasian skylark's popularity arises from its melodious song in flight—a high-pitched, sustained torrent of runs and trills as it hovers 200 feet in the air. Listen for it as you roam the park, especially in the area of South Beach and Pickett's Lane.

Mount Finlayson rises above South Beach.

ridge line to an abandoned gravel pit near Cattle Point Road. A faint trail leads northeast across a boulder-strewn meadow to an old overgrown road heading northwest into the trees and back into the park. Watch in the open old-growth timber for woodpeckers and brightly colored western tanagers. The road fades to a trail and ultimately joins an old road from Fish Creek near the east end of Third Lagoon.

Cattle Point Road Views

East of Pickett's Lane, Cattle Point Road traverses the open lower slopes of Mount Finlayson, providing astounding views south across the Strait of Juan de Fuca, east to Cattle Point Light on the end of San Juan Island, and beyond that to the rocky southern end of Lopez Island.

Within the sweep of the view are more public lands than can be seen from any other viewpoint in the United States. From the North Cascades to Mount Rainier, from the national forests spanning the Cascades to the onetime forts, now parks, of Admiralty Inlet and then to the heights of the Olympics are national wilderness treasures set aside for recreation and preservation. Two pull-outs along the road have interpretive plaques identifying these areas and paying credit to the legislative accomplishments of Senator Henry "Scoop" Jackson, who helped make these reserves possible.

CHAPTER SIX

NORTH FROM SPIEDEN CHANNEL AND PRESIDENT CHANNEL

Traveling north from the busy thoroughfares of Spieden Channel and President Channel, boaters encounter Spieden, Waldron, and Stuart islands and their associated smaller islands. These landfalls, which are similar geologically to the Sucia Islands group to the north, are composed of folded, eroded sedimentary beds with long ridges extending

Spieden Island (left) and Sentinel Island (right)

underwater as a network of reefs and shoals that make boat pilots wary, but beckon to fishermen and scuba divers.

Lying deep within the rain shadow of Vancouver Island, their climate is dry enough that the Cactus Islands do, indeed, support cactus. The brittle prickly pear cactus, *Opuntia fragilis,* the most northerly occurring species of cactus, blooms here with a delicate, yellow, tissue-like flower in early summer. Although more common in the prairies of the Great Plains, this cactus species is becoming rare in the San Juans; it is found in small colonies on only nine of the islands. The stress of invasions of other plants, a cooler climate, fire, and loss of habitat due to the invasion of humans may, sadly, drive it to extinction here.

These are islands to enjoy from the deck of your boat, for aside from the state parks on Stuart Island and Nature Conservancy reserves, all shore land is privately owned or held as a wildlife refuge, and there are no commercial developments.

SPIEDEN AND SENTINEL ISLANDS

The most striking in appearance of this northwestern group, 480-acre Spieden Island, with its long northern slope neatly forested and its southern side barren except for tawny grass, appears as if a prankish barber had been at work. Lying alongside to the south, 15-acre Sentinel Island is a miniature duplicate of its neighbor.

Spieden, which is the only large San Juan island without a bay or harbor of any sort, has not been commercially developed, and until recent years its life was pleasantly bucolic. In 1969 an abortive attempt was made to capitalize on its dry climate and open rangeland by transforming it into an African game farm and renaming it "Safari Island."

The island was stocked with ungulates such as Japanese sika deer, European fallow deer, Indian blackbuck antelope, and wild goats. No predators were brought, assuming that hunters who paid to come to the island would adequately keep the herds under control.

Immediately there was a loud outcry from conservationists protesting this "sitting duck" type of sportsmanship. Whether it was because of the voice of the conservationists, or because the project was ill conceived, the business went broke and the land was sold to other interests, but some of the wildlife remained.

Without any natural controls these animals increased to the point that they now number several hundred, on an island where the vegetation can sustain only about 50 such animals. They are seriously overgrazing the island's vegetation. A couple of attempts to round them up and relocate them have been unsuccessful, and thus far, despite all human efforts, these strange visitors from foreign lands remain. Passing boaters with binoculars can sometimes spot these exotic creatures.

Spieden Island was used for a time as a vacation resort for Alaska Airlines employees. It is currently leased to the Island Institute, a conservationist camp that conduct marine science classes in a natural setting. Classes are also offered in natural history, geology, astronomy, and native legends.

Sentinel Island, Spieden's small companion, was acquired by The Nature Conservancy in 1979 as a nature preserve. It is an active eagle-nesting area, it holds a nesting community of pigeon guillemots, and its rocky shores are used by harbor seals for resting and sunning. Unlike nearby Yellow Island, which is also owned by The Nature Conservancy, Sentinel Island is not open to public visitation.

FLATTOP ISLAND AND OTHER BIRD REFUGES

Sentinel Rock and Center Reef (both southwest of Spieden Island); Shag Rock, Gull Reef, and Ripple, Little Cactus, and Flattop islands (northeast of Spieden Island); and Gull and White rocks, and Mouatt Reef (between Flattop and Waldron islands) are all part of the San Juan Islands National Wildlife Refuge. They are nesting sites for glaucous-winged gulls, pelagic cormorants, black oystercatchers, and pigeon guillemots. Large flocks of harlequin ducks and occasionally some loons can be seen here in the summer.

Although in the past boaters have stopped at Flattop Island, the largest of these bird refuges, public recreational use of Flattop, as well as the less-hospitable rocks, is now prohibited in order to protect birds' nesting areas.

White Rock, near Waldron Island, is one of the islands of the San Juan Islands National Wildlife Refuge.

Disturbance of nesting birds by humans has a detrimental effect on the survival of the young, for when nests are abandoned, even for a short period of time, the unattended eggs may be broken by predatory birds or competing birds of the same species, or the eggs may chill and fail to hatch.

Nesting gulls are extremely territorial during this time and will viciously defend their foot-square domain against intrusion by other birds; if a parent gull is chased from her nest, the frightened chicks often scatter into foreign territory and are killed by rival birds. Boaters must recognize that it is imperative for the survival of the chicks that they stay away from the nesting grounds.

STUART ISLAND

Stuart Island thrusts deeply toward the Canadian border, only 3 miles from several of the Gulf Islands, making its protected harbors popular stops for B.C.-bound vacationers. Indeed, the outline of the island itself, ignoring its deep harbors, suggests a boat headed for Canadian waters, and Johns Island is its dinghy in tow. At 1,786 acres, the island is the eighth largest of the San Juan Islands, and it has 5,130 feet of shoreline on Haro Strait and Boundary Pass.

Stuart Island has a population of some forty permanent residents living in homes scattered about the island. A small private airfield on the

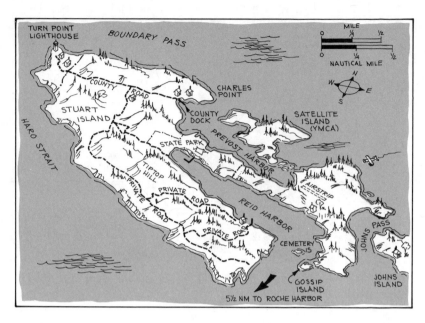

northwest tip of the island serves these residents. Fishing and farming have provided a livelihood for islanders since the days of early homesteading. The reef-netting site off the entrance to Reid Harbor has been fished by Indians and their descendants for six generations. Other residents are retirees or persons who can manage their jobs from here, with an occasional airplane commute.

Reid and Prevost harbors, the location of Stuart Island Marine State Park, provide fine overnight facilities for boaters. Those who stay a while longer enjoy the fishing, the beaches, and the shellfish, while the more energetic might even sample the forest hikes and pastoral road walks revealing the serene inner beauty of the island.

Stuart Island lies 3½ nautical miles north-northwest of San Juan Island's Roche Harbor. When planning a trip from Roche Harbor to Stuart Island in a small boat, consider strong tidal currents and shoal areas in Spieden Channel. The entrance to Reid Harbor is constricted by submerged rocks and shoals. Stay west of Gossip and Cemetery islands, in the middle of the channel or slightly to its west side to avoid running aground.

Boats cruising the north side of the island via Johns Pass should use care at the south entrance to the channel. Kelp marks several rocks and a ½-fathom shoal extending well out from the eastern tip of Stuart Island. Give all obstructions a wide berth. Check a good navigation chart for exact position of hazards.

Stuart Island is a fine destination for kayakers, with enough nooks and crannies to fill several days' worth of exploration; however, the distance and strength of tidal currents encountered en route to the island make this a trip only for experienced paddlers.

On the north side of Prevost Harbor, tucked behind the protective wing of Charles Point, lie a county dock and a few homes. No facilities or provisions are available there, so visitors should limit their stops to the state park docks.

The shores do not exhibit the sculptured sandstone cliffs so characteristic of the northern Sucia Islands group—instead the steep banks are heavily covered with vegetation almost down to waterline. The rounded, forested dome of Tiptop Hill, the highest point on the island, rises 640 feet above Reid Harbor.

Stuart Island Marine State Park

Park area: 88 acres; 4,130 feet of shoreline on Reid Harbor and Prevost Harbor

Access: Boat

Facilities: Floats, 23 mooring buoys, 19 primitive campsites, picnic tables, stoves, drinking water, pit toilets, composting toilets, marine pump-out station, hiking trails, portable-toilet dump (Designated Cascadia Marine Trail campsite)

Attractions: Camping, picnicking, clam digging, crabbing, fishing, paddling, hiking

The ½-mile recess of Reid Harbor is one of the best anchorages in the San Juans. The enclosing arms of the island drop off sharply to 5 fathoms, giving good anchorages almost up to the shoreline, while the gravel beach at the head of the bay is gradual enough for small craft to land easily.

A dock and float on the north shore, two floats anchored near the head of the bay, and 14 mooring buoys spaced about the harbor provide easy tie-ups for about 30 boats. The large blue-striped buoy in the center of the harbor is for use of Coast Guard vessels when stationed in the vicinity. The barge anchored to pilings about 100 yards south of the dock is a marine holding tank pump-out station.

On the north side, Prevost Harbor and its broader beaches offer a different perspective of the island. The only safe entrance to the harbor is by Charles Point, west of Satellite Island; do not attempt the channel on the east with boats of any draft, as it is dangerously rocky and shallow. The harbor contains a dock with float, 7 buoys, and good anchorages, although there may be some difficulty getting hooks to dig through the thick eelgrass at the bottom of the harbor.

Boats opting to anchor in the superb little bay on the north side of the harbor at Satellite Island should be aware of a large rock, submerged at tides above 8 feet, that lies near the center of the entrance. Satellite Island is owned by the YMCA, which maintains a summer camp there and does not encourage visitors. The tideland below mean high water is a public Department of Natural Resources beach, however, and is open for clam digging during favorable tides.

Nineteen campsites with fire grates are situated on a pleasant knob north of the Prevost Harbor dock, on the high rib between Prevost and Reid harbors, and on either side of the marsh at the head of Reid Harbor. All are pleasantly shaded by light timber. Water faucets are located at convenient spots throughout the campgrounds. Four spots at the head of the harbor are designated Cascadia Marine Trail campsites for kayakers.

The beaches of Prevost Harbor offer interesting low-tide exploration. Walk carefully to avoid crushing Dungeness and red rock crab that burrow in the eelgrass. Gentle (and cautious) probing of the grass may yield some of meal size. Any crabs left stranded in the sun may dry out and die; undersized and female Dungeness crabs should be returned to a protected, damp spot or put into the water.

The park's gravel beaches, especially the one at the head of Reid

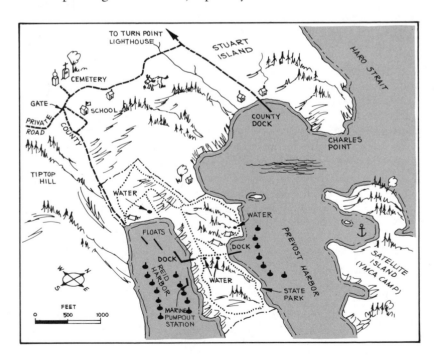

Harbor, provide first-rate clamming for littlenecks and butter clams. Those with the stamina to dig deep enough may claim some geoducks. Tidelands on Reid and Prevost harbors lying outside the park are privately owned and are posted.

A ½-mile trail connects the Prevost Dock with the head of Reid Harbor. Catch the cross-island trail northwest from the dock and follow it past the side trail to the toilets. In about 300 yards this trail joins another along the top of the high rocky bank above Reid Harbor, where twisted red-barked madronas frame pretty views of sleek boats bobbing at their moorings. Here, head south along the bank to return to the Reid Harbor dock, or drop down a switchbacking staircase to the beach at the head of Reid Harbor.

In another 300 yards to the north a sign marks the state park boundary. The trail turns sharply downhill for a short but extremely steep section (slippery when wet).

A young clam digger proudly displays her trophies.

At the bottom, in a marshy flat, bear left at a trail fork and head east for 300 yards, emerging at the campground at the northwest corner of Reid Harbor.

Cemetery and Gossip Islands

Lying on the east side of the Reid Harbor entrance are two undeveloped marine state park islands. The larger of the two, Gossip Island (also known as George Island), is about an acre of rock and grass and a few scruffy trees; at low tide it nearly joins Stuart Island. Smaller Cemetery Island, lying slightly farther into the harbor, is nearly barren. It gains its somber name from reported historical use of the island by natives as a burial site.

Both islands are closed to the public to preserve a variety of rare plants growing on them.

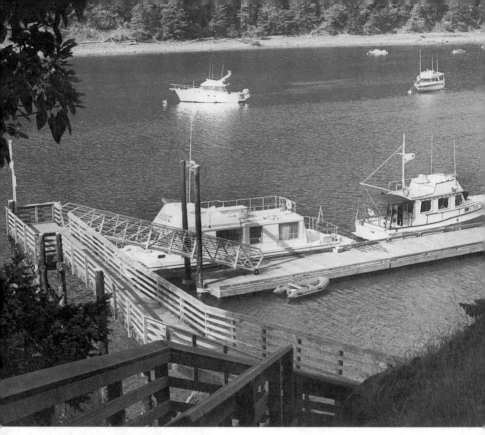

The state park float at Reid Harbor

The water surrounding the two islands is designated as an Underwater Marine Recreational Area for use by scuba divers.

Stuart Island School

An easy stretch of the legs gives visitors an opportunity to gain insight into the history and lives of the people who make this island their home.

Find the trail skirting the south boundary of the state park at the south end of the campground at the head of the bay. The route, along the county road, climbs gradually uphill. In about ½ mile watch for a fork on the right leading to the schoolyard in a clearing.

The county road can be reached by descending the switchbacking staircase from the bluff-top trail to the campsites at the head of Reid Harbor.

On the edge of the clearing is the classic, one-room, white clapboard schoolhouse that served generations of children living on Stuart, Johns, and Spieden islands. The building is presently used as a library for the more modern school nearby.

This is perhaps the most interesting school in the state; it has been featured on television. In early days the children from nearby islands would row to Stuart daily, in all weather, and then hike overland to school. Later, outboard motors made the trip easier, although still somewhat hazardous at times.

One December day in 1961, while all of the school's youngsters were on a boat outing, the boat sank in bad weather and all aboard were drowned. The school remained closed for sixteen years following the tragedy, and local children commuted to San Juan Island. In the fall of 1977, it reopened with an enrollment of eight. Growing population dictated the need for a larger, more modern facility, and in 1980 the new school standing nearby was opened. Although it is more spacious and its modern design provides a flood of cheery light, the

The historic schoolhouse on Stuart Island

building is still one room and is heated with wood stoves. Student enrollment usually numbers around a dozen.

Stuart Island Cemetery

To find the historic little Stuart Island Cemetery, continue west on the path past the school to its junction with a dirt road. Turn right, down the county road, and in 30 yards watch on the left for an unmarked, seldom-used road leading to the cemetery.

Spanning almost a century of island time, the gravestones tell the story of the many settlers who lived here for long years, and others who enjoyed this lovely, though sometimes harsh land for only a brief time. The land for the cemetery was originally donated by Chris Cook in memory of is mother Maria Cook, who was the first person buried at the site. The area was chosen because of its central location, beauty, and solitude.

When the deed was recorded in 1910, no one realized that the legal description was in error and described a spot in 200 feet of water in

Haro Strait. In the early 1980s, because of the description error, the islanders found out they did not own the cemetery when the actual property owners wanted it closed. The residents of Stuart Island then formed a cemetery district, with the power to tax, to purchase property, and/or to take the property through the power of eminent domain. Finally in 1989 a young woman who had purchased the land several years before "donated" the 480-square-foot site to the Cemetery District for the modest sum of $500.

In the past the cemetery had been protected only by a rusty fence. Recently the Cemetery Board has surrounded the area by a low chain-link fence, fronted by wide gates swinging from brick columns surmounted by cement lions. A nearby kiosk tells the story of the cemetery.

Examine the gravestones and speculate about the lives of these people, but remember to treat the cemetery with respect. Round trip from Reid Harbor to the cemetery is a little over 2½ miles.

Turn Point Lighthouse

Far on the western tip of Stuart Island, a lighthouse blinks warning to freighters, fishermen, and pleasure boaters traveling through the waters of Haro Strait. Turn Point Lighthouse, so named because it marks the point where boats must turn in the channel, was established in 1893 on a tract of land high atop a rocky cape, with a sweeping 300-degree view of the surrounding sea. The current concrete tower housing the light and a foghorn was built in 1936.

Originally this dramatically scenic point was home of Indians who fished nearby waters. After construction of the lighthouse a succession of lighthouse keepers lived here, raised their families, and often left their names imprinted on the history of the area. The fine, spacious home and idyllic island were an ideal place to raise a family. One of the lighthouse keepers was Edward Durgan.

In his book *Lighthouses of the Pacific* Jim Gibbs describes an incident that earned Durgan a certificate of merit. One February night in 1897 the tug *Enterprise* ran aground near Turn Point and the barge under tow was cast adrift with men still on its deck. As Durgan and his assistant, Peter Christiansen, were attempting to rescue both the men on the tug and those on the barge, one drunken member of the crew went berserk, attacking the lighthouse keeper with a knife. He was subdued by Durgan and Christiansen and the rescue was successfully carried out. By morning's light the crew was all safe in the lighthouse, and the drunken assailant was chained in the chicken house.

In 1974 the lighthouse was automated; it seems unfortunate at times that fine old traditions must give way to modern technology. The residence had fallen into disrepair, and although there were attempts to

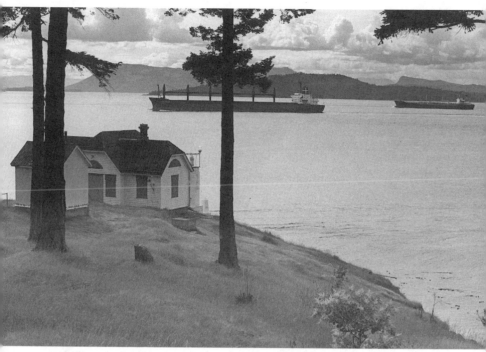

Freighters pass offshore from Turn Point Lighthouse on Stuart Island.

find someone to use the property and care for it, the buildings were finally boarded up to preserve them from vandalism. Treat this historic site with respect.

Turn Point is best reached by an overland hike from Reid or Prevost harbors. The steep cliffs below the point and the treacherous water offshore make landing a boat impractical. Catch either of the trails to the schoolyard described above, then continue a short distance past the school to the junction with a dirt county road. Follow the road north past a farmhouse and a barn. Walking the quiet, tree-shaded road is like stepping into time suspended. The nautical bustle of the harbors seems a planet away, and rarely is anyone seen along the deserted track. Even if some of the buildings appear unoccupied, all the land is private property; do not trespass.

About 1½ miles from Reid Harbor, the route intersects the Prevost road. Several homes can be seen down the road on the right; beyond is Satellite Island, and on a clear day Mount Baker hovers above. Turn left at the intersection and continue past rolling fields where cattle share pasturage with deer. To the left of the road are reminders of modern-day technology: several parked cars and tie-downs for aircraft that use the private strip to the southwest. At 2½ miles from the school, reach Turn Point Lighthouse.

Views spread in all directions across Haro Strait to Canadian islands and down the 50-foot cliff to the sea churning against the flanks of the point. Walk with care—the footing at the edge of the cliff can be insecure.

Take the hike in the late afternoon to enjoy the fiery sunset behind Vancouver Island and the crimson afterglow, but pack along a flashlight for the return trip through the forest. Fires and overnight camping are not permitted at Turn Point. The round trip from Reid Harbor is about 7 miles.

WALDRON ISLAND

Waldron is a staunchly individualistic island, defying categorization, either physically or socially, with any other in the San Juans. Although it is quite close to Orcas Island, lying only 2 nautical miles west of Orcas's West Beach, in reality it has little basic familial relationship.

The people of Waldron display this same individualism, along with a strong sense of self-sufficiency, for the island has no electricity, no water district, no telephones, stores, or regular ferry service, and most residents prefer it that way. This is not a totally primitive island, however, for many homes are modern, with either private gasoline generators or tanks of propane to power lights, radiotelephones, appliances, and furnaces.

The island is one of the more unusual pieces of topography to be found hereabouts. More than half the island is a marsh and meadow flatland covered by glacial drift, rarely more than 100 feet in elevation; however, at the southern tip the cliffs of Point Disney suddenly rush up to a height of over 600 feet. The imposing fortress-like walls of the point display beautiful banding of exposed fossil-bearing sandstone and conglomerate.

The walls of Point Disney drop off just as steeply underwater, providing an excellent dive site for scuba divers. This is a spot for the experienced, due to the strong current. Undersea walls and niches hold a colorful world of anemones, basket stars, and scallops. The nearest launch ramp is at West Beach on Orcas Island, 4½ nautical miles away.

Point Disney was the site of the island's only commercial enterprise—a sandstone quarry that operated here during the early 1900s. When concrete paving became favored over sandstone cobbles, the quarry closed. Some of the workmen departed, others remained to farm.

Waldron has less than a hundred year-round residents, with most homes located along the two broad bays of the northwest shore. The "village" of Waldron consists of a few abandoned buildings huddled around the county dock on Cowlitz Bay. There is a small float attached to the dock, but passing boaters rarely stop here as there are no onshore facilities and visitors are regarded with suspicion. The open bay is a marginal anchorage, even in good weather. Mouatt Reef, which is exposed at low tide, lies at the entrance to the bay, 300 yards off the end of the dock.

The island's only other harbor is rock-bound Mail Bay on the east side, which in early days was the local mail stop and is sometimes still used today by the mail boat when seas are too rough at Cowlitz Bay; obviously "neither rain, nor sleet, nor towering seas...." Mail Bay offers a few anchorages in 10 to 40 feet of water; skippers should be wary of submerged pilings, the remnants of earlier docks, along the north side of the bay.

Waldron Island Preserve

Preserve area: 478 acres; 4,000 feet of shoreline
Facilities: None
Attractions: Birdwatching

The Nature Conservancy has purchased 478 acres of beach, meadow, and marshland on the west side of Waldron Island, facing Cowlitz Bay, between Sandy Point and Point Disney. This purchase was fostered by

Silvered driftwood and American vetch on a Waldron Island beach

Eagles

Bald eagles are frequently seen in the San Juan Islands. (Photo: Bob and Ira Spring)

A black silhouette with a 6-foot wingspan, soaring, wheeling in the summer sky, its white head glinting in the sun, then swooping downward to alight in a skeletal tree snag—a bald eagle is one of the most spectacular sights in the San Juans. At times they seem so common that tourists become blasé about them, but those who understand the significance of their presence can never fail to be thrilled by sightings of those elegant raptors.

The San Juan Islands have the largest and healthiest concentration of nesting bald eagles in the continental United States, with about fifty pairs that are known to breed here. The local population thins briefly in the fall when spawning salmon lure them up inland rivers, although a few prefer their local diet and remain year-round. Other migratory bald eagles summer in the islands after nesting in Alaska and coastal British Columbia.

About 10 percent of the eagles found in the San Juans are golden eagles. Some of these also nest here, although they prefer more protected sites inland in trees and cliffs away from the water to the seaside snags that the bald eagles choose. The two birds are not closely related; golden eagles are considered true eagles, while bald eagles are sea eagles, as are ospreys.

Immature bald eagles are often mistaken for golden eagles, because they do not display their characteristic dark body and snowy white head until their third or fourth year. Young bald eagles are evenly brown-colored with white mottling as they mature, while golden eagles display patches or bands of light-colored feathers at the base of the tail and in the wing linings at the base of the primaries.

It is remarkable to find such a concentration of these strongly territorial birds in one area, along with large numbers of hawks, vultures, owls, and other predators with competitive feeding requirements. With the bountiful supply of rabbits, fish, and other favorite tidbits, coupled with the isolation of the islands and the current protective attitude of the residents, the eagles have modified their behavior to a more social existence. While golden eagles take large numbers of live rabbits, and thus are valuable to the islands in the control of these prolific rodents, bald eagles prefer fish, waterfowl, and carrion. They frequently will steal captured prey from other birds.

Eagles, which can be seen almost anyplace in the San Juans in spring and summer, are often spotted in snags of forested areas, surveying the sea from beach-front rocks, gliding low over quiet bays, or rising in concentric circles in the thermals above the mountains. Sometimes they are seen even near such busy places as Roche Harbor or Sucia Island.

A number of San Juan residents, assisted by The Nature Conservancy, have attempted to locate all bald eagle nesting sites in the islands, and have taken steps to protect them by obtaining conservation easements of 20 to 40 acres as a "buffer zone" around each nest tree, to prevent logging or public disturbance of the site. The trees are surveyed by air and boat each year to determine activity. About fifty chicks are believed to be successfully raised in San Juan nests each year.

In addition to the serious threat of loss of nesting sites by human encroachment, the birds also succumb to such natural hazards as storms, disease, and predatory raccoons, crows, and hawks. Although they are placed on the list of threatened animal species and are protected from being killed (except in Alaska), they are occasionally shot by irresponsible hunters. Stiff penalties can result from killing or disturbing eagles. In the 1980s some persons who deliberately cut down a tree containing a nest subsequently paid $10,000 in fines.

Still another threat to these majestic birds are the poisons in the environment. Because they have exceptional longevity, being known to live up to thirty years in the wild, all the while absorbing agricultural and industrial toxins in air, plants, and water, and in addition eating large quantities of carrion that may itself have died as a result of such poisoning, the eagles' bodies become storehouses of

DDT, dieldrin, PCBs, and mercury. These poisons, if they do not kill the bird outright, can cause sterility, thinning of eggshells, failure of eggs to hatch, and weakened chicks, ending the reproductive capabilities of the adult.

It is imperative that bald eagles be given every possible protection if the species is to survive. Visitors to the San Juans should stay well away from nesting sites, enjoying these birds from a distance with field glasses.

Bald eagle nesting sites are selected with a definite goal of overseeing territory. The birds choose the tallest tree and construct a platform of sticks, moss, shredded bark, and mud. Nests are re-used from year to year, and eventually are used by the eagles' offspring. Each year the nest is redecorated and expanded with additions of sticks and mud until, over a period of decades, it can become many feet across and weigh more than a ton. Such huge nests have been known to have come crashing down during storms, or to fall from their own sheer weight.

One to three eggs are laid in the nest, and in early April the downy chicks appear, although usually only one will survive. While the female may desert her nest if disturbed during the incubation period, she rarely will abandon it once the eggs are hatched. In about twelve weeks (about mid-July), the young have feathered out and are ready to leave home. Just prior to this time they can be seen teetering awkwardly on the edge of the nest, exercising their wings.

Nesting eagles in the San Juans have been known to be quite accustomed to island residents, but agitated by the presence of strangers. The best means of viewing them is from inside a car or boat, with binoculars.

Waldron residents who wanted to preserve it in its natural state. Especially important from an ecological standpoint are 52 acres of wetland that provide haven for migratory waterfowl and resident muskrats and river otters.

The area should be visited only by those seriously interested in viewing and studying the birds. Going ashore is permitted, subject to restrictions necessary to maintain this as a nature preserve: remain on designated trails; no pets, picnicking, camping, or fires; no collection of plants or animals; prior permission must be obtained for groups of more than six. To arrange for group access, call (206) 343-4344.

Douglas-fir, oak, and madrona forests attract colorful goldfinches, western tanagers, red crossbills, and nuthatches, while red-winged blackbirds, long-billed marsh wrens, and myriad other marsh birds inhabit the wetlands. Ponds are resting grounds for migratory freshwater ducks such

Murres, such as these seen in President Channel, nest on small rocks and islands in the San Juans.

as cinnamon, blue-winged, and green-winged teals, and occasional groups of whistling swans. Eagles nest in the forested heights above the island, as well as across President Channel on Orcas Island. The nesting sites are carefully protected by island residents and conservation organizations.

SKIPJACK AND BARE ISLANDS

Lying only 4½ miles from the northwest shore of Orcas Island, Skipjack Island has in the past been a popular destination for small boat adventurers. However, the island, along with a nearby unnamed rock and Bare Island, ¾ nautical mile to the east, is part of the San Juan Islands National Wildlife Refuge and now is closed to any public use. Landing on the islands is prohibited, except by special permit.

The islands, which lie due north of Waldron Island, support large rookeries of glaucous-winged gulls, pigeon guillemots, black oystercatchers, auklets, and other pelagic birds. As man's use of the other San Juan Islands increases, it is vitally important that some of these islands be reserved exclusively as refuges. *Any* intrusion by man, no matter how cautiously done or well-intentioned, can frighten birds from their nests, leaving their eggs and young open to predation by rival birds. Even after the nesting season, it is important that the birds have rocks on which to rest undisturbed.

The waters south and east of the islands are popular salmon fishing grounds, and the long underwater reefs nearby are popular with scuba divers. Boaters engaged in these activities should stay well away from the bird refuges.

CHAPTER SEVEN

ORCAS ISLAND

Orcas Island is unique among the San Juans, with its three long inlets thrusting deep into the interior of the land, giving it more shoreline and more protected waters than any of its neighboring islands. In addition, it has taller mountains and more surface area than any of the others. However, it exceeds San Juan Island in area by a mere 1½ square miles.

Proud residents can certainly boast that it has more of everything, including the largest park, Moran State Park; but with all this bounty Orcas Island has only limited saltwater lands open to public use. With the exception of the hike-in park at Obstruction Pass, public waterfront is limited to a few meager road ends at Cormorant Bay, Buck Bay, West Beach, and near Smugglers Villa on the north shore.

Although initially one might think that Orcas Island was named for the orca whales that are so abundant in the surrounding waters, it was in fact named by Francisco Eliza in 1792 for the viceroy of Mexico. It is doubtful this early Spanish explorer deliberately chose the name for its double meaning, for the major landfalls such as this were always named after important political figures, not for any wildlife, which at the time were taken quite for granted.

Islanders today, however, care little for Don Juan Vincente de Guemes Pacheco y Padilla Orcasitees y Aguayo Conde de Revilla Gigedo (yes, all that was his title), and generally prefer to relate the island to the magnificent mammal. Eliza further honored his patron by giving the name Isla y Archipelago de San Juan (Islands and Archipelago of Saint John) to the entire group of rocks. Guemes Island and Padilla Bay to the east also honor him.

While San Juan and Lopez islands have had, since the time of early settlement, a history of bustling industry and agriculture, Orcas holds a

Opposite: *The town of Eastsound graces the north end of Orcas Island's East Sound.*

long tradition as a vacation land. Ever since the 1890s, when ferries first made runs to the San Juans, mainlanders have flocked here to summer at gracious inns, or to rough it in canvas tents set up at beaches around the island. Several of the original inns have been modernized and are still in operation today, while newer resorts have accommodations ranging from rustic beach cabins to modern apartments.

Today Orcas Island is served by the Washington State ferry from Anacortes (about a one-hour trip), or from Sidney, B.C., on Vancouver Island (about two hours away). The Orcas Island Airport, which is 1 mile north of Eastsound, is a daily stop on the schedule of West Isle Air and Harbor Airlines. Charter air services also provide flights to the islands.

Hamlets at Orcas Landing, Eastsound, West Sound, and Deer Harbor have groceries, general stores, and interesting shops, while outstanding meals can be had at a number of restaurants. Daily or weekly lodging is available at resorts, inns, and bed-and-breakfast inns ranging from rustic to posh. In summer, reservations are a strongly recommended.

The only public camping areas are at Moran State Park and a small hike-in campground at Obstruction Pass. Private resorts at Doe Bay and West Beach also have some camping space. In summer, campsites

Bicyclers unload from the ferry at Orcas Landing.

fill rapidly; be sure of overnight accommodations before planning to camp on the island. Most campgrounds accept reservations.

The major marinas are at Deer Harbor and West Sound. Orcas Landing, West Beach, and Bartwood Lodge also have some boating facilities, although of a more limited nature.

Bicycling is a favorite mode of travel on Orcas Island, as anyone can testify who has witnessed the droves of bicycles exiting from the ferry in summer. Orcas roads, however, are two-lane affairs with limited shoulders and plenty of ups and downs and curves. Although auto traffic often is light, cyclists should use both care and courtesy when traveling here. Do not let traffic back up behind a slow-moving party of cyclists; pull over at a safe place and let cars go by. Do not stop on a curve or the crest of a hill where drivers may have difficulty seeing you. Travel single-file and make yourself visible with a bike flag, reflectors, lights, and bright clothing. Finally, respect private property. Do not trespass for a lunch stop or bathroom break. Public restrooms are available in Eastsound.

Nearly all island roads are blacktopped, and they wind through forest and farmland, at times edging some of the many miles of shoreline. Until recently, few of the roads carried names, and those that did changed their names seemingly at random. Most roads are now named and signed, a concession to the growing population and the need for emergency crews to quickly and correctly locate places. However, locals giving directions still refer to landmarks and names that do not appear on either maps or signs, such as "OPALCO Road" (which, incidentally, means the road where Orcas Power and Light Company is located—it's signed as Mount Baker Road).

Many of the old directional signs remain at intersections, pointing to one destination or another. The one reassuring thing is that one cannot get seriously lost on the island. If you do end up wandering a bit, you will probably discover a pretty corner of the island you otherwise might not have found.

You are sure to see waterfowl at any time of year, although their numbers are far greater during the winter migratory season. A startled deer may dash across the road, then pause to stare back curiously at passerby. The greatest scenic sight of all, whether by bicycle, foot, or car, is the road to the top of Mount Constitution in Moran State Park, with the culminating view out to a sea of islands. This park is so stupendous that in this book it is covered in a chapter by itself.

Orcas Landing

Access: Ferry to Orcas, boat
Facilities: Float, guest moorage, gas, diesel, water, groceries, fishing, tackle, bait, marine supplies, bicycle rentals, restrooms, shops, restaurants, hotel

A small collection of stores clustered near the ferry landing caters to tourists waiting for the ferry and visiting boats stopping to fuel up and resupply ship's stores. The marina adjacent to the west side of the ferry

The Orcas Hotel is on the National Register of Historic Places.

landing is equipped to meet most boating needs, while the grocery store has provisions for land or water visitors. The marina has some limited overnight moorage in the summer along its 300-foot-long float.

A number of gift shops and snack bars line the road on the slope above the ferry ramp, offering tourists pleasant places to browse, pass time, and purchase a few remembrances of the island while their cars sit in line.

Most interesting of the buildings at Orcas is the three-story, Victorian-era Orcas Hotel overlooking the bay. It attests to the longtime role of the island as a resort center. Constructed in 1900, it began accommodating vacationers in 1904 and did a flourishing business for many years. Extensively restored in 1985 and remodeled in 1994, the Orcas Hotel has guest rooms furnished in the style of the original hotel, as well as a restaurant and bar. The hotel is now on the National Register of Historical Places.

Ferry line parking, which once crowded the meager space along the highway at Orcas Landing, has been relocated to a large lot uphill from the Orcas Hotel, where there is ample space for cars awaiting the ferry, plus restrooms and revamped traffic patterns. Finding parking at the shops and hotel area can still be quite difficult in summer, however. An open grassy area adjacent to the stairs that lead from the lot to the terminal has a few picnic tables for open-air relaxation. In summer the wait for the ferry may still be long, but at least it is more enjoyable.

Killebrew Lake

Area: 13 acres
Facilities: Public float
Attractions: Fishing, paddling, birdwatching

A lily-pad lake, its quiet waters reflecting cattails, skunk cabbage, pussy willows, and fir trees along its margins. Although land bordering the lake is owned by the state Department of Fish and Wildlife, there are no developed public facilities. A short float on the northeast shore, patched and somewhat the worse for wear, provides the only access; the marshy nature of the shoreline limits any approach from other sides.

To reach Killebrew Lake, turn right immediately after leaving the ferry and follow Killebrew Lake Road east. The road first parallels the shore, then winds through thick forest, arriving in 2¾ miles at a Y intersection where White Beach Road continues on the right, and the lake and a small pull-off loop are to the left. The south end of the loop is quite overgrown, and it is better accessed from the north. There is parking space for a number of cars along the pull-off; RV camping is permitted, although there are no toilets or drinking water.

Boats must be hand carried for launching. Spend some time paddling about the lake, floating and watching the array of birds that visit the marsh and the dragonflies darting among the lily pads, or fish for the cutthroat trout with which the lake is stocked. Boats with gasoline motors are not permitted.

Grindstone Harbor

Grindstone Harbor has no public facilities from either land or sea, but it is a secure anchorage worth trying. Lying on the north side of Harney Channel, 2 nautical miles east of the Orcas ferry landing, the small, deeply indented cove has space for just a few boats to drop a hook.

A wicked reef, just below the surface in all but minus tides, lies in the center of the entrance 300 yards offshore. Its slightly more obvious companion reef lies just inside the entrance on the east. A slow and cautious approach, somewhat favoring the west side of the harbor, leads past a channel-pinching point to the pleasant inner harbor and anchorages in 10 to 15 feet of water. The upper end of the bay is quite shallow. Respect the privacy of the shoreline.

The harbor received its name because Paul Hubbs, an early settler who lived there, owned a grindstone. He was often called upon to sharpen the axes, knives, and other tools of neighboring pioneers.

More recently, Grindstone Harbor achieved notoriety when the (then) captain of the ferry *Elwha* attempted to steer the 382-foot vessel close to the entrance to the harbor while showing a lady friend the sights, and hung the ferry up on a reef. The event has since been immortalized in story, song, and a local bar drink called *"Elwha* on the Rocks." The reef has now been officially named Elwha Rock.

DEER HARBOR

Access: Ferry to Orcas Island, boat
Facilities (at the marina and resort): Guest moorage, power, water, diesel, gas, marine supplies, restrooms, showers, laundromat, inn, cabins, swimming pool, groceries, stores, restaurants, kayak rentals, charters
Attractions: Boating, fishing, paddling, crabbing

Smallest of the Orcas Island inlets, Deer Harbor indents the western lobe of the island for a mere mile. The marina and resort at the head of the bay is a handy stop for boaters seeking to avoid the long trek into Eastsound for supplies, and is a tourist attraction for both mariners and land-bound visitors.

Deer Harbor lies 6 nautical miles north of Friday Harbor, along a route threading through the interesting "rock pile" of the Wasp Islands.

The post office at Deer Harbor has been in operation since 1883.

Good anchorages can be had in the bay, although its extreme head is quite shallow. A little wooded islet, appropriately named Fawn Island, lies near the entrance; passage can safely be made on either side of it, although a shoal extends from its southern end.

To reach Deer Harbor by land, drive 2½ miles north from the ferry landing on the Horseshoe Highway to the Deer Harbor Road intersection. Turn left here and follow the road as it curves around West Sound, then heads south to Deer Harbor, 4 miles from the community of West Sound.

Landlubbers and seafarers mingle in the shops and restaurants of the charming little resort. Several of the neat clapboard buildings date from the 1890s, when it was first established. Adding to the atmosphere, all types of interesting boats tie up at the docks, ranging from shiny plastic runabouts to beautiful old classic sailing vessels.

All of Deer Harbor Resort is private property and is restricted to the use of patrons. The owners have a right to charge people for putting in kayaks or other hand-carried boats, parking, or other use of the facilities. The resort has its own water supply, and during an extremely dry summer, shortages may limit water use to essential needs only.

Kayakers with experience in handling tidal currents can paddle 2 nautical miles west from Deer Harbor to Jones Island Marine State Park, investigating Fawn Island en route, or can head southeast for 1¼ nautical miles to Pole Pass, then on around Caldwell Point into the expanse of West Sound. The current can be strong in Pole Pass; refer to a tidal current chart for the best time to attempt the channel. There is no boat launch ramp on the bay. Hand-carried boats can be put in at the resort for a fee.

Frank Richardson Wildlife Preserve

Facilities: None
Attractions: Birdwatching

The Frank Richardson Wildlife Preserve encompasses portions of a 20-acre marsh on top of the hill west of Deer Harbor. The marshland teems with bird life year-round. In spring look for hooded mergansers, cinnamon teals, mallards, and American coots with their broods. Marsh wrens and red-winged blackbirds call from the rushes.

To reach the preserve, take Sunset Beach Road west at the head of Deer Harbor. The road curves around the bay, then heads steeply uphill. In 1¼ miles from the Deer Harbor Road intersection the marshland lies on the right. The narrow road has no shoulders and

Ducks snooze at Frank Richardson Wildlife Preserve.

no parking alongside the preserve; find pull-offs at either end of the marsh and walk the road to observe the birds.

Frank Richardson was a professor of zoology at the University of Washington. He resided on Orcas Island from shortly after the time of his retirement until his death in 1985. The preserve was established to honor him and his important contributions to the study of wildlife.

WEST SOUND

Access: Ferry to Orcas Island, Kenmore Air float plane, boat
Facilities (at West Sound Marina): Guest moorage with power, water, diesel, gas, restrooms, showers, marine supplies and repair, groceries, boat launch (sling) (fee)
Attractions: Boating, paddling, shrimping

The "middle" of Orcas Island's three main inlets, West Sound is both middle in size and middle in location, located between East Sound and

Sailing is excellent on West Sound. The Turtleback Range, with the "head" of the turtle on the left, is in the distance.

Deer Harbor, and running north for 3 miles to the base of the Turtleback Range. Prevailing northerly or southerly winds make the waterway a favorite with sailors who happily leave the busy traffic of Harney Channel for brisk sails up the sound.

The remarkable outline of the Turtleback Range, with the "shell" formed by 1,500-foot Turtleback Mountain and the "head" created by Orcas Knob, is easily recognized from the waters of West Sound. Another good view of the turtle can be had from the north end of President Channel, northwest of Orcas Island.

A long rock at the entrance to Massacre Bay, midway between Haida Point and Indian Point, is marked by a daybeacon. At high tide considerable portions of the rock are submerged—give it a wide berth.

On the eastern "thumb" of West Sound is the village of West Sound, where there is a marina, yacht club, store, and county dock. The southernmost dock at West Sound is the property of the yacht club. Immediately north of this private dock is the county dock with a 50-foot float, which is accessible to the public for day use only. A staircase at the head of the dock provides access to the beach.

The marina, tucked behind Sheep Island, is the largest and best on Orcas Island, with both permanent and guest moorage, fuel, repair and maintenance services, haul-out, and chandlery.

Boats planning to drop a hook for the night will find Massacre Bay quite shallow and open to southerly winds; the most protected anchorage is on the northwest side of Double Island, near the entrance to the sound.

To reach West Sound by land from the ferry landing, follow the Horse-shoe Highway north for 2½ miles to Deer Harbor Road and turn left. The village is one mile farther.

The inlet offers little to the land-bound visitor aside from the very scenic drive around Haida Point. Pretty little Skull Island is visible from the road near the head of Massacre Bay, but once the road rounds the head of West Sound, it ducks into timber and all marine views are lost. In winter, Massacre Bay fills with great rafts of all kinds of migratory waterfowl—buffleheads, scaups, goldeneyes, grebes, and scoters—squawking and skittering about uneasily at every imagined menace from shore. When startled by the sight of a human or a stopping car, they depart in huge flocks of whirring wings, to alight farther down the sound.

Skull Island and Victim Island Marine State Parks

Park area: Skull Island, 2½ acres; Victim Island, 3 acres
Access: Boat
Attractions: Picnicking, paddling, crabbing

Skull and Victim islands bear grisly names for such innocuous bits of land, but rather than any recent problem, they, along with Massacre Bay, recall the area's history of bloody Indian raids.

Located only 400 feet off the shore of West Sound, Victim Island lies a third of the way up the sound, just north of Double Island, while Skull Island is near the head of Massacre Bay. Although they lie within arm's length of the nearby shore, there is no access to the parks from land.

The islands are small ("intimate" if you prefer) and rocky, with a few picturesquely scrubby trees. After a day of paddle exploration of the shore of West Sound, either is a fine spot to pause for a snack or a snooze. These are undeveloped parks, thus there are no amenities such as water, toilets, or garbage cans. Fires or overnight camping are not permitted; please take all garbage home with you.

The shoreline of West Sound wanders in and out, forming coves and bays ideal for small boat perusal and peaceful anchorages. The only public tidelands in West Sound are those surrounding Sheep (Picnic), Skull, Victim, Double, and Oak islands. Uplands are private except for Skull, Victim, and Oak islands and a small rock north of Sheep Island.

EAST SOUND

More than 7 miles long and a mile wide, the long, blunt inlet of East Sound nearly carves Orcas Island in two. Hills rise steeply along both sides of the fjord-like bay, and then suddenly drop down to the flat at the head of the bay. This is a small inland sea in itself, on which sailors can spend hours cruising about or drop in at its three diminutive ports

Indian History

Lummi Indians claimed the San Juan Islands as their tribal territory, and large numbers of them summered here, gathering berries, bird eggs, and roots of camas and other plants, then returning to the protection of mainland longhouses to wait out the dreary rains of fall and winter. They established permanent villages on San Juan Island at Friday Harbor, Fisherman Bay on Lopez Island, and West Sound on Orcas Island. The West Sound village, located at the head of the bay, is reported to have been named Elelung, and included a large permanent longhouse. Temporary shelters were wooden frameworks covered with woven mats that were removed when the tribe moved elsewhere.

The bounty of the islands provided the Lummis with all they required: fish, shellfish, deer, birds, and other small animals for meat; berries and a wide variety of other plants for food (some nutritionists believe that the Coast Indians had a diet superior in vitamins to modern man's); animal skins for clothing; and an abundant supply of cedar trees, which were utilized for nearly every purpose from homes and canoes, made from the wood, to clothing and baby diapers made from shredded bark.

With only the most basic materials, the Indians developed ingenious means of harvesting food. Nets and fishing lines were fashioned from incredibly thin strips of bark and plant fibers that were braided for strength. Fishhooks had hinged barbs or gates to prevent the escape of the catch. At Pole Pass, between Crane and Orcas islands at the mouth of Deer Harbor, the Indians were known to stretch nets supported by tall poles (hence the name) across the 200-foot channel to knock down low-flying flocks of birds. Reef netting, invented by ancestors of the Lummis, is still effective as a commercial fishing method today.

These Indians practiced the unusual custom of binding flat boards to the foreheads of their babies to permanently shape them with a broad, flat forehead and high crown, considered at the time to be quite beautiful. It is believed that a group of Coast Indians, traveling in the eastern prairies, were the ones sighted by explorers Lewis and Clark, causing them to erroneously name the local Indians the Flathead Tribe—the native Montana tribe was never known to practice the custom.

The Lummis were generally peaceful people, content with the abundance of their land. Nevertheless they occasionally suffered at the hands of war parties from the fierce tribes of the north, and they would retaliate. Territorial acquisition was not the intent; such raids were primarily for the purpose of taking slaves, who were usually used later for ceremonial sacrifices or killed at the whim of their captors.

The most vicious of these raids in recorded history occurred in 1856, when a party of Haida Indians from the north swept down on the West Sound village and slaughtered most of the inhabitants, taking the rest for slaves and completely destroying the settlement. More than a hundred Indians were reported to have been killed in the raid—and since that time Massacre Bay has borne its lurid name.

Roots of nodding onion (left) and great camas (right) were staple foods of early Lummi Indians in the San Juans Islands.

of call. East Sound is so large that it can "make its own weather." Twenty-knot northerlies that flow over the flat at the head of the bay can become 40-knot winds by they time they reach its south end. The same effect can occur with southerlies. These "gap winds" that occur here are caused by relatively mild winds that enter the channel increasing in velocity as they are constrained by the steep hills that edge it.

With a smooth shoreline and beaches dropping off steeply along its sides, anchorages are few. Only at Buck Bay, Cascade Bay, and Fishing Bay at the head of the sound are the waters shallow and protected enough to permit an overnight stay.

Olga

Access: Ferry to Orcas Island, boat
Facilities: Float, guest moorage, restaurant, water

This small settlement on Buck Bay, near the mouth of East Sound, has a dock and float providing some space for visiting boaters. Although it is owned by the Washington State Parks Commission, the dock is operated and maintained by the Olga Community Club, which charges a small fee for overnight stays.

The dock has no power outlets, but there is a water line out to the float, which is removed in the winter. The Olga grocery store, when and if open, is a possible sustenance stop for touring bicyclists; however, bowing to economic realities like many small island businesses, it usually is open during summer and closed during winter. An excellent restaurant and gift shop is at the road intersection ¼ mile to the north (also open only in summer).

In calm weather some anchorages are possible along the shore to the south. The lagoon at the head of the bay dries at low tide. Be cautious of a large rock in the center of the bay that is submerged at high tide.

To reach Olga by land, follow the Horseshoe Highway north from the ferry landing and through the town of Eastsound. Continue through Moran State Park and south to the village. Total distance from Orcas Landing is about 17 miles.

Rosario

Access: Ferry or airplane to Orcas Island, boat
Facilities: Docks and floats, guest moorage with electrical and water hookups, mooring buoys (fee), restrooms, showers, laundromat, diesel, gas, groceries, fishing tackle and bait, boat launch (ramp) (fee), hotel, restaurant, coffee shop, lounge, spa, convention center, swimming pools, tennis courts, moped rental, boat rental, car rental
Attractions: Boating, fishing, hiking, swimming (pools), sightseeing, historical landmarks, beachcombing, tennis, museum

Unquestionably the most outstanding historical landmark of the San Juans, Rosario has gained nationwide recognition as a fine resort and convention center. It effectively melds the quiet grandeur of a turn-of-the-century estate with the posh slickness of a modern marine resort.

The Rosario estate was built in 1904 by Robert Moran, a Seattle mayor who was a shipbuilder, millionaire, and man of unlimited talent and energy. Illness forced Moran to sell his shipbuilding enterprises in Seattle and retire to Orcas Island, where he purchased land enclosing Cascade Bay on East Sound and designed and supervised the building of his mansion, Rosario.

Moran built his home as solidly as he had built his ships, anchoring it on solid bedrock with concrete walls and inch-thick plate glass windows. The fifty-four-room main building required six years to complete; it is said that two years alone were consumed laying the wooden parquet floor of the interior.

The care lavished on the structure was also extended to the home's furnishings and to the grounds of the estate. An organ with 1,972 pipes, installed by Moran, is still played regularly, and visitors still admire an imported stained glass window. A figurehead salvaged from an old clipper ship that was wrecked in the San Juans was set up on the grounds and remains there today, a symbol for this elegant resort. Carved in 1874 from a solid pine log for the sailing ship *America*, the figure uses the motif of the Liberty silver dollar used during this period.

Moran left his mark not only on this quiet bay, but on all of Orcas Island. He purchased large quantities of property on the island, and eventually donated 3,600 acres of mountainous land, clothed with forests and lakes, to the state of Washington to be used as the park that

Materials salvaged from ships decorate Rosario Resort: left, figurehead from the America; *right, fence made from anchor chain.*

today bears his name. In addition he helped build roads, develop water systems, and provide much-needed jobs for the islanders during the Great Depression years of the 1930s.

Following the death of his wife, Moran sold Rosario in 1938. Another local ex-mayor, Gilbert Geiser of Mountlake Terrace, purchased the property in 1960. With energy and expertise possibly matching Moran's, he transformed the unique estate into a modern resort that attracts vacationers, seminars, and conventions year-round. The resort has changed ownership several times recently.

All of the original buildings of Rosario were named to the National Register of Historical Places in 1979, assuring their preservation in their original state with only necessary modernization. The second floor of the mansion holds an interesting walk-through museum.

To reach Rosario by land, follow the Horseshoe Highway east from Eastsound, bearing right at an intersection 1 mile east of town. In 3¼ miles more, a prominent sign points down the road to the right to Rosario Resort, 1½ miles away.

By boat, Rosario lies on Cascade Bay, halfway into East Sound along the eastern shore. Rosario Point reaches out to enclose the broadly curving bay, with a jetty-created moorage basin. Nearly any time of the year reservations are necessary for an overnight stay at the floats or in the hotel. A fee is charged for use of buoys placed in the bay. Boats unable to secure moorage can usually find space to anchor in the bay.

Because this is private property, a landing fee is charged for coming ashore from anchored boats or buoys. The fee also covers the water taxi to the resort and use of selected resort facilities, including the restaurant. A meal in the resort's outstanding dining room makes a stop at the resort a vacation highlight for any galley slave.

Rosario Lagoon Trail

If guests at Rosario become sated with the multitude of attractions the resort offers and feel the urge to stretch their legs, a path leads up the steep hillside to the tennis courts beside Rosario Lagoon, where a trail continues to Cascade Lake in Moran State Park.

Walk past the concrete lagoon and generator building of the Rosario estate to find the trailhead opposite Discovery House—and what a trailhead! Every bit in keeping with the elegance of the resort, the rustic path is planked at its start, and protected by a roof of cedar shakes. It zigzags briefly up the hillside through shadowed woods, stopping at a tiny pavilion, an ideal spot for resting, picnicking, or a romantic tryst.

From the pavilion, the path follows a road between resort villas to the Satellite Hall. Here follow the dirt road on the uphill side of the hall to its intersection with a higher paved road near the Cascade Creek drainage. Turn left, and in 100 feet find the signed trailhead next to the steel aqueduct carrying water to the Rosario power generators. From here the trail climbs steadily—rising 350 feet in about a mile, keeping close to the aqueduct. Fragments of an older aqueduct can be seen below the trail, along with the cascading stream that gives Cascade Bay its name.

Finally the trail crosses two bridges and emerges on a road at an unmarked trailhead opposite the sluice gate of the Rosario Lagoon dam; tennis courts are to the left. Trails at either side of the dam circle the shores of the lagoon, reaching Cascade Lake and the Moran State Park boundary in about ¼ mile. See chapter 8 for further descriptions of the state park.

Eastsound

Access: Ferry or airplane to Orcas Island, boat
Facilities: Groceries, stores, fuel, hotels, restaurants, movie theater, restrooms, dock (nearby)
Attractions: Shopping, sightseeing, museum

Since the 1880s, Eastsound has served as the main business area for Orcas Island. At that time the few stores located here sold axes, seeds, flour, blankets, and horse collars to settlers, a blacksmith shod their horses, and a gracious inn provided meals and lodging to vacationing mainlanders. The town has not grown up much since that time—in fact, some of the original buildings are still there—but today there is a service station instead of a blacksmith shop and the general store has a deli and is stocked like any modern grocery store. The beautiful little Emmanuel Episcopal Church, built in 1886, still opens its doors to worshippers each Sunday morning.

As in early times, stores along Main Street and North Beach Road are interspersed with private residences, although some of these homes have been converted to shops selling antiques, fine art, crafts, and gift items to visitors. Outlook Inn, which still provides overnight accommodations and fine meals, advertises that it has been in operation since 1883, making it one of the earliest such establishments in the San Juan Islands.

By land, the town is reached from the ferry landing by following the main road, Horseshoe Highway, north to the head of the sound, a distance of 9 miles. The Orcas Island airport is less than a mile due north of the town, on North Beach Road.

Eastsound's greatest drawback is that, even though it faces on a major waterway, it is difficult to reach by boat. The long shallow tide flat at the head of the bay makes it necessary for large boats to anchor well out in Fishing Bay and dinghy to shore. The possibility of a public dock with floats and a breakwater at the head of the bay has long been considered; unfortunately the problems involved in building a structure that could withstand the severe storms that occasionally sweep up the long sound make the project costly. The closest boat access is at Madrona Point.

Madrona Point

The last unspoiled peninsula on East Sound, Madrona Point was scheduled for condominium development in 1989. However, the land was a sacred burial ground of the Lummi tribe, which lobbied heavily for federal funds to purchase the land and preserve it from

Red-barked madronas on Madrona Point

desecration. As bulldozers pressed at the boundaries, Congress approved a bill that authorized purchase of the point and its transfer to the Lummis as a preservation area.

Today the area is open to public day use, courtesy of the tribe. The rocky, madrona-clad headlands offer spectacular views of Fishing and Ship bays, and occasional rock-rib accesses to stony beaches. Enjoy the beauty, and respect and revere this solemn point as much as the original inhabitants did. Camping and fires are not permitted.

A day-use-only dock and float at the northwest edge of Madrona Point provides boat access to Eastsound. Boaters can tie up here, or anchor nearby and row to the dock to visit the village, which is an easy leg-stretching ¼ mile to the north, down the road.

Orcas Island Historical Museum

A major highlight of a visit to Eastsound is its interesting Historical Museum, located two blocks north of Main Street on North Beach Road. Six old log cabins, originally built elsewhere on the island, were brought to Eastsound and reassembled into the structure that now houses the museum. Displaying a variety of construction methods ranging from massive hand-hewn, dovetailed boards to the traditional "round log" style, the building is nearly as interesting as the collection it houses.

The Orcas Island Historical Museum is housed in historic log cabins.

The museum has an outstanding display of Indian and pioneer artifacts and mementos from early island days. Many of the Indian objects were collected by Ethan Allen, a Waldron Island resident who was the county superintendent of schools during the early 1900s. The Allen collection, which is so valuable that it is housed in a fireproof vault, includes about 20 glass-framed wall displays containing countless Indian arrowheads.

Also on display is Allen's handmade boat, in which he rowed from island to island visiting the one-room schools in his district. In 1898 there were 27 such schools scattered around the San Juan Islands. The museum features other special exhibits during the summer, such as the work of historic island artists, the history of fruit farming, and 1940s summer resorts.

Behind the main structure is a shed housing an interesting collection of antique farm machinery. The museum, operated by the Orcas Island Historical Society, is open from 1:00 P.M. to 4:00 P.M., Monday through Saturday in the summer, and Friday and Saturday at other times.

Fishing Bay Waterfront Park

Although Eastsound faces on Fishing Bay, it has in the past lacked a real orientation to the water. Some of the waterfront restaurants and businesses have patio decks on their waterfront side, but public access to the waterfront is limited.

Beach access has been achieved with shoreline easements east from the small park on the northwest corner of the bay. The park property sits on a low bank above the bay. A few gigantic old Douglas-firs provide shade to the grassy meadow. The park consists of only a few primitive picnic tables and an open swath of grass. There is very little parking in the vicinity. Even with rustic amenities, it is still a lovely site to have a beach picnic, with its unobstructed views all the way down the long fjord of East Sound.

Just 200 yards offshore lies inviting little Indian Island, which is owned by the state and open to the public. At minus tides a sandbar links the islet to the mainland.

THE NORTHWEST SHORE

On the "outer shore" of Orcas Island, the gentle uplands roll smoothly to the sea, interrupted only by small rocky points and the long finger of Point Doughty. Broad sandy beaches provide some of the best recreation on Orcas Island; however, there are no public accesses, aside from a few road ends.

Several commercial resorts along this shore of the island have varying facilities, and also have varying reactions to the wander-in public, depending on the nature of the resort. Because this shoreline provides the closest access to the popular marine state parks lying to the north, there are frequent demands on these businesses to launch boats and put in kayaks. Even though they are commercial businesses offering services to the public, they have every right to limit use of their land and facilities to paying customers.

Resorts along the shore are reached by land from roads branching from West Beach and Mount Baker roads. All are well signed. By boat, West Beach is 10 nautical miles northeast of Roche Harbor, while North Beach is about 3 nautical miles farther.

Small boats or canoes launched from this side of Orcas Island can spend hours investigating the shoreline, stopping at Freeman Island and Point Doughty. Sucia Island is a tempting destination, lying only 4 nautical miles to the northeast, but is recommended only for those experienced with open water hazards, for there are reefs and tide rips along the way.

These same reefs and tide rips make this a popular salmon fishing grounds, where many anglers troll during summer months. The offshore reefs attract scuba divers who dive from boats at Parker Reef, Point Doughty, Raccoon Point, and along President Channel, finding swimming scallops and exceptionally large lingcod and cabazon. Free diving and snorkeling are good near the docks and bays of the resorts, and on a series of rocky ledges between Freeman Island and the Orcas Island shore.

Freeman Island State Park, which lies along Orcas Island's northwest shore, is a favorite site for scuba diving.

North Shore Resorts

Access: Ferry or airplane to Orcas Island, boat
Facilities (at Bartwood Lodge): Restrooms, boat launch (ramp) (fee), gas, groceries, restaurant
Attractions: Boating, fishing, beachcombing, scuba diving, kayaking

The only spot on the north side that has boat launching is Bartwood Lodge. To reach it, take North Beach Road north from Eastsound to Brandts Landing Road. Here turn east and in $3/4$ mile reach Bartwood Estates. The former resort has been converted mostly to residential development; however, it has retained its dock, launch ramp, fuel supply, store, restaurant, and several rooms for rent.

Two other resorts, Smuggler's Villa and North Beach, lie west along the shore. Facilities are only for registered guests.

North Beach Road End

A public road end lies just east of the Orcas Island airport and Smuggler's Villa Resort. To reach it, take North Beach Road north from Eastsound; ¼ mile from its intersection with Mount Baker Road, the road ends at a sand and cobble beach signed "Public shore. No overnight parking or camping." There is room here to park a half-dozen cars. The beach on either side of the road end is private. The gentle beach is suitable for launching hand-carried boats to explore the northern shoreline.

For the more skilled and adventurous, cross to Sucia Island, a scant 2 nautical miles away, beyond the menace of Parker Reef. Unfortunately, because cars may not park overnight by the roadside, kayakers must make plans to park elsewhere if they plan extended trips.

West Shore Resorts

Access: Ferry or airplane to Orcas Island, boat
Facilities (at West Beach): Dock with float, boat launch (ramp) (fee), groceries, gas, fishing tackle and bait, guest moorage, cabins, campground, RV hookups, restrooms, showers, laundromat, picnic tables, fireplaces, cabins, boat rental, scuba air
Attractions: Camping, boating, fishing, paddling, scuba diving, beachcombing

A resort on the west side of Orcas Island provides facilities for boaters headed for offshore fishing grounds, scuba diving sites, or a day's recreation at Sucia Island and points beyond.

The resort is especially popular with scuba divers, who dive north to

Point Doughty and south along the shoreline to Lover's Cove. The small moorage basin is protected by a log breakwater that gives some respite from waves off President Channel.

A resort to the north, Beach Haven, has facilities only for its guests.

Point Doughty Recreation Site

Access: Boat only
Area: 60 acres, 1½ miles of shoreline
Facilities: Picnic tables, fire rings, campsites, pit toilets; *no water* (Designated Cascadia Marine Trail campsite)
Attractions: Camping, picnicking, fishing, scuba diving, tidepools, beachcombing

It isn't an appealing anchorage, with kelp beds, tide rips, and submerged rocks in the vicinity, but for small boats that can be hauled up on the beach, Point Doughty offers go-ashore camping near some of the best scuba diving to be found in the Northwest.

The Department of Natural Resources area is accessible to the public only by boat. A public trail from above was proposed at one time, but the idea was abandoned for fear that heavy public use of such a trail would disturb eagles nesting in the area. An overland path does reach the point from YMCA Camp Orkila, down the beach to the south, but that route is restricted to use by youngsters from the camp.

A few campsites perch on the grassy slope above the beach, with stunning views across President Channel out to Boundary Pass. Offshore rocks can make landing boats on the beach a bit tricky; be prepared to wade. Bluff erosion can also make a scramble uphill to the campsites difficult.

Several generations of Northwest youngsters have had their first taste of the San Juans at YMCA Camp Orkila, which is on the west shore, just south of Point Doughty. Since 1906, when the camp was founded, up to 3,000 children each year have fished, swum, beachcombed, sailed, canoed, hiked, and had wilderness camp-outs here, and have grown to love the islands.

Freeman Island State Park

Park area: Less than 1 acre
Access: Boat
Facilities: None
Attractions: Beachcombing, tidepools, scuba diving, fishing

This undeveloped state park is an eroded, narrow ridge of an island, with a fringe of gnarled old trees. Perhaps eventually it will all wash away, but for now enjoy the meager little island, made beautiful by ravages of weather and time.

Freeman Island lies just 300 yards offshore of Orcas Island. Boaters frequently take day excursions to the island from West Beach Resort, Beach Haven, or Camp Orkila, all less than a mile away.

The shores are very rocky; boat landing is best on the south side and west end. Scuba divers often dive in the reef extending to the west.

Fires and overnight camping are not permitted. Please do not litter; if you picnic, take your garbage home with you.

OBSTRUCTION AND PEAVINE PASSES

Among an entire album of scenic treasures, Obstruction and Peavine passes rank as sublime. On clear days ferry travelers in Harney Channel are treated to the sight of the ethereal cone of Mount Baker floating above Peavine Pass, with blue-gray layers of islands and hills stretching between.

Lying near the end of Rosario Strait, this doorway in the eastern wall of the San Juans serves boaters approaching the islands from Bellingham, which is 18 nautical miles northeast, and Vancouver, B.C. Obstruction Pass doglegs around Obstruction Island and has submerged rocks lying near the edge of the channel; Peavine Pass on the south, although narrower, is straight and easier to navigate.

A county boat-launch ramp on Obstruction Pass provides the closest put-in for trailered boats seeking access to the east side of Orcas Island. To reach it, follow the Horseshoe Highway to Olga, turning east on

Point Lawrence Road ¼ mile before reaching Olga; the road is signed to Doe Bay. Follow this road, turning south in another ½ mile onto Obstruction Pass Road.

The road meanders down valleys and around hills, finally reaching Obstruction Pass 2 miles from the Point Lawrence Road intersection. A 125-foot-wide parking lot adjacent to the fire station has a concrete ramp at its west side, and an excellent county dock and float at its east side. The dock is for loading and unloading only—no overnight moorage. Property on either side of the launching facility is private, although that to the west contains a marina, resort, and small grocery store.

Boats put in here can explore westward to the DNR campground at the point, and on into Buck Bay and East Sound. The small rock-walled bay immediately east of Obstruction Point is Spring Bay. The spectacular bed-and-breakfast inn that graces the shore includes guided kayak cruises as part of their accommodations package.

Eastward and north are Doe Island Marine State Park and Peapod Rocks. Brown Rock, lying in Obstruction Pass, is a bird sanctuary of the San Juan Islands National Wildlife Refuge.

Currents in Obstruction and Peavine passes can run in excess of 4 knots, and heavy tide rips occur east of Obstruction Island. Use care in small boats.

Obstruction Pass Campground

Park area: 80 acres, 400 feet of public tidelands
Access: Ferry to Orcas Island, boat
Facilities: 9 campsites, picnic tables, fireplaces, latrines, 2 mooring buoys; *no water* (Designated Cascadia Marine Trail campsite)
Attractions: Camping, picnicking, boating, paddling, fishing, shrimping, hiking, beachcombing

A forested point of land facing on Obstruction Pass gives backpackers and boaters alike an opportunity to camp in seclusion above a quiet beach. This Department of Natural Resources facility has campsites, picnic tables, and group picnic areas scattered about a timbered flat, some within view of the water. If hikers are looking for more exercise after the walk in, a loop trail circles the area, through lush ferns and undergrowth.

To reach the trailhead to the campground by land, turn east off Horseshoe Highway onto Point Lawrence Road ¼ mile before reaching Olga. In ½ mile turn south on the Obstruction Pass Road, which winds around an open valley, then circles a wooded hillside and heads south. As it curves east again 1 mile from the Point Lawrence Road intersection, a gravel road branching right is signed to the Obstruction Pass DNR Recreation Site. Turn on this bone-jarringly rough, narrow road and follow it for 1 more mile to the parking area at the trailhead (space here for

A survival training camp for a group of Explorer Scouts at Obstruction Pass Campground

about 30 cars). Overnight camping at the trailhead is not permitted.

The nearly level trail wanders for ½ mile through timber and along steep bluffs above East Sound before reaching the campground. Occasional short side spurs lead to rocky outlooks on cliffs above the water.

By water, the park lies 1 nautical mile south of Olga on East Sound, and ½ nautical mile west of the boat ramp on Obstruction Pass. There are two mooring buoys in the bay, and space for several more boats to drop anchor in the gravel bottom. It's a pleasant spot, with a nighttime view of brightly lit ferries in Harney Channel; however, during a strong southerly it might be a bit rough. The pebbled beach slopes sharply into the bay, but offers a fine place to draw up small boats. It is a favorite kayaking destination. At low water explore tidepools along the rocky beaches framing either side of the bay.

Doe Island Marine State Park

Park area: 6 acres, 2,050 feet of shoreline on Rosario Strait
Access: Boat
Facilities: 5 campsites, picnic tables, pit toilet, dock with float, *no water, no garbage collection*
Attractions: Camping, picnicking, boating, paddling, hiking, fishing, beachcombing, scuba diving

Compared to the more spacious facilities of Sucia, Stuart, or Jones islands, Doe Island is a "minipark," but it is a delight nonetheless. The nearest boat launch is at Obstruction Pass, 2½ nautical miles to the south. Doe Bay Resort is a mere ½ mile away, making the island a favorite stop for kayak tours originating there.

Deep-draft boats should approach the island from the east, as a tideflat extends out from Orcas Island toward the west end of Doe Island. A dock with a 30-foot float sits on the north shore of the island. A portion of the dock is reserved for dinghy moorage. Water depth at the dock is 8 feet at mean low water, adequate for most craft except at very low tide. Buoys placed in the channel between Doe and Orcas islands are private, not for public use; however, there is space to anchor. Small boats and kayaks can easily be landed behind the east point and on the gentle beaches of the park's south side, but be wary of rocks just offshore.

A rocky cave can be found on the south side of Doe Island.

Campsites with fireplaces are spaced about the island—three in the timber and two in sunny clearings just above the south shore with views across Rosario Strait to Cypress Island. A latrine is located near the dock.

A trail circling the island on the bank above the beach leads to a rocky point that is festooned with flowers in spring. On the south side the bluff has been undercut by waves, forming an interesting cave to explore. Gulls and other seabirds often gather on the wave-washed beach rocks, flying in startled flocks when approached too closely.

Doe Bay

Access: Ferry to Orcas Island, boat
Facilities: Cabins, mineral springs, sauna, meeting halls, campsites, restrooms with showers, store, guest kitchen, volleyball courts, cafe (breakfast and dinner), kayak rentals, guided kayak tours
Attractions: Camping, picnicking, mineral baths, sunbathing, hiking, kayaking, beachcombing

Doe Bay Resort has for years been an on-again, off-again operation, sometimes public, sometimes private, always marching to its own

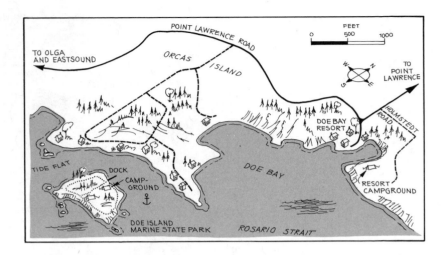

drummer. At present the resort is open to the public, in its own laid-back style. It still retains a flavor of days past when it belonged to the Polarity Institute, which was concerned with esoteric meditation, natural foods and purgatives, and merging opposing positive and negative forces within the body.

The resort has walk-in tent camping on a large bluff to the north, and in trees and an open field uphill to the west. A mineral spring bath and a sauna sit alongside a pretty little stream in a gully just northwest of the office. Cabins line the head of a grass bluff above the beach. The resort has a willingness to cram overflow campers into whatever flat space is left. Part of the resort's ambiance is a "clothing optional" attitude in the sauna and the more secluded campsites.

A shop at water's edge offers kayak rentals, guided kayak tours, and various levels of paddling instruction. For visitors arriving by boat, a few good anchorages can be found in the bay.

To reach Doe Bay by land, follow the Horseshoe for 8 miles east, then south from Eastsound. Near Olga turn north on Point Lawrence Road, and follow it for another 2¾ miles to the resort.

Peapod Rocks

This mile-long chain of islets serves two "levels" of interest. Below the sea is a State Parks Underwater Recreation Area, frequently used by scuba divers, while the grassy rocks protruding above water are a part of the San Juan Islands National Wildlife Refuge, attracting flocks of seabirds who congregate and nest there. Bald eagles also frequent the rocks.

The underwater area from Doe Bay to Peapod Rocks is highly regarded among scuba divers for its wide range of terrain and difficulty,

A pair of bald eagles survey their kingdom from the top of Peapod Rocks.

from the protected waters of the bay to the deep, current-swept walls of the rocks.

The largest of the islands is North Peapod, which has a navigational beacon. At the opposite end of the chain is, appropriately, South Peapod Rock. Stretching in between is an assortment of rocks that appear and disappear with the tide.

Landing boats on the rocks is prohibited, because such intrusion is disturbing to nesting birds. This is a favorite haul-out area for seals and sea lions, which can often be spotted sunning on the rocks or in the water nearby. Again, too-close observation by man can startle the animals and cause them to leave their resting and warming grounds.

CHAPTER EIGHT

MORAN STATE PARK

Park area: 5,249 acres; 1,800 feet of saltwater shoreline on the Strait of Georgia, 8½ milesof freshwater lake shoreline

Access: Ferry or airplane to Orcas Island, boat via Rosario Resort

Facilities: 151 standard campsites, 15 primitive bicycle campsites, picnic tables, stoves, kitchen shelters, drinking water, restrooms, showers, vault toilets, RV dump station, 2 unguarded swimming beaches (freshwater), 2 boat launches (freshwater), boat rentals, interpretive displays, 31 miles of hiking trails; Environmental Learning Center with dining hall, 9 cabins, restrooms, and infirmary.

Attractions: Camping, picnicking, hiking, fishing (freshwater), swimming (freshwater), boating (gasoline motors not permitted), view tower, birdwatching, horseback riding

Drive, bike, or hike—no matter how you get there, Moran State Park is a "must see" for anyone touring the San Juan Islands. Oddly, though, on this water-oriented island there is no easy way for people arriving via pleasure boat to reach the park. Unless they are willing to make the steep hike up from Rosario or rent cars or motor scooters at the resort, they must be content with the many magnificent views of Mount Constitution visible from the waterways.

From the northern reaches of Rosario Strait, the lookout tower on the 2,407-foot-high summit is visible to the naked eye. Boaters can gaze up and admire the scenic mountain and realize that landlubbers in the tower are admiring *their* scenic craft cutting the blue waters.

By land the park is reached via ferry from Anacortes or Sidney, B.C., to Orcas Island. From Orcas Landing travel north on the Horseshoe Highway to the village of Eastsound, loop around the end of the sound, and head south again. The route is well signed. Distance from Orcas Landing to the park entrance is 13 miles. Access to the park from Rosario is described in chapter 7.

Moran is ranked as the fourth largest Washington State park. Thirty-six hundred acres of park land was a gift to the state in 1920 by wealthy shipbuilder Robert Moran, who built his lavish estate, Rosario, on Cascade Bay, just below. Over time, additional property was acquired until today the park contains more than 5,000 acres. Much of the park development, including the picturesque old timber and stone picnic shelters, was accomplished in the 1930s by the Depression-era Civilian Conservation Corps (CCC).

Camping

Located on Cascade and Mountain lakes are four pleasant car-camping areas with a total of 151 campsites; an additional 15 sites are in a primitive camping area east of Cascade Lake.

Because of the ferry trip, many visitors to the park stay several days, and campgrounds are usually filled every night throughout the summer. Reservations are accepted from Memorial Day to Labor Day. With over 60,000 campers per month in prime season, without a reservation chances of finding an empty campsite during this period are slim.

Information regarding state park reservations is published in many newspapers in spring and summer, or can be obtained by calling the

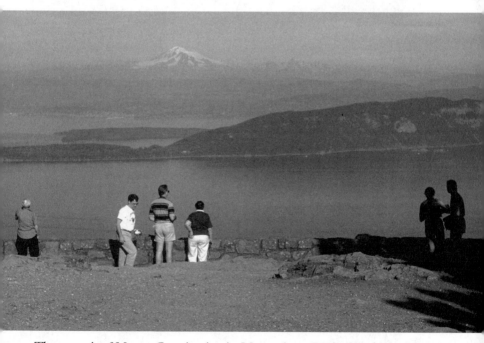

The summit of Mount Constitution in Moran State Park offers high views of Mount Baker, mainland Washington, and the San Juan Islands.

state parks information number listed in appendix A. When park campgrounds are full, a notice is usually posted at the Anacortes ferry terminal. If this occurs, go elsewhere on the mainland, or telephone ahead from the ferry terminal to find accommodations at commercial campgrounds or motels on one of the islands. *Do not travel to the San Juans in summer unless you are sure of overnight lodging.*

A group camp, the Environmental Learning Center (ELC), near the south end of Cascade Lake, is available for large organized parties (by reservation only). This camp can accommodate up to 155 persons; a fee is charged for its use. The ELC has a kitchen, dining hall, restrooms, showers, cabins with bunks, and its own stretch of beach with a dock on the lake.

Bicycles in the Park

Moran State Park is popular with bicyclists and, although the steep Mount Constitution road would severely tax someone who's out of shape, many cyclists do make the trip to the top (some cheat a bit by having a truck tote the cycles to the summit). Brakes must be in good condition for the downhill run. Drinking water is available at Cascade Lake, Mountain Lake Landing, and the summit. Some trails are closed to mountain bikes year-round or seasonally. Check with the park rangers for current restrictions. The Mount Pickett trail is open for equestrian use in all seasons except the summer.

Park Wildlife

Over twenty different mammals and a hundred species of birds are found in the state park. On occasion rabbits, wild turkeys (which were introduced), or raccoons can be seen near the roads, campgrounds, and lake. Black-tailed deer occasionally cross roads; drive carefully to avoid hitting them.

Black-tailed deer are often seen in Moran State Park.

For the best wildlife viewing, take to the trails and walk quietly, watching and listening for telltale movement, the chattering of squirrels, and the calls of birds. There are no bears or poisonous snakes. Lakeshore trails are excellent places to spot river otter, muskrat, and mink, especially at dusk. Watch for burrows, tunnels, and otter slides at the water's edge.

For the safety of wildlife and the convenience of other park visitors, pets must be on a leash no longer than 8 feet, and under control at all times while in the park, *including in the backcountry*. Pets illegally unleashed on trails have killed fawns and other wild animals. The best idea is to leave your pet at home and improve the outdoor experience for everyone.

Hiking Trails

Over 30 miles of trails lace Moran State Park. Most are enclosed by forest, but at times, especially on the upper trails, the timber opens and rocky, moss-covered bluffs protrude to give superb views north, west, or south. Matia, Barnes, Clark, Lummi, Cypress, Blakely, and Lopez islands lie below, and on clear days the snowy mass of Mount Baker rises above in the distance. All trails in the park are described in this chapter.

Most are described the easy way—beginning at the top and hiking downhill. Many variations are possible, with side trails leading to alternate destinations. One nice advantage of trails in the park is that groups of hikers with varied stamina, such as families with several children, can hike together for a distance, then some can choose an easy exit back to civilization while those with more endurance can continue on a more demanding route.

Trail maintenance at Moran State Park is done as crews are available from state and federally funded youth corps. Maintenance is sporadic on the less popular trails. In marshy areas, brush and nettles may overgrow the path and in some spots hikers may encounter downed timber. Before hiking the more remote trail segments, check with park rangers.

Many trips described here are one-way, beginning at one point on the road and emerging farther along. Hikers who do not wish to retrace their route may be able to arrange transportation with a friend. The lower park road between the two park entrances also serves as a main Orcas Island county road, connecting Eastsound with Olga and Doe Bay. Traffic on the county road travels fast, even during busy summer times; use great care when walking alongside the road or crossing it.

Overnight camping is not permitted anywhere in the park except at established campgrounds. On long hikes carry water, as there is no safe drinking water on any of the trails; stream and lake water may contain harmful bacteria or microorganisms. When nettles and brushbeating are anticipated, wear long pants and carry a stick to push vegetation aside.

The fire hazard can be extreme, especially in open meadows; be sure all cigarettes are properly extinguished, do not smoke while moving on trails, and do not toss cigarettes from cars. During periods of severe fire danger the park may prohibit all open fires, and cooking in campgrounds is restricted to barbecues or camp stoves.

CASCADE LAKE

Usually the busiest place in Moran State Park, Cascade Lake boasts the park's three largest campgrounds (North End, Midway, and South End) and a day-use recreation center. All the campgrounds have spacious, level campsites with fire grates and picnic tables. Restrooms and water faucets are centrally located; Midway and North End campgrounds have showers.

North End Campground, with 52 campsites, is ¼ mile inside the park's west entrance on a rise above the road and lake. Just beyond the campground is the park registration booth, manned during periods when reservations are accepted. At other times campers must self-register at Midway Campground.

A few hundred feet down the road from North End campground, facing on Cascade Lake, are the picnic area and recreation center where there are picnic tables, children's play equipment, and rustic picnic shelters with stoves. A beach with roped-off sections for wading and swimming has a float and diving board, although there are no lifeguards. On hot summer days the swimming area is crowded, and parking in the vicinity is difficult.

Rowboats and foot-operated paddle boats are available for rent at Cascade Lake in summer. Private boats may be launched at a ramp at lower Midway Campground; only electric motors are permitted. Visitors usually enjoy an exploratory paddle of the lake, peeking into tiny bays and gazing up at the heights of surrounding

Heavy-timbered picnic shelters, such as this one at Cascade Lake, were built during the Depression by the CCC.

cliffs. Trout fishing is popular, either from boat or shore; the bridge across Rosario Lagoon, reached by trail from either end of Cascade Lake, is sometimes a successful spot. The lake is stocked with rainbows, cutthroats, and silvers every June. Observe state Department of Fish and Wildlife regulations on licenses, season, and limits.

Midway Campground, ¾ mile farther south along the lake shore, has 49 campsites lining both sides of the road, with some along the lake shore. Smaller South End Campground, located on a spur road around the far end of the lake, has 17 campsites, some of them walk-in for bicyclers and backpackers.

A primitive camp area, with 15 informal sites for bicycle and walk-in camping, is located away from the lake on the north side of the Mount Constitution road, ¼ mile east of the county road intersection. This campground has no drinking water, and has only pit toilets.

Forest Recovery Display

On January 24, 1972, a violent storm with winds up to 100 mph wracked the San Juan Islands. At Moran State Park hundreds of trees were downed, some of them century-old patriarchs. Park personnel spent months in clean-up and repair of facilities and trails. Near Cascade Lake

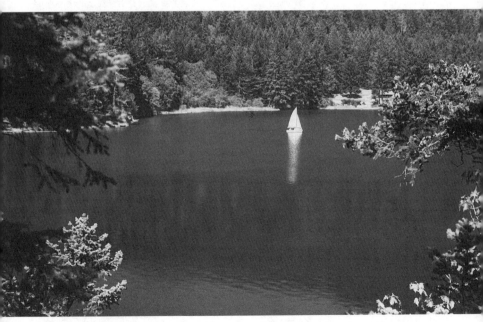

Cascade Lake

a 200-foot, 200-year-old western red cedar toppled by the winds has been left undisturbed as a reminder of the storm and an illustration of forest recovery.

Find the interpretive exhibit behind the registration booth and north of the large picnic shelter. A billboard display describes the storm. The giant tree is a progressive exhibit; visit it from time to time over the years to witness how nature, the original "ecological recycler," reclaims its own products.

Cascade Lake Loop Trail

This nearly level hike with ever-changing perspectives of the lake and mountain is enjoyable whether done only in part, or walked as a 2½-mile trail and road circuit. The trail circles the southwest side of the lake on a bank 30 feet above the water, with very few accesses to the lake itself.

Begin the hike west of the picnic area at Cascade Lake, passing through a marshy area bordered by a picturesque split-rail fence. The trail splits, one path high and one low, then reconnects and wanders along a rocky bluff where weathered Douglas-firs frame the lake views and droop low over the water. At a fork in a few hundred yards a spur heads west to the Rosario Resort road. At another fork less than 1¼ mile beyond, the right-hand trail described in the following section, goes along the edge of Rosario Lagoon.

Another 300 yards down the lakeshore a rustic log bridge spans the mouth of the lagoon. Farther south along the lake are good views of the mountain summit. Belted kingfishers and shy, long-legged great blue herons may be spotted along the shore; watch also for signs of muskrat and otter. Muskrat burrows, which resemble those of a beaver, can be seen in the water. A large snail found in abundance along the shores of Cascade Lake is a dietary staple for these muskrats; look for piles of empty shells.

Reach South End Campground 1½ miles from the trailhead. Follow the road past the ELC and service buildings to the junction with the paved county road. Here a short spur trail heads uphill to meet the Picnic Area-to-Cascade Falls Trail. Follow this trail west to return to the picnic area. Total distance around the lake is 2½ miles, with an elevation gain of 50 feet.

For a slightly longer loop hike, pick up the Cascade Creek Trail by campsite 17 of South End Campground and follow it for about 3½ miles until it emerges at the county road. Cross the road and catch the trail that continues uphill for an additional ¼ mile to Cascade Falls. A left-hand fork leads to the Cascade Falls parking area.

At the parking area, cross the Mount Constitution road and pick up the east end of the Picnic Area-to-Cascade Falls Trail as it heads west, traverses a steep sidehill past the primitive camping area, and continues on to upper Midway Campground. From here the trail proceeds west to reach the road near the registration booth opposite the picnic area. Total round-trip distance for this hike, including the trail around the lake is about 4 miles.

Rosario Lagoon

Detour from the Cascade Lake Loop onto a path by the quiet arm of the lake that includes probably the best birdwatching in the park, as waterfowl often congregate on the peaceful lagoon. The trail, sometimes used by fishermen, is unmaintained but easy to follow. Hike the Cascade Lake Trail around the north end of the lake to an unmarked trail fork ¾ mile from the picnic area. Rosario Lagoon can be seen through the trees on the right.

The right-hand fork of the trail leads along the north edge of the lagoon. The quiet water is a popular stopover for migratory waterfowl; mergansers, goldeneyes, buffleheads, and ring-necked ducks are but a few of the many birds that call at the lagoon in fall, winter, and spring.

As the trail nears the end of the lagoon, a jeep track goes straight ahead, terminating in a parking lot north of the Rosario Resort tennis courts. Continue left along the shore to a large concrete dam, ¼ mile from the Cascade Lake Trail intersection. Many years ago Cascade Lake was only a large marshy area. Before the turn of the century the dam that created the lake was built to provide hydroelectric power for Rosario, below.

At the dam the trail reaches a paved road; walk down the road to the east side of the dam. On the right a trail can be seen dropping down the steep slope to Rosario before paralleling a steel aqueduct. A small sign to the left of the road points to the trail that continues around the lagoon. If the route is lost in the brush at the outlet of the lagoon, follow close to the water's edge until it again becomes clear.

Lake water laps at the hiker's boots; salal and sword fern crowd the trail. Rejoin the Cascade Lake Trail at the log bridge. Total distance of the detour loop around the lagoon is about ¾ mile.

Sunrise Rock

A short but steep climb leads to views down to the shimmering water of Cascade Lake and across to the lookout tower of Little Summit. In recent years this trail has received little maintenance and may require some route-finding; check with the ranger regarding its condition before attempting it.

Follow the Cascade Creek Trail out of South End Campground as previously described. In ¼ mile the Sunrise Rock Trail branches right, drops slightly downhill, then begins the climb to the viewpoint, gaining 350 feet in ¼ mile. In cool, virgin forest the trail passes several ancient Douglas-firs nearly 6 feet in diameter showing the ravages of forest fires, lightning, and woodpeckers.

Where the trail becomes sketchy, look for an apparent clearing in the trees around the hill on the right. A mossy ledge provides views of the lake and mountain. Distance from South End Campground to the viewpoint is about ½ mile; total elevation gain is 500 feet.

CASCADE CREEK

Flowing between Cascade and Mountain lakes, Cascade Creek offers scenic waterfalls, woodland flowers, and wildlife (perhaps) just a short distance from the road. Even novice hikers can negotiate the easy trails, although they are often muddy; wear sturdy shoes. The stream is closed to fishing.

The odd little American dipper or "water ouzel" may be seen here from September through April along the banks of the stream. The plump, slate-gray bird, slightly larger than a wren, dives into the swift-flowing water and walks along the creek bottom to catch aquatic insects, invertebrates, and small fish. A unique adaptation—flaps covering its nostrils—enables it to survive underwater.

Cascade Falls

A chain of waterfalls on Cascade Creek can be reached by a short spur trail from the road, or may be viewed as part of a longer scenic jaunt from Mountain Lake to Cascade Lake. For the shorter trip, park at the trailhead on the south side of the road, ½ mile from the Olga–Mount Constitution road intersection. Be careful not to block the service road that goes straight ahead. The trail sign directs hikers first to Rustic Falls; however, the unmarked abandoned road to the right of the trail sign can be followed directly to Cascade Falls in ½ mile.

Although the hike is worthwhile any time of the year, the waterfalls are at their best in winter and spring when rainfall swells the lakes and streams. By late summer of a dry year the falls may be reduced to a narrow trickle. At Cascade Falls, the most spectacular of the four, the water fans widely across a 100-foot cliff, dropping into a tiny pool at its base. For a head-on view of the cataract, cross the stream cautiously on slanting (and slippery) downed logs.

The trail switchbacks to the top of the falls, then levels out in the brushy valley of Cascade Creek, where salal and salmonberry overhang the stream. In spring you may find mushrooms and wildflowers along the trail, but by summer dense patches of nettles discourage off-trail wandering.

The upper falls are much smaller than Cascade Falls, but lovely nonetheless. Rustic Falls is about 500 feet from Cascade Falls, and ¼ mile farther is the narrow plume of Cavern Falls. Just beyond Cavern Falls, the trail merges with the dirt service road; continue on for ¼ mile to Hidden Falls, located below the footbridge at the Mountain Lake Trail intersection.

You can follow the service road back to the parking area on the return trip. Total distance of the loop hike is slightly over 1 mile; elevation gain is 200 feet.

Cascade Creek Trail

For the longer hike from Mountain Lake to Cascade Lake, find the signed trailhead at Mountain Lake Landing, across from the ranger's residence. The path heads south along the lakeshore and passes a spur trail from Mountain Lake Road.

Reach the concrete dam at the lake outlet ½ mile from the trailhead; drop down the side of the dam to the wooden footbridge crossing Cascade Creek and turn right at a signed trail intersection at the end of the

Opposite: Spectacular Cascade Falls fans across a cliff.

bridge. Downstream 200 yards is a pretty spot where the water cascades in foamy white rivulets and an unusual L-shaped bridge crosses the creek. From here the trail occasionally leaves the creek for short distances only to switchback steeply down the drainage and rejoin the creek. At a third bridge at Hidden Falls, 1½ miles from Mountain Lake Landing, join the Mount Pickett service road, then leave it in another ½ mile where the main trail branches left.

Pause to enjoy scenic Cavern, Rustic, and Cascade falls tumbling down the slope. Sections of an old wooden aqueduct still in evidence at spots along the trail are part of the park's original water system. The route crosses the county road near the south park entrance, 2 miles via trail from Mountain Lake Landing. Find the continuation of the trail, which may be unsigned, slightly up the road to the west.

Cascade Creek heads south out of the park, paralleling the county road, but the trail continues west through a timbered flat, passing giant, century-old Douglas-firs. Walk quietly and watch for Douglas squirrels, pileated woodpeckers, and black-tailed deer in the open forest.

Avoid an unmarked spur trail to the right leading to the group camp and continue on the left fork through brush and, in spring, colorful displays of wildflowers. A short distance before reaching the lake, signs at another trail intersection point left to Sunrise Rock, straight ahead to the Around-the-Lake Trail, and right to South End Campground. By taking the right-hand spur, you soon will see the inviting blue water of Cascade Lake and then shortly reach the campground, 2¾ miles from the start with 550 feet of elevation loss.

Energetic hikers may wish to extend the hike by continuing straight ahead at the last intersection and following the trail on the south side of Cascade Lake, arriving at the picnic area at the north end of the lake in another 1½ miles.

MOUNTAIN LAKE LANDING

Lying a bit off the main thoroughfare, Mountain Lake does not receive as much tourist attention as popular Cascade Lake. It therefore offers more solitude to those who are willing to leave their cars to enjoy its crystal waters and level, tree-cloaked shoreline.

To reach the lake, drive east in the park on the county road to the Olga–Mount Constitution road intersection and continue toward Mount Constitution; 2 miles from the intersection take a right-hand fork, which is signed to Mountain Lake Landing. The road ends in ½ mile at a small parking lot. A vehicle-accessible campground with 7 campsites lies in a hollow immediately west of the parking area; 11 additional walk-in sites are a short distance from the road on a small peninsula overlooking the lake.

The long lake fills a narrow green valley trough between Mount Pickett and Mount Constitution. Rainbow, cutthroat, silver, and Eastern brook trout stocked in the lake each spring make this a popular fishing spot. The best fishing is from boats; they may be rented at a boat dock below the parking area. Or bring your own for fishing—or just for a tranquil paddle and magnificent views of Mount Constitution. Launch boats on the north side of the peninsula at Mountain Lake Campground; gasoline motors are not permitted. Pack a lunch and go ashore on one of four miniature islands in the lake for an hour of quiet reverie.

Mountain Lake Loop

A nearly level hike circles the shore of Mountain Lake, highlighted by a unique view of the summit of Mount Constitution. A counterclockwise route around the lake is recommended so the prime views of the mountain lie ahead rather than at the hiker's back.

The trail begins south of Mountain Lake Campground, contours the lakeside, and in ½ mile crosses the outlet of the lake on a bridge below a concrete dam. Just beyond the dam a right-hand fork of the trail turns down Cascade Creek, while the main trail continues straight ahead along the shore. Avoid a spur, branching to the right a few hundred feet east of the dam, that joins the Mount Pickett Trail.

5. CASCADE CREEK TRAIL
6. MOUNTAIN LAKE LOOP
7. TWIN LAKES TRAIL
8. MOUNT PICKETT TRAVERSE
9. SOUTHEAST BOUNDARY TRAIL
11. MOUNT CONSTITUTION TO TWIN LAKES
16. LITTLE SUMMIT TO MOUNTAIN LAKE

Mountain Lake lies in a valley below the summit of Mount Constitution.

The long summit ridge of Mount Constitution rises above the lake. Little Summit can be seen on the left and the stone observation tower of the main summit far on the right. Below the summit, precipitous 1,000-foot cliffs show their dramatic profile.

Look for bald and golden eagles, hawks, and ospreys soaring in the up-drafts near the mountain. Several pairs of ospreys are believed to nest in the vicinity, although others summer here. The same factors of population, pollution, and pesticides that threaten bald eagles have severely reduced the osprey population. In addition, bald eagles frequently steal fish ospreys have caught and generally harass them, at times causing them to leave. Ospreys, which resemble small white-breasted eagles, favor the heights of Mount Constitution, with its remote nesting sites and fish-filled lakes.

At the north end of Mountain Lake, 2¼ miles from the trailhead, a trail branch goes right to Twin Lakes. Continue along the lakeshore, with views across the lake to wooded Mount Pickett, named for the commander of U.S. forces in the San Juans during the "Pig War" boundary dispute of 1859 to 1872.

Trail's end is reached at the parking lot at Mountain Lake Landing, 1¼ miles from the Twin Lakes Trail intersection. Total distance of the trip is 3½ miles. The only appreciable elevation gain of the hike is midway around the lake where the trail climbs 50 feet above the water to skirt a rocky cliff.

Twin Lakes

Tucked away on a timbered shoulder of Mount Constitution, a pair of small lakes are the destination for one of the park's most pleasant hikes. During fishing season anglers will want to take a fly rod to try for rainbow and cutthroat in the chilly spring-fed waters of the larger of the two lakes. The smaller lake is not stocked, and the stream joining the two lakes is too small for trout.

This trail and its continuation from Twin Lakes to the summit of Mount Constitution have been designated as the Bonnie Sliger Memorial Trail to honor a young woman who died in 1977 in a tragic fall at Doe Bay. She was a popular Youth Conservation Corps supervisor who had spent much time working with youngsters on trail maintenance in the park.

From the trailhead by the ranger's cabin north of Mountain Lake Campground, the wide, level path meanders along the lakeshore for 1¼ miles to the north end of the lake.

Leave the lake at a signed trail junction, following the Twin Lakes Trail along a brook. In a stand of alder you may find scattered remains of an ancient log cabin, possibly built by Civil War draft dodgers who are said to have lived in the area. Big Twin Lake is reached just short of a mile from the trail intersection. Total distance from Mountain Lake Landing to Big Twin Lake is 2½ miles; elevation gain is 200 feet.

Trails circle the shores of both lakes. The edges of the lakes are fairly overgrown with trees to the waterline, with only a few spots where the lakeshore itself is easily accessible. Breaks in the enclosing timber permit glimpses of the summit of Mount Constitution. The distance around Big Twin Lake is about ½ mile; around Little Twin Lake is slightly less.

Mount Pickett Traverse

A long trek combining a trail and an abandoned road can be used as a part of an ambitious around-the-park excursion. Check with park rangers for information on current trail conditions.

Begin the hike at the Cascade Falls pull-out on the Mount Constitution road, ½ mile east of the Horseshoe Highway intersection. Follow the dirt service road east past Hidden Falls and the intersection of the trail to Mountain Lake. The road first climbs gradually but steadily, then levels a bit at a flat near Mountain Lake, where a spur heads left to the Mountain Lake Trail. Here the road begins to climb in earnest, switchbacking up the steep arm of the mountain. Tall second-growth timber limits views to a few tantalizing glimpses between the trees of distant blue water.

The road again levels somewhat at 1,600 feet elevation, and near a large marsh on the left, a spur of the Southeast Boundary Trail branches to the east.

You finally reach the 1,750-foot summit of Mount Pickett 3½ miles from the Cascade Falls trailhead. Now the road continues steadily downhill to the northwest for another mile before narrowing into a footpath. The trail continues for ½ mile farther to the shore of Little Twin Lake.

The nature of the forest changes dramatically upon crossing the Mount Pickett summit. The south slope consists mainly of second-growth fir and cedar with typical Cascades-type underbrush. North of the summit a verdant carpet of moss coats the open ground between huge trunks of towering old-growth cedar, with stands of alder around marshy areas.

Total distance from Cascade Falls to Twin Lakes is 5 miles; elevation gain from the falls to the summit is 1,250 feet, with 650 feet lost on the descent to Twin Lakes. From Twin Lakes hikers can return to the road via the short but very steep trail to the summit of Mount Constitution (1½ miles), or the gentle but somewhat longer Mountain Lake Trail (2¼ miles). For those who prefer the downhill to the uphill, hike the trail in the opposite direction, starting at either Mountain Lake or the summit of Mount Constitution.

Southeast Boundary Trail

One of the longest and most strenuous trails in the park lay overgrown for years. It was originally built during the 1930s by the CCC, but after many years of disuse was reclaimed by trail crews in 1987.

A lush understory of ferns and moss surrounds a Moran State Park trail.

The upper trailhead for the Southeast Boundary Trail heads east from the Mount Pickett Trail at a switchback a hundred yards south of the top of Mount Pickett, as described previously. The path swings around the east side of the mountain summit, dropping through a forest of open old-growth cedar. In ½ mile the route swings to the southeast and begins a long traverse south, descending gradually at first then more abruptly as it crosses steep sidehills supporting thick stands of western hemlock. Splendid views north and east at a few outcroppings reveal a scattering of islands below and Mount Baker towering in the distance.

In a clearing at the head of a drainage, 1¾ miles from the trailhead, the trail meets a short spur descending from the Mount Pickett road. This spur leaves the Mount Pickett road near a large marsh on the lower shoulder south of the summit, and then picks its way down a precipitous hillside to join the main Southeast Boundary Trail. Total length of the spur trail is ½ mile; elevation loss is 600 feet.

From this junction, the Southeast Boundary Trail continues south through a series of ups and downs (mainly downs) to arrive at the park's southeast boundary, 1¼ miles from the spur trail intersection. Here is a choice, as the trail offers two forks—unfortunately both climb relentlessly uphill. The right fork ascends 550 feet in little over a mile to join the Mount Pickett road 100 yards uphill from its intersection with the Mountain Lake spur trail.

The left fork climbs westward along the southern boundary of the park. At 1¾ miles from the trail fork it reaches a junction with a path leading north to the Cascade Falls parking area. In another ¼ mile the trail reaches its southern terminus at the county road at the park's east boundary.

Total distance of the longest trail choice is 5 miles, not including the 3½ mile hike up the Mount Pickett Trail to reach the Southeast Boundary trailhead. Elevation difference is 1,300 feet, with much more elevation gained and lost en route.

MOUNT CONSTITUTION

Rising nearly half a mile above the surrounding sea, Mount Constitution is a dramatic landmark recognizable from many points throughout the San Juan Islands. The expansive view from the summit and the fascinating old stone tower make it the culmination of most tourists' visits to the San Juans.

The U.S. Exploration Expedition of 1838–1842, commanded by Charles Wilkes, named the mountain after the famous American frigate. In a fit of patriotism, Wilkes chose to name all of the San Juan Islands "the Navy Archipelago," and began flinging names commemorating the officers and ships of the War of 1812 at every bit of land and water in sight. It may be that he was unaware of the Spanish and British names already given to many of the landmarks, or (more likely) he felt American names were more suitable, because the United States was attempting to establish claim to the region.

In Wilkes's scheme, Lopez and Orcas islands were named Chauncy and Hull islands in honor of two U.S. Navy commodores. East Sound was designated Old Ironsides Inlet after the ship Hull commanded, and West Sound was Guerrier Bay, for the British warship that Hull defeated.

Five years later a British surveying expedition led by Captain Henry Kellett restored many of the original Spanish and British names. A number of Wilkes's names were retained, however, including Blakely, Decatur, James, Jones, Frost, Shaw, Clark, and Watmough (all honoring U.S. naval officers)—and also, of course, Mount Constitution. Old Ironside Inlet, fortunately, did not survive.

From October to April the road to the top of the mountain is gated at the Olga road intersection at 5:00 P.M., except during fishing season, when it is blocked above Mountain Lake, allowing early-morning access to the lake for anglers. From June through August the road is kept open until 10:00 P.M. to accommodate late-day hikers and tourists who stay on the mountain to enjoy spectacular sunsets from the summit.

The Mount Constitution road leaves the county road 1¼ miles east of the main park entrance; in another mile it begins the upward climb to the top of the mountain. Narrow, with steep switchbacks and hairpin curves, it is not recommended for trailers, buses, or large mobile homes. Halfway up, at the end of a switchback, is a small pull-out space with

*A pullout on the Mount Constitution road provides dramatic views of
Entrance Mountain and (when weather is clear) the San Juan Islands.*

dramatic views down to Cascade Lake, the twin summits of Entrance
Mountain, East Sound, and Spencer Spit on Lopez Island.

At Little Summit the road levels out and traverses the long plateau
leading to the true summit. Total distance from the park entrance to the
summit parking lot is 6 miles. Buildings and radio towers just below the
observation tower are relay facilities for KVOS-TV, Bellingham.

Little Summit

Views rivaling those from the observation tower on the higher main
summit look down to Cascade Lake and Rosario Resort and out to the
symmetrical humps of Entrance Mountain. Beyond are Shaw, San Juan,
and Lopez islands, and in the far distance, above the Strait of Juan de
Fuca, the white peaks of the Olympic Mountains.

As the Mount Constitution road completes its last switchback and
reaches the summit plateau, a pull-off on the east side of the road provides parking space for a few cars. Walk 500 feet up the trail to an open
viewpoint.

A latrine and a few picnic tables are situated in the adjacent meadow.
Rest on the stone and log bench and enjoy the scene, or wander across
the open slopes for ever-widening perspectives—lovely even on foggy
days when the mists swirl around the islands, encompassing, then suddenly revealing bits of the marine view.

Summit Lake

This long marshy lake near the mountain's summit is only about 10 feet deep at its maximum. During winter it sometimes freezes over and islanders go ice-skating here. There is only enough space to park two or three cars along the road where it meets the lake; be careful not to block the road or obstruct the vision of drivers.

Drop a canoe or inflatable boat into the water to commune with the frogs and explore the half-mile-long lake, or drift quietly and watch for eagles, hawks, and waterfowl. There are no fish. The marshy shoreline makes hiking around the lake impossible.

Summit Observation Tower

Perched atop the hard-rock, 2,407-foot summit of Mount Constitution, the stone lookout tower is one of the most unusual and interesting features of Moran State Park. Children especially delight in climbing the many flights of stairs inside the tower, exploring the cell-like rooms, peering out the narrow window slits barred with wrought iron, and firing imaginary crossbows at imaginary armored knights (or laser guns at alien intruders) in the forest below.

The summit observation tower on Mount Constitution

Originally designed as both a fire lookout and a public observation tower, the 50-foot-high structure is a facsimile of the military fortifications built by mountain tribes in the Caucasus Mountains of Russia during the twelfth century, Orcas Island quarries supplied the sandstone blocks for the CCC crews that erected the tower in 1936. A display just inside the tower tells of its history.

From the top, the highest point in the San Juan Islands, views spread in all directions; displays identify visible landmarks. Look down to Twin and Mountain lakes shimmering below, surrounded by dense green forest. Look out in all directions to the array of green and brown islands scattered in the azure fabric of the sound. Especially striking is the stratified geological pattern of the northern San Juans and Canadian Gulf Islands. Toylike boats dot the water, their silver wakes remaining as long streaks on the smooth surface. To the east massive Mount Baker looms, and to the south, through the smog of civilization, Mount Rainier.

From the viewing area at the base of the tower peer over the stone railing for an added thrill—a dizzying view straight down the precipitous 1,000-foot face of the mountain.

Little Summit Trail

Hike from north to south along the mountain rim, looking downward into lakes and forest, outward to islands and sea—but take time to enjoy the quiet forest, too. The character of the vegetation changes rapidly as the trail traverses the gradually sloping summit plateau. It is thought the abrupt changes in the timber are caused by localized variations in the depth and permeability of the soil.

At one time a number of small ponds dotted the summit; many of these filled in with organic material and are now meadows. Hemlock and fir edge these former marshes, sustained by water seeping in the soft peat. In areas where sandy soil covers the hard summit rock, crowded stands of lodgepole pine with shallow root systems grow, but most reach only 15 feet in height and 2 to 3 inches in diameter. Thickets of manzanita growing in the loose sandy soil attract birds who feast on their tiny apple-like fruit.

Near the brow of the plateau where dirt lodges in the spaces between rock outcroppings, mountain hemlock and Rocky Mountain juniper with tenacious roots grow. Strong winds buffeting the face of the mountain twist these trees into beautiful Japanese "bonsai" shapes. In the valley of Paul Creek near Little Summit, moistness creates another forest type—the soaring, big-trunked timber of western red cedar and western hemlock.

The signed trail departs from the top of the mountain behind the KVOS-TV buildings. Watch the route carefully at the beginning as there are several confusing side trails. After two downhill switchbacks and a short traverse, a spur trail leads to an open rock with limited views to the south. The main trail descends steeply to a larger moss-covered rock, ¼ mile from the start, with a 180-degree outlook encompassing the nearby summit cliffs and the distant shores of the mainland.

From vantage points such as this look for eagles and ospreys circling on updrafts, and swallows and flocks of swifts performing high-speed aerial acrobatics. Common nighthawks, who dart about at dusk captur-

Osprey frequent the heights of Moran State Park. (Photo: Bob and Ira Spring)

ing night-flying insects, nest in thickets along the top of the summit.

Views change as the route edges along the brow of the summit. The final open vista is southeast down to Mountain Lake, then the route turns west into the forest. At about ¾ mile the trail crosses a trickling stream on a crude log bridge; the dam at the outlet of Summit Lake can be seen through the trees on the right. The Cold Springs Trail intersects in another ¼ mile, 1 mile from the summit trailhead.

Continuing southeast toward Little Summit, the trail passes east of False Summit, barely noticeable through the trees, and then descends for some distance to a grassy knoll with an eagle's-eye view down to Mountain Lake. Here the lowest point of the trail is reached, some 400 feet in elevation below the summit.

The trail continues on, traversing a sidehill and climbing slightly. In ¼ mile watch carefully for another trail intersection that is signed, but easily could be missed. The trail to the left heads downhill above the gully of Paul Creek, following the path of an old telephone line through heavy timber to emerge at the kitchen shelter at Mountain Lake Campground. The desired route to Little Summit turns right sharply at the intersection, contouring the slope.

The path, almost a road now, crosses Paul Creek and in a short distance reaches Little Summit, 2¼ miles from the trailhead with an elevation loss of 400 feet.

Mount Constitution to Twin Lakes

One of the steepest trails in the park, losing over 1,000 feet in a mile, but what scenery! Leave the hoards of car-bound tourists at the summit for challenging trails and rugged vistas.

Find the signed trail on the north side of the turn-around loop at the summit. After a few switchbacks it crosses a wooded flat and zigzags down again to the end of a switchback where an opening looks north to

Matia Island and Canada. The trail now turns eastward, traversing a saddle. Occasional glimpses through the trees reveal the craggy face of Mount Constitution rising above.

At ¾ mile a short side trail on the right leads to an east-oriented rock outcropping, with the long outlines of Barnes and Clark islands seen just below, Lummi Island farther in the distance, and Mount Baker on the horizon. Another ¼ mile down the main route a second spur trail leads right to the last viewpoint, the most spectacular of all. These two spurs are actually the ends of a short, overgrown side loop south of the present main trail. There is space here to rest and picnic, enjoying the wide views east and south—Mountain Lake, Obstruction Pass at the tip of Orcas Island, the mid-channel hump of Obstruction Island, thickly forested Blakely Island beyond, and to the far right an impressive view upward of the vertical summit cliffs.

More switchbacks reach a gully with a signed trail junction with the North Side Trail. Take the fork on the right, arriving at Big Twin Lake in another 500 yards. Total distance from the summit is 1½ miles; elevation loss is 1,240 feet.

North Side Trail

Swing wide around the north flank of Mount Constitution through cool forest, past marshes and ponds. Views are few, but majestic eagles and hawks can frequently be seen in this oft-ignored section of the park. The trail is not heavily used and not regularly maintained; route finding in brushy areas may pose a problem.

Begin the hike on the Twin Lakes Trail from the top of the mountain. At the trail junction 1¼ miles below the summit, turn left onto the trail signed to Cold Springs. The route heads northwest through open second growth, maintaining a gradual but steady ascent. As it swings over a ridgeline and heads west, watch for an impressive grove of cedar below, along a stream bed. The trail then switchbacks uphill, occasionally obscured by growths of short fir.

Just beyond a marsh on the right, the trail is clear again and a long traverse begins. Suddenly, an incongruous sight beside the trail—a deteriorating park bench of hewn logs. Perhaps Robin Hood and his merry men gather here to plot their next foray against the Sheriff of Nottingham!

The trail slowly climbs, traversing steep slopes covered with an open stand of tall hemlock, and 2 miles from the Mount Constitution–Twin Lakes intersection it crosses a rough jeep road that can be followed downhill (for no particular reason) to the park boundary; private property lies beyond.

The trail continues its traverse and in 300 yards crosses a power line right-of-way that is the north end of the West Boundary Trail. At this point the trail turns south along the edge of a section of private property lying within the park boundary. Beyond a lake and marsh the trail takes a short switchback up a rise. At a concrete post marking the corner of the private land the route turns southeast along the crest of Hidden Ridge.

The way is virtually flat now, through alder, fir, and sword fern, to the intersection 4 miles from the starting point. The right-hand fork switchbacks steeply down to Cascade Lake. Bear left here, continuing along the level plateau of Hidden Ridge to Cold Springs and the road.

Total distance is 4¾ miles. Elevation loss from the summit to the Twin Lakes Trail intersection is 1,000 feet; elevation gain from that intersection to Cold Springs is 650 feet. For a mostly downhill trip, reverse the route, starting at Cold Springs; at the lower intersection continue downhill to Twin Lakes and then on to Mountain Lake Landing. Total distance is 5½ miles; elevation loss is 1,130 feet.

Cold Springs and Hidden Ridge

An isolated picnic area in open forest is reached by driving 3¾ miles up the mountain from the Horseshoe Highway–Mount Constitution road intersection to a gate at an old service road. There is parking space for a couple of cars at the gate and along the roadside. Just inside the barrier is a rustic shelter with picnic tables and a stove, and downhill, south of the shelter, a log-and-cedar-shake gazebo protects what was once Cold Springs. At one time this area was a campground, but it has been closed to overnight use for some time. The old-fashioned hand pump that supplied spring water was so frequently vandalized that park rangers gave up efforts to keep it operational and capped the spring. Picnickers must now supply their own water.

West of Cold Springs a trail wanders out to Hidden Ridge through a cool marsh with cedar, hemlock, alder, and maple. Ferns thickly cover the forest floor, and in season trilliums, skunk cabbage, and marsh marigolds brighten the green carpet with their blossoms. Several ponds along the way are nearly dry in summer, but during the wet season they offer sanctuary for migrating waterfowl. In the forest look for varied thrush and several species of warblers.

The trail is broad and gentle for nearly a mile as it meanders the length of Hidden Ridge. It continues on to join the North Side Trail.

Cold Creek Trail

Zigzag downhill, crossing and recrossing the branches of Cold Creek; or for a real workout begin at Cascade Lake and hike uphill, gaining 1,700 feet of elevation in 2 miles.

For the downhill route, find the trailhead by the Cold Springs shelter on the south side of the picnic area. Hike west through the swampy flat to a trail intersection in ½ mile; bear left on the trail signed to Cascade Lake.

As the steep descent begins, the vegetation immediately changes from wetland to dry, open forest. Curious squirrels edge headfirst down trees, circling out of sight around the trunk when hikers approach.

An open, moss-covered bluff ½ mile from the trail intersection is a good place to rest, break out the chocolate bars, and enjoy the view of Cascade Lake, Rosario Resort, and points beyond. Aside from occasional glimpses of scenery through the trees while on the trail, this is the only viewpoint along the route.

In about 1¼ miles the trail crosses two branches of Cold Creek on log bridges. A traverse begins and the trailside growth changes from open forest to tangled vine maple, berry bushes, and nettles. At the end of the final switchback, just below the North End Campground, the creek cascades prettily over water-worn boulders overhung with ferns. Cold Creek is a natural spawning ground for native trout; fishing is not permitted.

The trail reaches Cascade Lake recreation center 2¾ miles from the Cold Creek trailhead; elevation loss is 1,700 feet.

Sunlight filters through the dense forest along a Moran State Park trail.

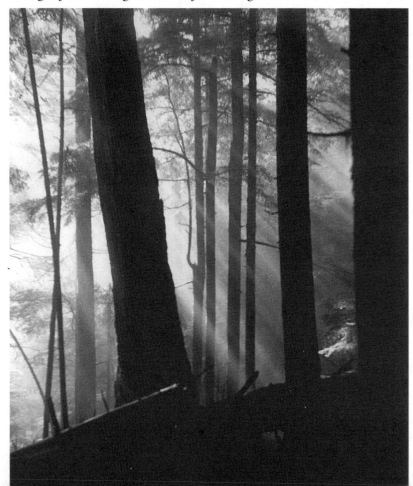

West Boundary Trail

This is not really a trail per se, but a jeep road along a power line going up to the radio towers at the summit of Mount Constitution. Because the West Boundary Trail is extremely steep throughout its entire length, with little in the way of scenery except glimpses northwest through trees on top of steep cliffs forming the west bastion of the mountain, its primary appeal is to hard-core hikers seeking a remote wilderness experience in the heart of civilized Orcas Island.

The upper end of the trail starts at its intersection with the North Side Trail 1¾ miles north of Cold Springs. The power line drops briefly to the west, then heads south near the top of a 600-foot-high cliff. In ½ mile the head of the west fork of Cold Creek is reached, and the road and power line start an uninterrupted 1 mile drop down the drainage— very steep in places.

In another 1¼ mile the trail heads west, then south another ¼ mile to meet the county road at the northwest park entrance. Total distance from Cold Springs to Cascade Lake is 4½ miles. Elevation loss is 1,700 feet.

AROUND THE MOUNTAIN

Although Moran State Park's trails were designed for day hikes, and backcountry camping restrictions preclude tenting by the trail, a determined hiker can complete a circuit of the park by planning ahead to stay in one of the established campgrounds where the trail meets the road. In summer make reservations in advance for campsites, and check in with the ranger. Remember that dogs must be kept on leash, even in the backcountry, so it might be best to leave your best friend at home.

Two possible routes are listed here, although a number of variations are available. Hikers can choose the shorter, somewhat easier scenic route, or opt for the more challenging, less traveled outer loop, which may involve some brush beating and trail-finding problems, and along with it, more solitude. Either circuit could be completed in one day by a seasoned hiker, with little time taken for sightseeing. Specific sections of trail are described earlier in this chapter.

Carry water and, in case of backcountry emergency, a rucksack with the Ten Essentials: extra clothing, sunglasses, first-aid kit, extra food, flashlight (and extra batteries), map, compass, matches in a waterproof container, firestarter, and pocketknife.

Both hikes described here begin and end at the top of the mountain, with overnight stops at South End Campground on Cascade Lake. Cars may not be left overnight at the summit, so hikers must park at the campground and prearrange transportation up and down the road with a friend, or resort to the expedient of an extended thumb.

Elevation loss via each route on the first day is slightly over 2,000 feet, all of which is regained the following day.

Route A: The Scenic Circuit

From the parking lot below the observation tower, take the Little Summit Trail south and turn right onto the trail spur to Cold Springs. Follow the Cold Springs Trail along Hidden Ridge to the junction in ½ mile and head downhill to the Cascade Lake recreation center. Cross the road and turn right onto the trail circling the north and west sides of Cascade Lake, finally reaching the South End Campground, the first night's destination. Total day's distance is 5¾ miles.

Begin the second day with a hike along Cascade Creek from Cascade Lake to Mountain Lake, reaching the dam at Mountain Lake outlet. At the trail intersection turn right along the east side of the lake, and at the north end head up-valley to Twin Lakes. From Twin Lakes, climb the trail back to Mount Constitution's summit. Total day's distance is 5½ miles; total distance of the circuit is 11¼ miles.

Route B: Far from the Madding Crowd

Begin the hike on the trail descending to Twin Lakes from the observation tower parking lot. Just before reaching the lakes turn left onto the North Side Trail, which is signed to Cold Springs. The route swings around the northwest corner of the park, reaching the intersection with the Hidden Ridge Trail, which eventually joins the Cold Springs Trail. From here hike downhill to Cascade Lake, then turn right onto the trail around the north and west shores of the lake, arriving at the night's destination at South End Campground. Total day's distance is 7½ miles.

On the second day, take the trail on the west side of the campground signed to Mountain Lake and follow it along Cascade Creek to the point where it joins the dirt service road over the top of Mount Pickett. Beyond Mount Pickett the road narrows to a trail as it approaches Twin Lakes. End the day by returning to the main road via the steep trail from Twin Lakes up to the summit. Total day's distance is 7¾ miles; total distance of the circuit is 15¼ miles.

CHAPTER ❖ NINE ❖

THE NORTHERN BOUNDARY

Dotting the sea like scattered gems of a broken necklace, a scenic string of islands—Patos, Sucia, Matia, Clark, Barnes, and their attendant smaller islets and rocks—form the northern boundary of the San Juans. Although early settlers lived on the larger of these islands from time to time, none were ever officially opened for homesteading. In early days, cobblestone for Seattle streets was quarried on Sucia, and later foxes were commercially raised there and on Matia.

During the late 1800s, after the settlement of the boundary dispute with Britain, the U.S. government set aside some of the islands as light-

Eroded sandstone, such as this fantastic form at Ewing Cove on Sucia Island, is typical of the northern San Juan Islands.

house reservations or military reserves for coastal defense. When modern warfare made the concept of fixed coastal defense fortifications obsolete, many of the islands were converted to wildlife sanctuaries and state marine parks. Sucia, made available for private development in the 1950s, was purchased in part by the state and in part by an association of boating clubs under the leadership of Ev G. Henry, and was turned over to the State Parks and Recreation Commission for use as a marine park.

These two dozen islands and rocks share a common geological history. Tilted beds of shale and sandstone, believed to have been deposited as a river estuary 75 million years ago during the Cretaceous period, were covered by layers of gravelly till from glaciers that twice covered this region in more recent times. Sea animals such as clams, snails, and ammonites that were buried in the sediment of the estuary became the well-known fossils of Fossil Bay. Erosion of the folded beds of alternating hard and soft material accounts for the long parallel ridges enclosing slender bays.

The glacial till provides good support for vegetation, thus the larger islands are thickly covered with trees and brush. One of the most common is the Pacific madrone, with broad evergreen leaves and peeling red bark. Its gracefully twisted trunks overhang many of the islands' shores, picturesquely framing marine views. Sandstone beds exposed on the edges of the islands have been eroded to fantastic shapes and patterns lovely enough to make a sculptor envious. Caves formed were used by early-day smugglers and today delight beach explorers.

All or part of Patos, Sucia, Matia, and Clark islands are now state parks, with mooring and camping facilities for visiting boaters. Camping is permitted only in designated sites—a stiff fine may result for those

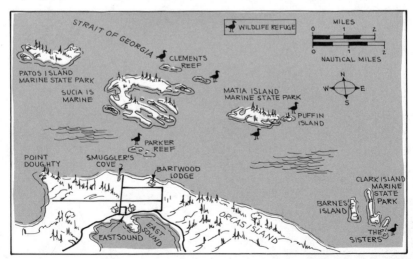

Sucia Wildlife

The pitted sandstone of the islands that makes them such a scenic delight provides nesting areas for a variety of marine birds, such as pelagic cormorants and pigeon guillemots, while seals and sea lions haul out on the smooth, sun-warmed rocks of the more secluded beaches and nearby reefs.

Curious river otters at Sucia Island

Birdwatchers can often spot bald eagles, ospreys, or turkey vultures perched high atop scraggly fir trees or soaring the skies above them. Although quite rare, brown pelicans have been seen here, foraging the shores. Cormorants, known colloquially as "shags," sit on rocks or vacant buoys, overseeing the harbor.

Cormorants are not completely waterproof, thus they must perch with wings hanging loosely or slightly outspread to dry their "sails." Their lack of oily waterproofing makes them less buoyant, enabling them to dive underwater to depths of several hundred feet to capture food. When winds are high, pelagic cormorants can be seen with their long black bodies plastered against sandstone cliffs; in good weather they frequently fly as flocks in sinuous V-formations.

Observant visitors may spot otters swimming along the shores. One evening in early June the authors watched an otter diligently foraging for seafood in Sucia Island's Shallow Bay. With its stomach finally filled, the otter scrambled up the beach and rolled in the soft sand like an ecstatic puppy before finally sauntering into the forest. The following day we watched a pair of otters fishing along the shore in Fossil Bay.

Although this is the ocean, the animals seen in the San Juans are river otters, ranging 2 to 3 feet long (with another 1 to 1½ feet of length for their tail), and weighing 10 to 25 pounds. Sea otters have a larger, heavier body (but shorter tail), and weigh 30 to 85 pounds. Sea otters were so heavily hunted for their fur during the late 1800s that they very nearly became extinct in the Pacific Northwest; they are making a slow comeback along the Pacific coast.

who pitch tents in unauthorized areas. There is no garbage collection at Patos, Matia, and Clark islands; while Sucia does have containers, visitors are encouraged to take their trash with them to ease the problem of garbage disposal.

The marine parks are accessible only by boat. Sucia Island, which generally is the major destination for boaters, lies 2 nautical miles north of the north shore of Orcas Island. Active Cove on Patos Island is 2½ nautical miles northwest of Sucia's Shallow Bay. To the east, Matia lies 2¼ nautical miles from Fossil Bay on Sucia, while Clark is 4 nautical miles farther southeast.

The nearest put-in for small craft is at Bartwood Lodge, 2 nautical miles away on the north shore of Orcas Island; a fee is charged for launching. Tidal current in the channel can be strong, and rough water may occur near the middle at Parker Reef. In a small or unpowered boat, crossing at slack tide is recommended, with a careful eye to the weather as the crossing can be quite risky when the direction of the wind opposes that of the current. Once Sucia Island is reached, small boats can island-hop, timing their open-water adventures for favorable tides. Strong tidal currents and tide rips occur at many points on these passages; kayakers should not attempt these trips unless trained and experienced in open-water paddling. West Beach Resort on Orcas Island, which also has a launch ramp, is about 4½ miles from Sucia. Clark and Matia islands are approximately 14 nautical miles from launch ramps at Bellingham on the mainland.

Patos Island Marine State Park

Island area: 209 acres
Park area: 207½ acres; 4½ miles of shoreline on the Strait of Georgia
Access: Boat
Facilities: 5 primitive campsites, picnic tables, fireplaces, pit toilets, 2
    mooring buoys, 1½ miles of hiking trail, *no water, no garbage collection*
Attractions: Camping, picnicking, fishing, hiking, beachcombing,
    tidepools

Patos Island, the northern outpost of the San Juan Islands, commands sweeping views of Canadian lands and of boundary waters heavily plied by commercial vessels. A lighthouse occupies 2 acres of the western tip at Alden Point; the remainder of the mile-long island is a marine state park. On the eastern end, parallel ridges of erosion-resistant rock extend far out into the water like toes on a foot, thus the name Toe Point. Slightly removed from the pleasure-boating mainstream and lacking the many protected anchorages of Sucia and Stuart, Patos attracts few boaters, and the beaches are uncrowded.

Patos Island's Active Cove offers protected anchorages.

Patos can be reached only by boat; the nearest launching area is at West Beach Resort on the north side of Orcas Island, 5 nautical miles across President Channel. Heavy tide rips occur off Alden Point, along the north side of the island, and around Toe Point.

The east entrance to Active Cove, the only protected harbor on the island, is narrow, shallow, and filled with large rocks, so entry should be made from the west. The deep, narrow cove holds two mooring buoys and has room for a few additional boats to drop anchor. At the head of the cove on a grassy spit are three campsites and a few picnic tables; one more site is located farther back in the trees. Pit toilets are nearby. A "penthouse" campsite is located on a cleared flat area on the bluff west of the beach, just off of the island loop trail.

There is also a reasonably well protected anchorage in the cove at Toe Point; however there are no on-shore facilities.

Patos Lighthouse was established in 1893; the present structure was built fifteen years later. The light is now automated, as are all such navigational warning devices throughout the San Juans.

Patos Island is the setting for Helene Glidden's book *The Light on the Island*. Mrs. Glidden lived here as a child at the turn of the century when her father was lighthouse keeper; her book is based on her childhood adventures and the early history of the San Juans. The vivid accounts of smugglers, Indians, visits by Col. Teddy Roosevelt, rowing to Bellingham in a skiff, and the day-to-day routine on this far outpost give readers insight into early life in the islands. The book is now out of print, but is available in many public libraries.

Eagles seem to have become quite accustomed to visitors at Patos Island, and sometimes can be seen sitting on rocky points as they calmly watch passing boaters. Such apparent acceptance of humans should not be interpreted as domesticity, however. The birds are very susceptible to

Patos Lighthouse

disturbance during nesting season, and should not be harassed, even in the spirit of curiosity.

Beaches and Trail

Eroded sandstone cliffs 10 to 20 feet high edge the south side of the island, making beach walking there difficult except on the rock benches immediately east of Active Cove. In contrast, the north-side beaches are a true delight. These beaches can be walked at all but an extreme high tide, when the headlands have to be crossed by short inland scrambles. At the west end of the north shore, eroded, kelp-covered rock beaches offer tidepools; eastward, gravel beaches separated by small headlands of sandstone and conglomerate stretch along the shore to Toe Point. Watch for seals fishing the turbulent waters of offshore tide rips or hauled out on offshore rocks.

Beaches on the north side of the island can be reached from a loop trail that heads east from the campground along the bluff edge above the south shore. In ¼ mile the trail turns inland, continuing east through dense alder, fir, cedar, and shoulder-high sword fern. The nearly level trail skirts east of the highest point of Patos (100 feet), then swings north and west, as wild rose and thimbleberry crowd its edges. The path finally emerges near mid-island at north beach accesses. After paralleling the north shore, sometimes making short inland digressions, the trail completes its loop with a short climb over the west end of the center island rib, reaching an unmarked intersection with an overgrown service road connecting the lighthouse area to the campground at the head of Active Cove. Total trail loop is about 1½ miles.

SUCIA ISLAND MARINE STATE PARK

Islands' area: 749 acres
Park area: 564 acres; 13¾ miles of shoreline on the Strait of Georgia
Access: Boat
Facilities: 55 campsites, picnic tables, 2 reservation group camps, picnic shelters, fireplaces, water, composting toilets, pit toilets, underwater marine park, 2 docks with floats, 48 mooring buoys, 6¼ miles of trail and 3½ miles of service road, portable-toilet dump
Attractions: Camping, picnicking, beachcombing, fossils, clamming, crabbing, swimming, hiking, fishing, scuba diving, birdwatching

Mile-long rocky fingers protecting shallow bays form the group of eleven islands known as the Sucias. Over a twenty-year period beginning

An amazing mushroom-shaped rock on the shore at Fox Cove

in 1952, portions of the present park land were purchased by the state for recreational use. During the 1960s, 319 acres were bought by the Puget Sound Interclub Association of boaters and entrusted to the care of the State Parks and Recreation Commission for use as a marine park. All of Sucia Island, Little Sucia, Ewing, and the Cluster Islands are now park property.

With nearly 9 miles of waterfront, 6 bays, and extensive boat and camping accommodations, Sucia Island State Park provides one of the best public marine recreational facilities in the San Juans. Located 2 nautical miles north of Orcas Island, the nearest point where boats can be rented or launched, Sucia is inviting to boaters in vessels ranging from kayaks to luxury yachts. Two docks with floats in Fossil Bay and 48 mooring buoys scattered around the island are heavily used by boaters. Small boats can be beached at the head of any of the bays.

Boaters in small craft will need to exercise caution en route from Orcas or points beyond, carefully considering the weather and tidal currents. Heavy summer traffic or larger boats can also be a hazard. The trip is recommended only for experienced sea kayakers and canoeists.

During summer, facilities can be very crowded at Sucia, with well over 100,000 visits by boaters annually. Be prepared to anchor if necessary. Buoys and floats are first-come, first-served and the practice of

A delicate tracery of madrona branches frames Echo Bay.

"reserving" a buoy or float space by tying a dinghy to it for the later arrival of a friend or for the return of the mother craft is neither courteous nor legal; it can result in your tender being cast adrift. A fee is charged for on-shore camping and for moorage on either floats or buoys after 3:00 P.M.

Camping areas, connected by trails or service roads, are situated around Sucia Island at Fossil Bay, Echo Bay, Shallow Bay, Snoring Bay, and Ewing Cove, for a grand total of 55 sites. Camping is permitted only in designated sites. In the summer, drinking water is available at Fossil Bay, Fox Cove, and Shallow Bay; however, from November through March all water pipes except those at Fossil Bay are shut off to protect against freezing.

The Spanish name "Sucia" is correctly pronounced *Su-SEE-ah*, although few people (even residents) say it that way. The common pronunciation is *SU-shuh*—not as melodious, but perhaps more logical to an Anglicized tongue. The name, meaning "dirty" or "foul water," was given to the island by early explorers who noted the dangerous rocks and reefs near the shores. Boaters today should take warning from the name and be wary of submerged rocks offshore and in the bays. Deep draft boats should be especially careful that they have enough depth throughout the swing of their anchorage during low tide.

Sucia has some of the finest examples of the eroded cliffs that are typical of these northern San Juan Islands. The rocks are sculpted by the chemical action of salt water on sandstone, assisted by the wearing action of wind and waves. Low-level wearing of the beaches here and on many of the other San Juan Islands is limited by tide rips offshore; only at high tide do storm waves reach shore without being broken up by tide rips; beaches at the high tide level demonstrate the cutting action of the waves.

The fierce wave action can occasionally present problems to boaters at Sucia. When a southeaster blows into any of the bays on the southeast side of the island, the anchorages are at best uncomfortable, and possibly dangerous. West-facing Shallow Bay offers the best protection during these conditions. It may be necessary to go elsewhere if it is impossible to secure a safe moorage.

The fashion once was to spray-paint the name of visiting boats on the sandstone cliffs of the island. All this graffiti has been cleaned from the rocks, and the fad hopefully is now past, so that today visitors can enjoy the natural beauty rather than the ugly scrawls of insensitive visitors.

Sucia Bays

Fossil and Mud bays. Fossil Bay is the hub of park activity, with its 2 floats and 15 buoys filled nearly every night of the summer season. A small picnic shelter and campsites with water, picnic tables, and fire grates can be found in the sparse trees near the docks, while more sites are nearby on the sandspit between Fossil Bay and Fox Cove and on the finger on the south side of the cove.

Mud Bay, offset from Fossil Bay, nearly empties at low tide; other times the water is just deep enough for dinghying. Harnden Island at the entrance to Mud Bay is private property.

Fox Cove. Across a low sandspit from Fossil Bay, Fox Cove faces westward, sheltered by Little Sucia Island. Worn cliffs on the north side of the bay form marvelous shapes, including an 8-foot-high rock mushroom where children can pretend to be in Alice's Wonderland. There are four mooring buoys in Fox Cove. It can be entered via either a narrow rocky channel on the south end of Little Sucia, or a much wider and safer passageway on the east side of that island; nervous skippers should choose the latter. The sandy beach at the head of the cove is one of the best on the island for wading and swimming.

Little Sucia, on the west side of Fox Cove, is a wildlife refuge, and is seasonally closed to public use from January 1 to August 15. The remainder of the year it is open for day use only. Currents in the channel between the islands can be strong; use care.

Shallow Bay. Indenting the western end of the horseshoe-shaped island, Shallow Bay has three distinct sandy beaches with a campground on each, separated by rocky headlands. Enter the bay with care, as submerged rocks extend out from the points at either side of the entrance. The channel is marked by daybeacons. Seven buoys and numerous good anchorages attract boaters. However, the bay is extremely shallow; check water depth and the predicted tides before settling down for the night.

Shallow Bay offers driftwood, clams, and crabs to beachcombers. Large cockles may be picked up right on the surface at low tide, while other clams hide deeper in the sand. Dungeness crabs lurking in the eelgrass of the cove can be trapped with crab pots in deep water or routed out of the seaweed (carefully) during a minus tide.

Chinaman Rock is said to have at one time been used to hide illegal aliens.

Observe size and sex restrictions on Dungeness crabs. Return undersized crabs to the water or to a spot where they can burrow for protection. Crabs left unprotected in the air quickly dry out and die. In any place in the San Juan Islands it is illegal to collect or kill any live marine animal except for food use.

Chinaman Rock, on the northeast side of Shallow Bay, is a striking example of the wave- and chemical-eroded sandstone and subsequent uplifting so characteristic of these northern isles. The rock is mostly obscured by a growth of trees, but can be found by going to the east end of the northernmost beach, then walking into the trees at the edge of the cliff.

Body-sized hollows have obviously been geologically uplifted at least 30 feet since they were formed. Legend is that during the late 1800s Chinese aliens smuggled into the United States from Canada often hid in the recesses from patrolling immigration officials. Do not scratch names or deface the rock, so that others may enjoy this fascinating spot in its natural state.

Echo Bay. The largest bay on the island, Echo contains 12 mooring buoys with ample space for additional boats to swing at anchor. The large blue-striped buoy in the center of the bay is reserved for Coast Guard boats when they are stationed in the area. Because this is the most open of Sucia's anchorages, it is exposed to waves and surges and can be uncomfortable during some wind and tide conditions. The two large, long, forested islands in the bay, appropriately named North Finger and South Finger, are privately owned.

The eastern half of the tiny island at the western tip of South Finger Island is a recent park addition. The property was turned over to the state in 1986 after previously being confiscated by U.S. marshals when the owner was convicted of running a drug-smuggling operation there. When the would-be smuggler scouted and purchased the island in winter, the deserted island seemed the perfect spot for clandestine activities. He hadn't realized it was smack-dab in the middle of the state's most popular marine state park. Surprise!

The 2-acre island, now appropriately called "Justice Island," is a nesting area for bald eagles and pupping ground for seals, so public use is prohibited. The western half of the island is privately owned.

Snoring Bay. Tiny Snoring Bay on the south side of Johnson Point, generally scorned by powerboaters, is a haven for kayakers seeking refuge from the noise and fumes of motors. The story goes that the bay received its name when park officials visiting the island discovered a ranger there enjoying a siesta. Snoring Bay has two mooring buoys and two campsites.

Ewing Cove. Boaters seeking privacy may find it in Ewing Cove, on the north side of Echo Bay, snuggled between Ewing Island and the Cluster Islands. The long narrow cove boasts sandy beaches and exquisite examples of the worn sandstone that makes the rest of the island so popular. Approach the cove from the east, favoring the Ewing Island side of the channel, where the shore drops off rapidly to 50 to 75 feet of water; avoid rocks and shoals that extend out from Cluster Islands. Do not try to enter the cove via the narrow channel on the west end of Ewing Island; it is shoal, laced with rocks, and suffers from fast and unpredictable tidal currents.

Four mooring buoys are available in 25 feet of water, and three campsites and a pit toilet are located above the beach at the west end of the cove. A buoy near the east end of the cove marks the site of an underwater marine park area. Three sunken vessels are below the buoy and several yards to the east in 45 feet of water. When entering the cove, stay reasonably close to Ewing Island (within 100 yards, or so), and keep a sharp eye out for submerged rocks and reefs that lie on the southwest side of the channel.

At Ewing Cove an added bonus for birdwatchers is Clements Reef and adjoining rocks, part of the San Juan Islands National Wilderness Refuge, lying less than ½ mile to the north. Hundreds of seabirds congregate here, some of them nesting on Sucia and Matia, others merely resting on their migratory flights. Be content to identify them with strong binoculars from shore, for waters around the reef can be treacherous and any approach by man disturbs the birds. Seals and sea lions, too, can be seen on the reefs in large numbers, snoozing in the sun or warily eyeing passing boaters.

Hiking Trails

A dirt service road loops through the wooded main section of the island, with branch trails stretching from it to all ends of the island fingers. Except for park service equipment, motorized vehicles and bicycles are prohibited on park roads and trails. The rock quarry near the head of one dock at Fossil Bay is particularly dangerous; visitors should stay out of the area.

Fox Cove and Ev Henry Finger. The trail around the north side of Fox Cove follows the high edge of the bluff above the bay, while paths

Fantastic scenery is typical of Ewing Cove.

on Ev Henry Finger, Johnson Point, and the northern edge of Echo Bay skirt the water. Wear sturdy shoes on any long hike; deck "tennies" or sandals do not provide adequate footing on steep, slippery trails. Search shoreline rocks, especially on Ev Henry Finger, for fossilized clams, snails, and ammonites 75 million years old. Such specimens may be collected if they are loose, but digging in the banks with pick, shovel, or any other device is illegal.

Lawson Bluff. A short but very scenic loop trail skirts the edge of Lawson Bluff on the northwest side of the island. Find the signed trail out of the northernmost campsite at Shallow Bay, near the latrines. A network of side paths leading to open viewpoints confuses the route as it rounds the point north of the Shallow Bay entrance. All paths

Saltwater erosion creates fascinating patterns in Sucia Island sandstone.

eventually lead back to the main route along the edge of the bluff. The way climbs gradually, staying just above the precipitous cliffs of Lawson Bluff. Keep a hand on the kids—the trail is easy enough, but in places it is so near the edge that a misstep could cause a bad fall.

Aerial views stretch down the sheer cliff to the ocean glimmering 100 feet below, and north to the long stretches of Patos Island and the rugged outlines of the Canadian Gulf Islands. After about ½ mile the trail turns inland, joining the northernmost loop of the service road at a signed trailhead in another 200 yards. Turn right to return to Shallow Bay, left to reach the head of Echo Bay (the easiest return to Fossil Bay). Total distance of loop hike from Shallow Bay is about ¾ mile.

Ewing Cove. The most beautiful hike on Sucia, and possibly in the entire San Juans Islands, is the 2-mile trail along the north side of Echo Bay to Ewing Cove. This is a "three-or-more rolls of film" hike for photography buffs. The signed trailhead leaves the park service road about 300 yards east of its spur to Chinaman Rock.

After a few hundred yards of meandering through thick brush, the path breaks out to the edge of the bluff above Echo Bay, which it follows for the remainder of the hike. At a few points inland, detours have

The Ewing Cove trail skirts numerous small coves.

been created to avoid dangerously eroded sections of trail falling off the bluff above 75-foot cliffs—take the detours.

There is no beach access at first, as the trail winds along the 100-foot-high cliffs whose eroded sandstone cavities are used as nesting sites by darting swallows. In ¼ mile a grassy knob, so tempting that is must be signed "No Camping," provides views down the sinuous waterways between the Finger Islands.

Pocket coves have steep, somewhat hazardous scrambles down to beaches framed by wave-sculpted sandstone. Graceful madronas and gnarled, silver, long-dead junipers frame pictures of the myriad shapes and forms carved in the soft rock. Small rocks and islets just offshore await the visit of kayakers.

Note in places where the tread is on sandstone that this rock shows the same pock-marking of saltwater erosion as does the beach a hundred feet below, indicating it was once at water level and has, over time, been uplifted.

Incessantly cawing crows warn eagles, woodpeckers, and gulls of a hiker's pending arrival. As the trail nears its destination at Ewing Cove, the cliffs moderate and ready beach access is available. Not moderated, however, is the fantasy of wave-carved sandstone forms continuing out along the Cluster Island chain. The cove itself is a remote and peaceful retreat—difficult to leave for the trip back to the hubbub of the main island campgrounds.

MATIA ISLAND MARINE STATE PARK
AND WILDLIFE REFUGE

Island area: 145 acres; 3¾ miles of shoreline on the Strait of Georgia
Park area: 5 acres
Access: Boat
Facilities: 6 campsites, dock with float, 2 mooring buoys, picnic tables, fireplaces, composting toilet, *no water*
Attractions: Camping, picnicking, clamming, crabbing, tidepools, fishing, beachcombing, hiking, birdwatching

Although Matia may well be the loveliest of these jewel-like northern isles, it is often passed over by visiting boaters as it has limited overnight space. Only 5 acres facing Rolfe Cove on the west side of the island are open to camping; the remainder of the island is designated as national wildlife refuge and a wilderness area.

The U.S. Fish and Wildlife Service permits use of this small area of the island as a state park, in hopes that such limited use of the land will be compatible with wildlife preservation. If the presence of the public on Matia ever becomes a threat to the birds and mammals living there or on nearby Puffin Island, all human intruders will be asked to pull up their tent stakes and anchors and go elsewhere. Treat the land with tender, loving care and strictly observe all regulations, or risk losing it.

The composting toilet at Matia Island is an engineering curiosity.

Matia Island is 2½ nautical miles northeast of Bartwood Lodge on the north shore of Orcas Island, where boats may be launched for a fee. For day excursions, small boats can be beached in any of several coves on the island; however camping is allowed only on state park land.

Rolfe Cove holds a dock with a 45-foot float and two mooring buoys, with room for only a few more boats to drop a hook. Hovering at the mouth of the cove, a rocky islet gives some protection from northerly wind, but it also causes peculiar current flows that disrupt confident anchoring. The bottom of Rolfe Cove is deep and quite rocky; in a strong blow it may be difficult to secure a safe anchorage. The float is removed during the winter months to prevent damage from storms.

On the bank at the head of the cove are picnic tables, garbage cans, six campsites, and an ingenious composting toilet; a portable-toilet dump is also provided to preserve the composting toilet from chemicals that would destroy its effectiveness. A sign tells you all you ever wanted to know about composting toilets—and then some. Drinking water once was available from a nearby pump; it was capped because federal standards would require expensive purification, so bring your own.

The exposed walls of the coves at Matia Island are naturally sculpted masterpieces. Hollowed and smoothed by wind and waves, the stony banks are accentuated by banded patterns of layered conglomerate.

Boats also may anchor in a long narrow bay on the southeast end of the island; however, the end of the bay is extremely shoal at low water. Several rocks lying in the entrance are an additional hazard. Going ashore is permitted at the head of the bay. The north shore and south shores are posted as wildlife refuges.

"Matia" has undoubtedly the most varied and disputed pronunciation of any San Juan Island. The Spanish pronunciation of the word, meaning "no protection," is *Mah-TEE-ah*. However the name is often corrupted as *May-shuh*, *May-tee*, or *Mat-ty*.

The state park float at Rolfe Cove can accommodate several boats.

The Hermit of Matia

In early years this island was the longtime home of the San Juans' most interesting character, known as the "hermit of Matia." His name was Elvin Smith, and even though local newspapers of the day referred to him as a hermit, he was in truth not antisocial, for every week, in all but the foulest of weather, he rowed his skiff to North Beach on Orcas Island. From there he hiked a 2-mile trail to Eastsound to collect his mail, buy supplies, and gossip with his cronies.

The pioneer recluse had gained a reputation as a mystic and a mail-order faith healer. His weekly mail included dozens of letters, and sometimes money, from supplicants all over the country seeking his assistance. At home, on the retreat of his island, Smith claimed to spend many hours each day in prayer on behalf of his correspondents.

Elvin Smith lived for nearly thirty years in this briny paradise. From time to time other pioneers showed interest in the land, but one occupant on a 150-acre island was considered quite crowded enough for the time, so they settled elsewhere. One stormy February in 1921, Smith (who was then 86) and a visiting friend, their boat heavily laden with supplies, cast off from Orcas for a return trip to Matia. They were never seen again. Stones marking two vacant graves in an Orcas Island cemetery commemorate their lives.

A wilderness loop trail on the island passes remnants of Smith's early settlement. A wide path leaves the dock at Rolfe Cove and heads south near the edge of the cove. After reaching a marshy area on the south side of the island, the path continues eastward, shaded by second-growth maple and Douglas-fir.

Look sharply along this section of trail to spot faint skeletons of ancient fences. Although Smith was a vegetarian, he kept sheep for wool, chickens for eggs, and rabbits, perhaps for companionship.

Matia Island Trails

Near the head of the southeast bay a faint spur trail heads out along the edge of the finger of land framing the south side of the bay. Here are terrific views west over a tiny cove and south to Orcas Island and Mount Constitution. In about ¼ mile is a sign reading "National Wilderness Area." End your hike here.

The main loop trail turns north, passes the head of the southeast bay, then bends west for its return to Rolfe Cove. Here a glance at the rock cliff just west of the trail clearly illustrates the geological origins of the island. Two wide dark bands of conglomerate are sandwiched between bands of sandstone, and the whole layer cake is tilted upward at about a 60-degree angle, clearly demonstrating the upthrusting that created the island.

A sign at the east end of the loop trail indicates that the remainder of the island is closed to public access; respect it. As the trail heads west, the nature of the forest changes to huge old-growth trees—predominately cedar, but with a sprinkling of Douglas-fir, hemlock, and alder.

Puffin Island

Puffin Island is just a stone's throw offshore from the east end of Matia. This steep, rocky island, topped with a scraggly pompadour of trees and grass, is one of the islands of the San Juan Islands National Wildlife Refuge; going ashore is prohibited. Seals and sea lions can often be seen lolling about in the warmth of the sun, and, with binoculars, squawking gossipy seabirds can be identified: ungainly murres and auklets, and shy pigeon guillemots.

From mid-March to mid-September these birds gather in colonies and lay their eggs in rock clefts, tending them until the downy chicks feather out and are able to fly. During this nesting time any close approach by boats or people is disturbing to the families; if the birds become alarmed by your presence, you are too close.

Early day Lummi Indians from the Bellingham region paddled dugout canoes to Matia and Puffin islands to collect eggs, which they packed in the cool, moist leaves of sea lettuce to safeguard against spoilage and breakage. The sea lettuce, too, was later eaten or dried for winter use. Today visitors may sample the green, tissuey seaweed (if they do not go near the birds to collect it), but Uncle Sam protects the eggs.

CLARK ISLAND MARINE STATE PARK

Park area: 55 acres; 2 miles of shoreline on the Strait of Georgia
Access: Boat
Facilities: 7 campsites, picnic tables, fire rings, pit toilets, 9 mooring buoys, *no water, no garbage collection*
Attractions: Camping, picnicking, clamming, mussels, beachcombing, scuba diving, fishing, tidepools, birdwatching

Swept by the waters of the Strait of Georgia, shadowed by the mountains of Orcas Island, a group of rocks and islands cluster together like a family. On the southwest, the smaller, barren rocks are known as The Sisters, with the southernmost wedge-shaped rock named Little Sister.

The largest of the rocks once sported a single pine tree, prompting the name Lone Tree Island, but the tree has long since surrendered to the sea, leaving the islet to some tenacious grass and hundreds of nesting birds. The rock is now marked by a navigational light.

The Sisters are included in the San Juan Islands National Wildlife Refuge. In spring and summer, cormorants, pigeon guillemots, glaucous-winged gulls, and other pelagic birds nest here. At other seasons

A kayaker's campsite at Clark Island

gulls gather on the rocks, occasionally in enormous numbers, for reasons known only to them—perhaps an approaching storm, perhaps feeding is poor, or perhaps for an afternoon coffee (or herring) klatch. Whatever the reason, the cacophony of their conversation at such times is overwhelming, even on the shores of Clark Island.

Barnes Island, second in size of the island group, lies on the west. While the uplands at Barnes are private, all the surrounding tidelands below the mean high water level are public. Do not stray above the driftwood level onto private property.

Less than ½ mile east of Barnes is the largest of the island family, 55-acre Clark Island, a marine state park. Although it is located less than 2 miles from the shores of Orcas Island, the nearest boat launching area is 5 nautical miles to the west at the resort at North Beach. The distance from populated areas, the lack of fresh water for campers, and the lack of protected anchorages make this one of the less frequented of the San Juan marine state parks.

The slender island is a mile in length, but scarcely 300 yards across at its widest point. Its southern end hooks sharply eastward to form a small broad bay; here six mooring buoys offer easy, although exposed, anchorages. Skippers approaching this bay should use care, as several rocks lie just beneath the surface along its east side; boats have been known to have run aground. Refer to a good navigational chart for location of hazards. A slight indentation on the opposite side of the island holds three additional mooring buoys, sheltered from the west by Barnes Island and from the southeast by the end of Clark.

Timber and impenetrable brush cover most of the island. Along the

Seagulls feeding on herring

edges graceful red-barked madronas lean over the ever-eroding banks.
Near the latrines, a single trail crosses the island. A bluff-top trail, accessible from the west side beach, can be followed around this end of the
island, with views down to the beaches and tiny steep-walled coves; side
trails drop down to the water.

Campers may pitch tents in one of five campsites snuggled in thick
wild rose at the beach on the east side of the island. Two more campsites
can be found in the trees along the cross-island trail connecting the two
anchorages. One of these inland sites is large enough to hold several
tents for a group gathering. The west beach, with a warm inviting sand
strip above a gradually tapering gravel beach, is a day-use picnic area.
Camping or building fires on the beach is prohibited in order to keep it
as natural as possible. A fire circle, surrounded by rough-hewn log
benches, is on the west side, above the beach.

Clark Island has some of the most varied beaches of any of these
northern island state parks. Sand and mud flats to the south, exposed at
low tide, are good for clamming and summertime wading; mussels cling
to protruding rocks. The steeper, rocky northern beaches, inaccessible
from land, hold an array of marine life—purple starfish, pastel sea anemones, barnacles, sea squirts, purple and green urchins, and more—to be
admired by scuba divers and tidepool explorers.

Mountains rising on the British Columbia mainland are visible from
campsites and anchorages on the east side of the island. Monstrous oil
tankers occasionally sail by in the distance, delivering their cargo from
Alaskan oil fields to the refinery at Cherry Point. At night the lights of
the refinery glimmer across the water.

APPENDICES

A. EMERGENCY PHONE NUMBERS AND LIST OF CONTACTS

Fire (Alarms Only)

Blakely Island—(360) 375-4151
Orcas Island—911
Shaw Island—911

Lopez Island—911
San Juan Island—911

For fires on remote islands, call the Department of Natural Resources—(800) 562-6010. (If calling by radio, notify the U.S. Coast Guard.)

Medical Emergencies

Blakely Island—(360) 375-4151
Orcas Island—911
Shaw Island—911

Lopez Island—911
San Juan Island—911

Poison Information Center—(800) 732-6985

Sheriff

Lopez and Shaw Islands
  Emergencies—911
  Other Business—(360) 468-2333

Orcas Island
  Emergencies—911
  Other Business—(360) 376-2207

San Juan Island
  Emergencies—911
  Other Business—(360) 378-4151

All other islands
  Emergencies—911
  Other Business—(360) 378-4151

U.S. Coast Guard

Marine and Air Emergency—(206) 286-5400

Hotlines (Toll Free)

Marine Toxins/PSP Hotline—(800) 562-5632
Whale Hotline—(800) 562-8832

Radio Contacts

Marine V.H.F.: Coast Guard distress and hailing—Channel 16
Marine V.H.F.: Coast Guard liaison—Channel 22A
Marine V.H.F.: Marine Operator; Bellingham—Channel 28, 85
Marine V.H.F.: Marine Operator; Victoria, B.C.—Channel 27
Citizens Band: Distress—Channel 9

To contact a boat via the marine telephone system: (800) 955-9025

U.S. Customs

Friday Harbor and Roche Harbor—(360) 378-2080
  (After hours—(800) 562-5943)

Washington State Ferries

Information—(800) 843-3779 (toll free; automated response only)
Seattle—(206) 464-6400
Anacortes terminal—(360) 293-8166
Lopez terminal—(360) 468-2252
Orcas terminal—(360) 376-2134
Friday Harbor terminal—(360) 378-4777
Shaw terminal—(360) 468-2142
Internet ferry information—www.wsdot.wa.gov

Parks

San Juan Island National Historical Park; P.O. Box 549, Friday Harbor, WA 98250. Phone—(360) 378-2240

Washington State Parks and Recreation Commission; 7150 Cleanwater Lane, Olympia, WA 98504. Phone—(360) 753-2027; www.parks.wa.gov

Spencer Spit State Park; Route 2, Box 3600, Lopez, WA 98261. Phone—(360) 468-2251

Moran State Park; Star Route 22, Eastsound, WA 98245. Phone—(360) 376-2326

All other San Juan State Parks (Patos I., Sucia I., Matia I., Clark I., Freeman I., Stuart I., Jones I., Posey I., Blind I., Turn I., Doe I., Lime Kiln Point, James I., Saddlebag I., Huckleberry I.); Sucia Island Marine State Park, Star Route, Box 177, Olga, WA 98279. Phone—(360) 378-2073

San Juan County Park; 380 West Side Road North, Friday Harbor, WA 98250. Phone—(360) 378-2992

Odlin County Park; Route 2, Box 3216, Lopez, WA 98261. Phone—(360) 468-2496

Museums

Lopez Island Historical Museum; P.O. Box 163, Lopez, WA 98261. Phone—(360) 468-2049

Orcas Island Historical Museum; Eastsound, WA 98245. Phone—(360) 376-4849

Pig War Museum; 620 Guard Street, Friday Harbor, WA 98250. Phone—(360) 378-6495

San Juan Island Historical Museum; 405 Price Street, Friday Harbor, WA 98250. Phone—(360) 378-3949

Shaw Island Historical Museum—Phone—(360) 468-2637

Whale Museum; 62 First Street North, Friday Harbor, WA 98250. Phone—(360) 378-4710

Other

University of Washington Marine Field Laboratories; 620 University Road, San Juan Island, WA 98250. Phone—(360) 378-2165

B. NAUTICAL CHARTS AND MAPS

Sketch maps for this book are intended for general orientation only. When traveling by boat on any of the San Juan waters it is imperative that the appropriate nautical charts be used. The following charts cover the area included in this book. They can be purchased at map stores or many marine supply centers.

NOAA Chart 18423, Bellingham to Everett, including the San Juan Islands (Scale 1:80,000—folio of charts including some detailed insets)

NOAA Chart 18421, Strait of Juan de Fuca to Strait of Georgia (Scale 1:80,000—covers all areas included in this book)

NOAA Chart 18429—Rosario Strait—southern part (Scale 1:25,000)

NOAA Chart 18430—Rosario Strait—northern part (Scale 1:25,000)

NOAA Chart 18431—Rosario Strait to Cherry Point (Scale 11:25,000)

NOAA Chart 18432—Boundary Pass (Scale 1:25,000)

NOAA Chart 18433—Haro Strait—Middle Bank to Stuart Island (Scale 1:25,000)

NOAA Chart 18434—San Juan Channel (Scale 1:25,000)

Although it would be difficult to get seriously lost on any of the islands, the USGS topographic maps listed below are useful and interesting.

7.5 " series maps—Mount Constitution, Blakely Island, Lopez Pass, Lummi Island, Eastsound, Shaw Island, Richardson, Waldron Island, Friday Harbor, False Bay, Sucia Island, Stuart Island, Roche Harbor.

C. SELECTED REFERENCES

History

Gibbs, Jim A. *Lighthouses of the Pacific.* West Chester, Pa.: Schiffer Publishing, Ltd., 1986.

Haskett, Patrick. *The Wilkes Expedition in Puget Sound—1841.* Olympia, Wash.: Western Interstate Commission for Higher Education and The State Capitol Museum, 1974.

Meany, Edmond S. *Vancouver's Discovery of Puget Sound.* New York: The Macmillan Company, 1907.

Murray, Keith. *The Pig War.* Tacoma, Wash.: Washington State Historical Society, 1968.

Richardson, David. *Pig War Islands.* Eastsound, Wash.: Orcas Publishing Company, 1971.

Beaches and Marine Life

Sheely, Terry W. *The Complete Handbook on Washington's Clams/Crabs/Shellfish.* Snohomish, Wash.: Osprey Press.

Washington State Department of Fish and Wildlife. *Puget Sound Public Shellfish Sites.* Olympia, Wash.: Washington State Department of Fish and Wildlife, 1978.

Washington State Department of Natural Resources. *Your Public Beaches, the San Juan Islands.* Olympia, Wash.: Washington State Department of Natural Resources, 1985.

Nature

Angell, Tony, and Kenneth C. Balcom III. *Marine Birds and Mammals of Puget Sound.* Seattle: Washington Sea Grant Program, 1982.

Atkinson, Scott, and Fred A. Sharpe. *Wild Plants of the San Juan Islands.* 2d ed. Seattle: The Mountaineers, 1993.

Lewis, Mark G., and Fred A. Sharpe. *Birding in the San Juan Islands.* Seattle: The Mountaineers, 1987.

Paulson, Dennis. Shorebirds of the Pacific Northwest. Seattle, Wash.:University of Washington Press, 1993.

Wahl, Terence R., and Dennis R. Paulson. *A Guide to Bird Finding in Washington.* Bellingham, Wash.: T.R. Wahl, 1981.

Boating, Paddling

U.S. Department of Commerce. *United States Coast Pilot: 7 (Pacific Coast: California, Oregon, Washington and Hawaii).* Washington, D.C.: U.S. Department of Commerce, published annually.

Washburne, Randel. *Kayaking Puget Sound, the San Juans, and Gulf Islands.* Seattle, Washington: The Mountaineers, 1990.

Western Marine Enterprises, Inc. *Pacific Boating Almanac: Pacific Northwest and Alaska.* Ventura, Calif.: Western Marine Enterprises, Inc., published annually.

Bicycling

Kirkendall, Tom, and Vicky Spring. *Bicycling the Pacific Coast.* 2d ed. Seattle: The Mountaineers, 1990.

Powers, Peter, and Renée Travis. *Touring the Islands: Bicycling in the San Juan, Gulf, and Vancouver Islands.* 2d ed. Eugene, Ore.: Terragraphics, 1989.

Woods, Erin, and Bill Woods. *Bicycling the Backroads around Puget Sound.* 3d ed. Seattle: The Mountaineers, 1989.

Hiking

Sterling, E. M. *Best Short Hikes in Washington's North Cascades and San Juan Islands.* Seattle: The Mountaineers, 1994.

Scuba Diving

Clark, Dareld, and Janine Clark. *Diving in the San Juans.* Seattle: Evergreen Pacific Publishing, 1988.

Fischnaller, Steve. *Northwest Shore Dives.* Edmonds, Wash.: Bio-Marine Images, 1986.

Pratt-Johnson, Betty. *141 Dives in the Protected Waters of Washington and British Columbia.* West Vancouver, Canada: Gordon Soules Book Publishers, 1990.

Weber, Edward. *Diving and Snorkeling Guide to the Pacific Northwest.* Houston: Pices Books, 1993.

Fishing

George, Don. *Jigging The San Juans.* Anacortes, Wash.: Ace in the Hole Publishing Company, 1991.

Haw, Frank, and Raymond M. Buckley. *Saltwater Fishing in Washington.*, 2d ed. Seattle: Stan Jones Publishing, Inc., 1981.

Olander, Doug. *Northwest Coastal Fishing Guide.* Seattle: The Writing Works, 1984.

General

Diamond, Lynnell and Marge Mueller. *Let's Discover the San Juan Islands.* Seattle: The Mountaineers, 1989.

Mueller, Marge, and Ted Mueller. *The Essential San Juan Islands Guide.* Medina, Wash.: JASI, 1994

D. QUICK REFERENCE TO FACILITIES AND RECREATION

Some kinds of marine facilities—such as boating, fishing, and beachcombing—are found throughout the San Juan Islands. Others, however, are more specific to particular areas. The following table provides a quick reference to needed facilities and specific activities in the major areas covered by this book.

Marine Services include marine supplies and repair; in some places they may be of a very limited nature.

Floats/Buoys refers to marinas that have transient moorage, as well as public facilities at marine parks.

Launch Facilities may be only a shore access for hand-carried boats. Hoists and slings are always at commercial marinas. Ramps may be at either commercial or public facilities.

Point of Interest includes historical or educational displays, museums, and self-guided nature tours.

Some facilities listed may be entirely at commercial resorts or marinas; some may close off-season. For detailed information read the description of specific areas in the text.

( ) = Nearby; [ ] = Freshwater
Fuel: D = On Dock; S = Service Station
Launch Facilities: R = Ramp; H = Hoist; C = Hand Carry
Camping: B = Bicycle Only
Walking/Hiking: BW = Beach Walk

	U.S. Customs	Fuel	Marine Services	Groceries/Shopping	Restaurants	Floats/Buoys	Launch Facilities	Fishing	Shellfish	Paddling	Scuba Diving	Swimming	Camping	Picnicking	Walking/Hiking	Point of Interest
1. THATCHER PASS																
Blakely Island	D	•	•			•		•						•		•
Decatur Island							R									
James Island Marine State Park						•		•		•	•		•	•	•	
2. LOPEZ ISLAND																
Odlin County Park						•	R	•	•	•	•	•	•	•	•	
Upright Channel Picnic Area						•		•	•	•		•		•	•	
Lopez Village	S		•	•	•											•
Fisherman Bay	D	•	(•)	•	•	•	R/H	•	•	•		•		•		
Otis Perkins Park							C	•		•				•	BW	
Hummel Lake						[R]	[•]			[•]						
Spencer Spit State Park						•	C	•	•	•		•	•	•	•	•
Hunter and Mud Bays						•	R	•	•	•					BW	
Islandale Bicycle Rest														•		
Shark Reef Recreation Area										•				•	•	•
Richardson	D/S								(•)		(•)	(•)				
Mackaye Harbor							R	•		•	•					
Agate Beach Picnic Area							C		•	•	•			•	BW	
Hughes Bay County Park										•	•				BW	
3. THE CENTRAL CHANNEL																
Shaw Landing	D/S		•			•	C			•						(•)
Blind Island Marine State Park						•		•		•			•	•		
South Beach County Park							R	•	•	•		•	•	•	•	
Yellow Island Preserve										•					•	•
Jones Island Marine State Park						•		•	•	•	•	•	•	•	•	
4. SAN JUAN ISLAND																
Friday Harbor	•	D/S	•	•	•	•	H			•			(•)	•		•
Whale Museum																•

	U.S. Customs	Fuel	Marine Services	Groceries/Shopping	Restaurants	Floats/Buoys	Launch Facilities	Fishing	Shellfish	Paddling	Scuba Diving	Swimming	Camping	Picnicking	Walking/Hiking	Point of Interest
San Juan Is. Historical Museum																•
The Pig War Museum																•
Turn Island Marine State Park						•		•	•	•	•	•	•	•	•	
Turn Point Road Access							C	•		•						
Jackson Beach							R	•		•		•			•	BW
Sportsman and Egg Lakes							[R]	[•]		[•]						
Lakedale Campground				•			[C]	[•]		[•]		[•]	•	•		
Reuben Tarte Picnic Area							C			•	•			•		
Roche Harbor	•	D/S	•	•	•	•	R			•		[•]		•	•	•
Posey Island Marine State Park								•		•	•		•	•		
Westcott Bay								•	•	•						
Mitchell Bay (Snug Harbor)	D	•	•			•	R			•			•	•		
San Juan County Park			•				R	•		•	•	•	•	•		•
Lime Kiln Point State Park								•		•	•			•	•	•
Pedal Inn Bicycle Camp													B			
Eagle Cove Public Access							C			•	•	•			•	BW
Griffin Bay Campground						•				•			•	•		
Cattle Beach Picnic Area														•	•	•
Cattle Point															•	•

5. SAN JUAN ISLAND NATIONAL HISTORICAL PARK

	U.S. Customs	Fuel	Marine Services	Groceries/Shopping	Restaurants	Floats/Buoys	Launch Facilities	Fishing	Shellfish	Paddling	Scuba Diving	Swimming	Camping	Picnicking	Walking/Hiking	Point of Interest
English Camp						•	C	•		•	•			•	•	•
American Camp							C	•		•	•			•	•	•

6. NORTH FROM SPIEDEN CHANNEL AND PRESIDENT CHANNEL

	U.S. Customs	Fuel	Marine Services	Groceries/Shopping	Restaurants	Floats/Buoys	Launch Facilities	Fishing	Shellfish	Paddling	Scuba Diving	Swimming	Camping	Picnicking	Walking/Hiking	Point of Interest
Stuart Island Marine State Park						•		•	•	•	•		•	•	•	
Stuart Island School															•	•
Stuart Island Cemetery															•	•
Turn Point Lighthouse														•	•	•
Waldron Island Preserve															•	•

	U.S. Customs	Fuel	Marine Services	Groceries/Shopping	Restaurants	Floats/Buoys	Launch Facilities	Fishing	Shellfish	Paddling	Scuba Diving	Swimming	Camping	Picnicking	Walking/Hiking	Point of Interest
7. ORCAS ISLAND																
Orcas Landing	D/S	•	•	•	•									•		•
Killebrew Lake							[C]	[•]		[•]						
Deer Harbor	D/S		•	•	•		C			•		[•]				•
Frank Richardson Preserve																•
West Sound (Marina)	D	•	•	•	(•)	•	H	•		•						
Skull and Victim Islands										•			•			
Olga				(•)	(•)	•				•						
Rosario	D	•	•	•	•	R				•		[•]			•	•
Eastsound	S		•	•	(•)		C			•				•		•
Madrona Point				(•)	(•)	•	C			•				•	BW	
Orcas Island Historical Museum				(•)	(•)									•	BW	•
Fishing Bay Waterfront Park				(•)	(•)		C			•				•	BW	
North Shore Resorts		•	•	•		R	•			•	•			•		
West Shore Resorts		•	•		•	R	•			•	•	•	•	•		
Point Doughty Recreation Site										•	•		•	•		
Freeman Island Marine State Park										•	•			•		
Obstruction Pass			•			•	R	•		•						
Obstruction Pass Campground						•		•		•	•	•	•	•	•	
Doe Island Marine State Park						•		•		•	•		•	•	•	
Doe Bay			•	•		C		•		•	•	•	•	•	•	•
8. MORAN STATE PARK																
Moran State Park						[•]	[R/C]	[•]		[•]		[•]	•	•	•	•
9. THE NORTHERN BOUNDARY																
Patos Island Marine State Park						•		•	•	•	•		•	•	•	•
Sucia Island Marine State Park						•		•	•	•	•	•	•	•	•	•
Matia Island Marine State Park						•		•	•	•	•		•	•	•	
Clark Island Marine State Park						•		•	•	•	•		•	•	•	

INDEX

ABOUT THE AUTHORS

MARGE and TED MUELLER are outdoor enthusiasts and environmentalists who have explored Washington State's waterways, mountains, forests, and deserts for nearly forty years. Ted has taught classes on cruising in Northwest waters, and both Marge and Ted have instructed mountain climbing through the University of Washington. They are members of The Mountaineers and The Nature Conservancy, and Ted is a board member of the Washington Water Trails Association.

Heidi Mueller

THE MOUNTAINEERS, founded in 1906, is a nonprofit outdoor activity and conservation club, whose mission is "to explore, study, preserve, and enjoy the natural beauty of the outdoors...." Based in Seattle, Washington, the club is now the third-largest such organization in the United States, with 15,000 members and five branches throughout Washington State.

The Mountaineers sponsors both classes and year-round outdoor activities in the Pacific Northwest, which include hiking, mountain climbing, ski-touring, snowshoeing, bicycling, camping, kayaking and canoeing, nature study, sailing, and adventure travel. The club's conservation division supports environmental causes through educational activities, sponsoring legislation, and presenting informational programs. All club activities are led by skilled, experienced volunteers, who are dedicated to promoting safe and responsible enjoyment and preservation of the outdoors.

The Mountaineers Books, an active, nonprofit publishing program of the club, produces guidebooks, instructional texts, historical works, natural history guides, and works on environmental conservation. All books produced by The Mountaineers are aimed at fulfilling the club's mission.

If you would like to participate in these organized outdoor activities or the club's other programs, consider a membership in The Mountaineers. For information and an application, write or call The Mountaineers, Club Headquarters, 300 Third Avenue West, Seattle, Washington 98119; (206) 284-6310; clubmail@mountaineers.org.

Send or call for our catalog of more than 300 outdoor titles:

The Mountaineers Books
1001 SW Klickitat Way, Suite 201
Seattle, WA 98134
1-800-553-4453 / e-mail: mbooks@mountaineers.org